TEACHERS
AS INTELLECTUALS

CRITICAL STUDIES IN EDUCATION SERIES
EDITED BY PAULO FREIRE & HENRY A. GIROUX

EDUCATION UNDER SIEGE
The Conservative, Liberal & Radical Debate Over Schooling
STANLEY ARONOWITZ & HENRY A. GIROUX

CRITICAL PEDAGOGY & CULTURAL POWER
DAVID W. LIVINGSTONE & CONTRIBUTORS

LITERACY
Reading The Word & The World
PAULO FREIRE & DONALDO MACEDO

THE POLITICS OF EDUCATION
Culture, Power & Liberation
PAULO FREIRE

WOMEN TEACHING FOR CHANGE
Gender, Class & Power
KATHLEEN WEILER

THE MORAL AND SPIRITUAL CRISIS IN EDUCATION
A Curriculum for Justice & Compassion in Education
DAVID PURPEL

BROKEN PROMISES
Reading Instruction in Twentieth-Century America
PATRICK SHANNON

EDUCATION & THE AMERICAN DREAM
Conservatives, Liberals & Radicals Debate the Future of Education
HARVEY HOLTZ & ASSOCIATES

POPULAR CULTURE & CRITICAL PEDAGOGY
Schooling & the Language of Everyday Life
HENRY GIROUX, ROGER SIMON & CONTRIBUTORS

TEACHERS
AS INTELLECTUALS

Toward A Critical Pedagogy
Of Learning

HENRY A. GIROUX

Introduction by Paulo Freire
Foreword by Peter McLaren

CRITICAL STUDIES IN EDUCATION SERIES

BERGIN & GARVEY PUBLISHERS, INC.
MASSACHUSETTS

First published in 1988 by
Bergin & Garvey Publishers, Inc.
670 Amherst Road
Granby, Massachusetts 01033

89 987654321

Printed in the United States of America

Library of Congress Cataloging-in-Publication Data

Giroux, Henry A.
Teachers as intellectuals: toward a critical pedagogy of learning
/ Henry A. Giroux; introduction by Paulo Freire; foreword by Peter
McLaren.
p.   cm. — (Critical studies in education series)
Bibliography: p.
Includes index.
ISBN 0-89789-157-0 (alk. paper): $39.95. ISBN 0-89789-156-2
(pbk.: alk. paper): $14.95
1. Education—United States—Aims and objectives. 2. Education—
United States—Philosophy. 3. Education—Political aspects—United
States. 4. Educational sociology—United States. 1. Title.
II. Series.
LA217.G57 1988   88-10433
370'.973–dc19   CIP

This book is dedicated to my three children, Jack, Chris, and Brett, who have provided me with a deeper understanding of what it means to struggle for a better future for all children.

It is also dedicated to my sister, Linda Barbery, whose courage is a constant source of inspiration for me, and to Donaldo Macedo, my brother and friend, whose intelligence and generosity of spirit provide me with a constant source of strength and pleasure.

Contents

Foreword: Critical Theory and the Meaning of Hope

By PETER MCLAREN

Henry Giroux's Pedagogy of the Concrete

The task of providing a comprehensive intellectual profile of Henry Giroux is not easy in such a short space. (Even under optimal conditions, critics would be hard pressed to do justice to the scope and critical depth of his work.) Therefore what follows is a more modest effort which highlights only some general aspects of Giroux's work, enough, I trust, to provide readers with a theoretical context in which to locate the chapters in this volume.

Giroux's work has, over the past ten years, continued to address issues of theoretical, political, and pedagogical importance. The cumulative effect of his writings has virtually dismantled the received notion of schooling and its relationship to the wider society as one of uninterrupted accord and mutually advantageous arrangement. By arguing against the traditional view of classroom instruction and learning as a neutral or transparent process removed from the juncture of power, history, and social context, Giroux has managed to provide the generative foundations for a critical social theory of schooling which offers a singular challenge to educators, politicians, social theorists, and students alike.[1]

Critically appropriating new advances in social theory, and developing at the same time new categories of theoretical inquiry, Giroux has effectively challenged the dominant assumption that schools function as one of the major mechanisms for the development of the democratic and egalitarian social order. His analysis of the neoconservative resurgence in education has helped to uncover the logic by which the excellence movement has been able to camouflage its retreat on issues of equity and social reform. In addition, his criticisms of progressives have revealed how many accepted practices among liberal educators—such as institutionalized tracking and structuring the curriculum in accordance with the imperatives of industry—undermine the very democratic values that serve as a basis for the liberal position. Consequently we are shown how the priorities developed by both conservative and liberal educators are often belied by the inequality and hierarchy at the root of the ideologies they so cherish.

What Giroux has accomplished, both politically and pedagogically, has been to unmask the structured inequality of competing self-interests within a social order. He has revealed how the fundamental public services that Americans generally associate with schooling, such as the meritocratic empowerment of all individuals regardless of race, class, faith, or gender, are subverted by the very contradictions which constitute them. In sum, Giroux's work is fundamentally bent on obstructing those prevailing ideological and social practices in schools which are at odds with the goals of preparing all students to be active, critical, and risk-taking citizens. Spanning the wide range of Giroux's interests has been an abiding constant, a liberating intention to empower those who have been bypassed on the road to educational success, those for whom history has exercised a cruel and premature closure on hope. These include both the disaffected and the indigent, together with those whose more privileged class position renders them too insensitive and powerless to take a stand against the inequities and injustices of society.

Giroux's work represents much more than an historical contribution to critical educational theory. For he also has developed a highly original account of the political forms of contemporary schooling, an account which stems from an awareness of the strengths and inadequacies of critical educational theory and an acute sensitivity to the limitations and historical contingency of theory itself. While Giroux's writings disclose a deep theoretical erudition, there are grounds upon which they can and should be challenged and contested as part of an ongoing dialogue. Aspects of his work are not, to be sure, without their critics. This is not the place, however, to dwell on criticisms of Giroux's work as much as to explore it as a body of critical thought that must be read as part of an ongoing project of pedagogical struggle and political empowerment.

Although Giroux's writing did not begin as a serious political activity until the late 1970s, his work now constitutes a major discourse and foundation for developing and advancing a critical theory of education. The last few years have witnessed Giroux undertake significant forays into the wider terrain of social theory itself, resulting in a number of important contributions to the nascent discipline of cultural studies.[2] The overarching project of Giroux's work, illustrated by the range of material that appears in this volume, can be summarized as an attempt to formulate a critical pedagogy committed to the imperatives of empowering students and transforming the larger social order in the interests of a more just and equitable democracy. For Giroux, the central issue is the development of a language through which educators and others can unravel and comprehend the relationship among schooling, the wider social relations which inform it, and the historically constructed needs and competencies that students bring to schools. A critical grasp of this relationship becomes necessary if educators are to recognize how the dominant school culture is implicated in hegemonic practices that often silence subordinate groups of students as well as deskill and disempower those who teach them. Such an understanding can also enhance the ability of teachers to work critically with students from dominant and subordinate classes so that these students can come to recognize how and why it is that the dominant culture encourages both their complicity and their powerlessness. Of course, the major objective of critical pedagogy is to empower students to intervene in their own self-formation and to transform the oppressive features of the wider society that make such an intervention necessary. Giroux's final judgment on the cultural factions which exert such an enormous power over educational, cultural, and economic life, while damning, does not exclude the possibility of progressive change and reform. From Giroux's perspective, human agents possess the capacity to remake the world both through collective struggle in and on the material world and through the exercise of their social imagination.

There is a passion and indignation in Giroux's writings—one could also say a militant hope—which betray little of the detachment and academic smoothness of conventional scholarly work. The vitality and at times ferocity that mark Giroux's critical voice carry a legacy both of anger and of strength that derives, in part, from the frustration he experienced and the resistance and struggles he engaged in as a youth growing up in a working-class neighborhood in Rhode Island. Giroux's history has also been shaped by his involvement in the struggles of the 1960s, his work as a community organizer, and his seven years as a high school teacher. Giroux often refers to his university education as an historical accident. Had it not been for the basketball scholarship that helped transport him from the streetcorners of Smith Hill to the lecture halls of the university, his life undoubtedly would have taken a different and less advantageous turn.[3] It is both the lived sense of class difference which marked Giroux's early years and his subsequent struggle to understand the ways in which schooling empowers those with an early social advantage that bring to his writings the passion for justice and equality for which they have become known.

Giroux's work provides educators with a critical language to help them understand teaching as a form of cultural politics, that is, as a pedagogical enterprise that takes seriously relations of race, class, gender, and power in the production and legitimation of meaning and experience. The significance of such a language can be judged by how well it addresses certain issues and concerns which are germane to the construction of an emancipatory pedagogy. Some of the issues and concerns which have guided Giroux's work over the years can be formulated as a series of questions: What are the moral variants against which we shall construct ourselves as social agents of change? How can problems related to class, race, gender, and power be translated into questions of educational quality and excellence? In what way can we reposition ourselves as educators against the dominant culture in order to reconstitute our own identities and experiences and those of our students? How can educators construct a pedagogical project that legitimates a critical form of intellectual practice? How is it possible to acknowledge difference and multiple forms of identity and still address the issues of will and political struggle? What diversity do we silence in the name of a liberatory pedagogy? How can educators come to recognize injustices which have been perpetrated in the name of education? How can they come to face their own participation in the employ of an often oppressive system that appears to rob students of their basic rights? In what ways can teachers work to support a pedagogy responsible for collectively forging a democratic public culture? How can educators link a theory of schooling to a pedagogy of the body and desire?

What are the limits of the knowledge/power/subjectivity relation? How do we develop a public discourse that integrates the language of power and purpose with the language of intimacy, friendship, and caring? How do we speak in the name of emancipation without showing scorn for those who are caught in the grip of domination or ignorance, regardless of their class position? Since we don't know what is historically possible until it has been tried, how can educators begin to empower students to imagine a future in which hope becomes practical and where freedom can be dreamed, struggled for, and eventually won? Critical pedagogy speaks from questions such as these, whose answers are required to take as their point of departure the real, concrete problems facing students and teachers today. Questions raised by critical pedagogy—questions which are relevant and pertinent to the human condition, questions which are formulated as part of a larger struggle for human liberation—are those which must be asked of history itself.

There are, loosely speaking, two main periods to Giroux's work. The first is reflected in his essays on social class and schooling which were written in the late 1970s. During this time he was often associated with a small but influential group of educational theorists—which included such people as William Pinar, Jean Anyon, and Michael Apple—who produced some important analyses of schooling which now appear somewhat burdened by the language of political economy and a reductionistic concept of social reproduction.[4] While much of the work produced by the critical school at that time harbored a residual homage to causal determination and an economistic Marxism, Giroux soon began to envisage a more complex relationship between what transpired in classrooms and the political, social, moral, and economic arrangements within the larger society. Giroux became influenced to some extent by the new sociology of knowledge that grew out of the work of Michael Young and Basil Bernstein in England, by the writings of Raymond Williams, and by the highly innovative work on youth subcultures undertaken by Stuart Hall, Richard Johnson, Paul Willis, and others at the University of Birmingham's Center for Contemporary Cultural Studies. Giroux's theoretical interests soon gravitated towards the writings of the Italian theorist Antonio Gramsci, Brazilian educator Paulo Freire, and the Frankfurt School of critical theory—most notably Theodor Adorno, Max Horkheimer, Herbert Marcuse, and Walter Benjamin. Giroux's early bequest to the critical educational tradition, *Ideology, Culture, and the Process of Schooling,* was an inventive and successful attempt to forge a conceptual link among Gramsci's formulations of ideology and domination; Freire's concepts of culture and literacy; the Frankfurt School's critique of technocratic rationality, classical Marxism, and depth psychology; and work in the sociology of education and curriculum theory in United States, Canada, Great Britain, and Australia.[5] For Giroux, the concept of culture had to be politicized in order to remove it from the narrow categories of art, poetry, theatre, and high-status literature and theoretically recast as a terrain of ideological and material contestation. Such a reformulation of culture also helped Giroux reject the classical Marxist view of culture as merely the reflex of the economic base, a view which in various versions greatly influenced a number of Marxian analyses of schooling. Attempts to posit a mirrorlike correspondence between the economy and the curriculum failed, in Giroux's terms, either to account for or to explain the absorption of various cultural and ideological elements into our schools and wider society.

Theory and Resistance in Education marked another shift in direction for Giroux, as he further challenged theories of social and cultural reproduction which prevailed after the publication of *Schooling in Capitalist America* by Bowles and Gintis.[6] Here Giroux maintained that schools are more than simply sites of social and cultural reproduction; similarly, he challenged the notion that schools are defined exclusively by the logic of domination and teachers merely pawns of the ruling class. In Giroux's terms, this type of analysis is theoretically flawed, politically incorrect, and strategically paralyzing. According to Giroux, the tendency within orthodox Marxian discourse to regard the impulse of capital as the heartbeat of domination shifts critical attention away from the various ways in which culture, power, and ideology work as mutually informing apparatuses of domination to shape student subjectivities and maintain the hierarchical separation between dominant and subordinate groups. The work of Freire and Gramsci had, by this time, alerted Giroux to the various ways in which ideology gets established and legitimated by means of the multileveled and multidirectional mediations and determinations of culture, class, ethnicity, power, and gender. Giroux's understanding of the dialectical relationship between social structure and human agency militates against the idea that human subjects are reflections of some innate, ahistorical essence or that they are passive victims caught in the web of ideological formations. Giroux has endowed social agents with the ability to transcend the historical situatedness of their inherited culture. In the final instance, individuals do not succumb to the inevitablity of a tradition which holds them prisoners of fixed ideas and actions but rather are able to use critical knowledge to alter the course of historical events. Individuals, for Giroux, are *both* producers and products of history.

Giroux is particularly concerned that the lack of critical attention that traditional Marxist discourse gave to the concept of culture hampers a clear understanding of how meaning is produced, mediated, legitimated, and challenged within schools and other educational institutions. While the economic sphere and the social relations of production are still considered by Giroux to be important targets for critical analysis, these can no longer supplant the concepts of culture and power in accounting for the historical apparatuses of domination and struggle. At the same time, Giroux understands that to undervalue the existence of counterhegemonic struggle on the terrain of school culture makes educational critics generally appear as counsellors of despair. This brushed against the grain of what Giroux thinks should be the purpose of a truly critical analysis of schooling. To remake a phrase of Bertolt Brecht's, this means the type of analysis which goes beyond an explanation of what *is* in order to shape with hammers of critical thought what *could be.*

The second period of Giroux's writings is marked by his involvement, in the early 1980s, with the issue of agency and student resistance. Influenced at this time by the theoretical writings of Stanley Aronowitz and sociologist Anthony Giddens (not to mention Paul Willis's ethnography, *Learning to Labour*), Giroux began to argue that schools do not totally position students within a logic of seamless oppression in which even the most sweeping and innovative of reforms can achieve no more than a gentle modification of the most extreme instances of social pathology. Rather, there exist spaces and tensions within school sites which provide students with the possibility of resistance. While acknowledging the priority of capital and unequal relations of power as determinants of oppression, Giroux insists that they in no way obliterate completely the possibility of contestation and transformative struggle. In other words, it is to the process of resistance that Giroux believes critical educators must pay particular attention in laying the groundwork for educational reform. As part of a critical discourse of education, resistance theory is important because it signals the primacy of student experience as a central terrain for understanding how identity, politics, and meaning actively construct different interventions and mediations within the sphere of schooling. The category of resistance is not meant merely to supplement the formulaic insistence on social and cultural reproduction; it represents a theoretical reconstruction of how subjectivities are positioned, invested, and constructed as part of the intricacies of moral and political regulation. For Giroux, it is essential that schools be seen as sites of struggle and possibility and that teachers be supported in their efforts both to understand and to transform schools as institutions of democratic struggle.

Giroux also makes clear that, while it is virtually impossible to live outside of ideology, there is a pressing need to uncover ideology's rules of formation, its relation to necessity, to the politics of resistance, and to the manufacture of needs and desires. Ideology in this case is defined in the broader productive sense as a mobilization of meaning whose effects can be seen in the manner in which individuals sort through the contradictions and complexities of everyday life. Ideology is not merely an imposition that ties people to an imaginary relationship with the real world; it is an actively constructed and *fundamentally lived form of experience* connected to the ways in which meaning and power intersect in the social world. Ideology is conveyed by images, gestures, and linguistic expressions, related not only to how and what one thinks but also to how and what one feels and desires. Ideology is, in this view, involved in the production and self-generation of subjectivities within the private and public domains of everyday life. It is also central to understanding how fleeting the "subject" as the ground of agency actually is but at the same time offers the principal hope of creating a discourse in which individuals can act with conviction and political purpose.[7] Consequently, teachers need to discover in their students how meaning is actively constructed through the multiple formations of lived experience that give their lives a sense of hope and possibility.

Giroux argues that students should learn to understand the transformative possibilities of experience. In order to enhance this possibility, teachers must make classroom knowledge *relevant* to the lives of their students so that the students have a voice, that is, affirm student experience as part of the pedagogical encounter by providing curriculum content and pedagogical practices which resonate with the life experiences of the students. It is also important, in Giroux's view, that teachers go beyond making experience relevant to students by also making it *problematic and critical,* by interrogating such experience for its hidden assumptions. Critical direction is necessary to help students recognize the political and moral implications of their own experiences. Thus, teachers need to develop a pedagogical approach in which student experiences and actions will not be unqualifiedly endorsed at the expense of enabling students to recognize in their daily interactions with others undesirable instances of behavior such as racism and sexism. And finally, Giroux maintains that teachers ultimately must make knowledge and experience *emancipatory* by enabling students to develop a social imagination and civic courage capable of helping them to intervene in their own self-formation, in the formation of others, and in the socially reproductive cycle of life in general.

Education Under Siege, a work which Giroux co-authored with Stanley Aronowitz, first invoked the concept of schools as democratic public spheres.[8] Democratic public spheres encompass public networks such as schools, political organizations, churches, and social movements that help construct democratic principles and social practices through debate, dialogue, and exchange of opinion. While Giroux had already begun to develop this concept in the last chapter of *Theory and Resistance* (Aronowitz had also developed it in a previous work, *The Crisis in Historical Materialism*[9]), it now took on a marked importance. Democracy is a notoriously contested and admittedly complex concept, and Giroux's use of it altered slightly depending on the context. Generally speaking, democracy is defined at the level of social formations, political communities, and social practices which are regulated by principles of social justice, equality, and diversity. According to Giroux, schools play a significant role in establishing local democracy, but work best in collaboration with other democratic public spheres in the larger struggle for democracy at the state and federal levels of government. The first task of transforming schools into democratic public spheres becomes, for Giroux, one of developing a public language for educators—a critical vernacular of sorts—that will allow teachers and students to reconstruct public life in the interests of collective struggle and social justice. On the issue of language, Giroux is quite clear: Language is not merely an instrument that reflects social reality "out there" but also is partly constitutive of what in our society is considered "real."

Education Under Siege marks the point at which Giroux begins selectively to appropriate some of the theoretical advances of the French philosopher Michel Foucault, especially his concept of power/knowledge, a concept that would prove to be one of the central axes in some of Giroux's later work. The concept of power/knowledge is instrumental in Giroux's formulation of the role that teachers should play as critically engaged intellectuals. Knowledge can no longer be seen as objective, but has to be understood as part of the power relations that not only produce it but also those that benefit from it. Every form of knowledge can be located within specific power relations; as time passes certain forms of knowledge are transformed by ruling groups into "regimes of truth." According to Giroux, an essential step in helping teachers challenge existing "regimes of truth," especially as they influence curricular and pedagogical issues, can be best achieved if teachers assume the role of transformative intellectuals, who deliberately undertake socially transformative practice as against the exercise, under the guise of political neutrality, of arcane intelligence or specialized knowledge. In fact, Giroux is careful to sever the term "intellectual" from its traditional usage and its lingering notions of elitism, eccentricity, and manipulation of ideas. Quite clearly, the teacher as transformative intellectual must be committed to the following: teaching as an emancipatory practice; the creation of schools as democratic public spheres; the restoration of a community of shared progressive values; and the fostering of a common public discourse linked to the democratic imperatives of equality and social justice. Unlike hegemonic or accommodating intellectuals, whose labor is at the behest of those in power and whose critical insight remains in the service of the status quo, transformative intellectuals take seriously the primacy of ethics and politics in their critical engagement with students, administrators, and the surrounding community. They work relentlessly, dedicated to furthering democracy and enhancing the quality of human life.

One insight into Giroux's work can be taken from his view of scholarly writing. Giroux rejects the notion that critical scholarship should be objective or nonpartisan, a task he believes is both impossible and undesirable. That Giroux considers his own writings to be part of an ongoing political project reflects his longstanding efforts to link critical scholarship to broader forms of oppositional struggle. In Giroux's judgment, the social conscience of the scholar too often is supplanted by the will to power, the desire for security within the academy, personal success, and recognition. Scholarly research is thus compromised as it becomes assimilated into the status quo of the discipline, is written more and more for one's peers rather than the general public, and is judged according to the empirical rigor of its arguments and the (misplaced) concept of scientific neutrality. Consequently, Giroux refuses to discriminate between his responsibility as a public intellectual and his role as a university professor.

What is particularly striking about Giroux's work is that it inevitably remains unfettered by the rigid parameters of doctrinaire certainty. His refusal to allow his work to become indebted to any orthodoxy has granted him much theoretical flexibility and increased rigor; moreover, his efforts at cross-fertilizing ideas from a number of theoretical domains have promoted a continual refinement of his intellectual and political interests, leading to a fresh, integrated viewpoint. Giroux's ability to fuse the horizons of past and present theories with each other and with the horizon of his own perspective can be seen in his recent critical engagement with the works of John Dewey, George Counts, and C. Wright Mills, as well as with selected works drawn from feminist theory and liberation theology.

Today it is especially difficult to locate Giroux's work within any one school of thought since he rarely passes over the same conceptual terrain twice without deconstructing its boundaries and bringing to it a new and rich subtlety of insight.[10] Not interested in seeking ideal fathers in Marx, Gramsci, Foucault, or others, Giroux remains on the move. What has given his work such resiliency, from his earliest to his most recent writing, perhaps has been his continual effort to give pride of place to the dialectical nature of social life, more specifically to the mutually informing interaction of structure and agency, language and desire, and critique and hope.

Giroux's writings continue to bear the imprint of his deepest concerns and commitments. Most recently he has attempted to refine further his notion of schooling as a form of cultural politics, particularly with respect to the issue of pedagogy and student voice. He recognizes that pedagogy is fundamentally a political and ethical practice as well as a socially and historically situated construction; that it does not restrict itself to classrooms; that it is involved whenever there exist deliberative attempts to influence the production and construction of meaning or how and what knowledge and social identities are produced within and among particular sets of social relations.[11] Pedagogy is not only about teaching practices but also involves a recognition of the cultural politics such practices support.[12] That pedagogy is implicated in the social construction of knowledge and experience confirms for Giroux that a pedagogy of possibility is truly possible, for if the world of self and others has been socially constructed, it can likewise be dismantled, undone, and critically remade.

A critical pedagogy recognizes the contradictions which exist between the openness of human capacities that we encourage in a democratic society and the cultural forms that are provided and within which we live our lives.[13] Pedagogy never ceases so long as tensions and contradictions exist between what is and what ought to be. Few writers have been as constant as Giroux in arguing that educators need to articulate their purpose clearly, to set the goals, and to define the terms of public schooling as part of a wider democratic project. At the same time, Giroux is aware that the quest for self and social transformation must not seek out truth as an absolute category but as a situational and relational one. A pedagogy of liberation has no final answers. It is always in the making.

The writings that constitute this volume carry the trademark of much of Giroux's work. They are filled with prescient passages designed to promote the development of practical learning with an emancipatory intent. Examples from Giroux's earlier period retain much of their theoretical relevance today. The fact that Giroux has not banished some inconsistencies in no way diminishes their important challenge for teachers and researchers attempting to understand the complex interconnections among teaching, the construction of identity, the development of democratic social relations, and the challenge of social transformation. These chapters allow the reader to perceive Giroux's work as a set of historical practices; they portray a constant development of, and engagement with, various aspects of critical educational thought. Furthermore, they reveal both the structuring principles of Giroux's earlier work and his ongoing attempt to rethink in a more critical and dialectical fashion the theoretical basis and political project that inform his work.

In the final analysis, Giroux's work may be said to constitute a pedagogy of the concrete, in which what can be is already sown in the seeds of what is—in what is actual and real. Such a pedagogy attempts, in Jessica Benjamin's words, to "bring politics into the field of immanence."[14] Ultimately, it represents a concerted attempt *not* to exalt the abstract, universal principle over the individual concrete particularity of need.[15] It is a pedagogy which recognizes all regimes of truth to be temporary strategies of containment. The point, Giroux reminds us, is to purge what is considered truth of its oppressive and undemocratic effects. In a world such as ours, one which is decidedly hostile to the future, such a project of possibility is at odds with the standard referent by which most educators judge theoretical work: Will it enable *practice* in the classroom? The answer, of course, will depend on what is meant by practice. If what we mean by practice refers to a "cookbook" of "how to's," then the answer is a resounding "No." To understand practice in these terms is to be at the mercy of a domesticating discourse which establishes a false dichotomy between theory and practice, effectively collapsing its dialectical relation. Such a logic assumes that judgments of what educational practice should be are internal to the practicality of classroom work itself, thus undervaluing the transformative potential of pedagogy in favor of instrumental procedures that work regardless of their effects.[16] If, on the other hand, we mean practice to refer to a daily engagement in a more empowering language by which to think and act critically in the struggle for democratic social relations and human freedom, then "Yes," Giroux's work offers us the opportunity to effect a concrete, practical, transformation of our teaching. To assist educators in making such a distinction between instrumental practice and empowering practice is, of course, one of the purposes of this book.

Giroux continues to provide an important service to educators because he speaks directly to the problems and issues facing the future of our schools and our society at large. He raises questions that challenge the role schools have played—and continue to play—in furthering our nation's historical legacy of creating a just and democractic society for all. Giroux recognizes that if we ask history no questions it will remain silent. And it is under the cover of such a silence that history can be revisited with the injustices and inhumanity that have, in the past, placed the world in so much peril. Giroux's success at confronting history's structured silences and developing a new vision of a society grounded in hope and liberating struggle has made him one of the most challenging and significant theorists of education on the present scene, and certainly one of the most prolific and perceptive analysts of schooling writing today.

ACKNOWLEDGMENTS

When my friend and colleague, Peter McLaren, first suggested that I undertake the project that eventually became this book, I was hesistant. I had doubts about including early articles which I felt did not reflect adequately the comprehensiveness or theoretical interests of my current work, especially my recent writings on ethics, popular culture, and public philosophy. Despite my initial reservations, I decided to publish this collection of essays for a number of practical and political reasons.

On the practical side, for a number of years I have been receiving letters from public school teachers requesting many of the aricles that are collected in this book. Surprisingly, many of the teachers who have reacted to my work with respect to their own teaching have found my earlier work to be especially useful for their own development as critical educators and public intellectuals. This book is, in part, a response to these reactions and represents and attempt to further contribute to the public culture of the many teachers who exhibit on a daily basis in their classrooms the courage, dignity, and vision necessary to make a difference in the lives of their students. For them I have attempted to put together those essays that provide theoretically concrete and pedagogically practical insights for improving the daily task of teaching itself.

On the political side, it became increasingly important for me to demonstrate through my own work how a critical discourse about schooling is constructed historically. The language of education is not merely theroretical or practical, it is also relational and has to be understood in its genesis and development as part of a wider network of historical and contemporary traditions so that we can become self-conscious about the principles and social practices that give it meaning. The sense of where our language comes from, how it is sustained, and how it functions to name and construct particular experiences and social forms is a central aspect of the project of critical theory. This book demonstrates that principle by reflecting the theoretical evolution of my own work as a particular form of cultural politics. In doing so, I hope to provide the reader with an opportunity to analyze the different theoretical and political junctures which constitute one particular journey through the ideological mine field of contemporary schooling.

In retrospect, many of my earlier essays are marked by an overemphasis on the discourse of domination and reproduction. Similarly, there is a failure to analyze adequately issues related to the organization of experience, subjectivity, gender, and racially related forms of oppression, not to mention the broader issues of public philosophy and ethics. Yet there is much in them that I consider to be valuable, both theoretically and politically, for teachers. At the same time, when juxtaposed with my more recent essays, it becomes clear that no theoretical project is ever finished and that each essay has to be read anew for the insights it may provide at the present time. The chapters in this book make possible an opportunity for not only examining the historical evolution of a particular discourse, but also for exercising as teachers the dialectic of re-reading and re-appropriating elements of a body of work that resonates with contemporary concerns. Such an endeavor will, I hope, provide some critical signposts for both rexamining the work of teachers and, where necessary, transforming it in the interest of constructing both a more critical pedagogy and a more humane world.

A few special people have provided me with a great deal of support and encouragement in the writing and rewriting of this book. I am greatly indebted to Peter McLaren, who presented a convincing case for a retrospective look at my work. His argument was that some of my earlier writings would not only provide educators with an historical introduction to the theory and practice of critical pedagogy, it would also be helpful for those readers interested in pursuing more recent theoretical advances in the field. I am also warmly indebted to my friend and publisher, Jim Bergin, who has provided support from the very beginning of this project. My wife, Jeanne Brady, has once again generously provided me with encouragement and political insight. Stanley Aronowitz, Donaldo Macedo, Candy Mitchell, Richard Quantz, Ralph Page, Roger Simon, and Jim Giarelli always pushed me further to clarify issues central to my work. This book has also benefitted from the many teachers and students I have had the pleasure of working with in my classes, in correspondence, and in workshops and public discussions. Of course, I am solely responsible for the limitations of the work collected in this book.

I am indebted to the editors of the following journals for allowing me to publish in slightly modified or unaltered forms the following articles: Henry A. Giroux, "Teachers as Transformative Intellectuals," reprinted from *Social Education* with permission of the National Council for the Social Studies; Henry A. Giroux, "Crisis and Possibilities in Education," *Issues in Education* 11 (Summer 1984): 376–79, Copyright 1984, American Educational Research Association, Washington, D. C.; Henry A. Giroux and Anthony N. Penna, "Social Education in the Classroom: The Dynamics of the Hidden Curriculum," *Theory and Research in Social Education* 7 (Spring 1979): 21–42; Henry A. Giroux, "Toward a New Sociology of Curriculum," *Educational Leadership* (December 1979): 248–53, Reprinted with permission of the Association for Supervision and Curriculum Development and Henry A. Giroux, Copyright © 1979 by the Association for Supervision and Curriculum Development, All rights reserved; Henry A. Giroux, "Rethinking the Language of Schooling," *Language Arts* 61 (January 1984): 33–40, Reprinted with Permission from the National Council of Teachers of English; Henry A. Giroux, "Writing and Critical Thinking in the Social Studies," *Curriculum Inquiry* 8 (1978): 291–310; and Henry A. Giroux and Peter McLaren, "Reproducing Reproduction," *Metropolitan Review* 1 (Spring 1986): 108–18. Some of the chapters in this book appeared in substantially altered forms in the following journals: *Boston University Journal of Education, Dalhousie Review, The Review of Education, Interchange, Telos, Philosophy and Social Criticism, New Education,* and *Educational Forum.*

Editor's Introduction

By PAULO FREIRE

Henry Giroux is a thinker, as well as an excellent professor. This, in itself, would be sufficient enough to influence positively the numerous students who come into contact with his powerful critical discourse each semester. This affirmation may suggest, to someone who is less critical, the possibility that one could be an excellent professor, or simply a professor, without having to think profoundly about the relationship that the object of his or her teaching has with other objects. In fact, this is not possible. It is not viable to write or talk about contexts or themes, or to teach them in isolation, without seriously taking into account those cultural, social, and political forces that shape them.

More than his epistemological posture, which requires that we avoid the ingenuous mode of interaction with the object, what characterizes Giroux as a superb theorist is his insistence that we understand the complex relationships among objects. What characterizes him as a superb writer is his esthetically pleasing style, which keeps the reader attentive by the many brilliant metaphors that capture the essence of the context and content of the themes about which he writes. This epistemological posture, together with his agility and talent for language, mark Giroux as an intellectual who, by making thinking a precondition of existence, becomes a great thinker. We all think, but we are not necessarily thinkers.

Giroux's creativity, his openness to questions, his curiosity, his doubt, his uncertainty with respect to certainties, his courage to take risks, and his rigorous methodological and theoretical approaches to important themes characterize him as one of the great thinkers of his time not only in the United States, but also in many foreign countries where he is widely and critically read and where the force and clarity of his thinking have contributed to the shaping of current philosophical and educational discourse.

What I would like to highlight about Giroux and his total understanding of the world and its process of transformation is his view of history as a possibility. For Giroux there is no hope without a future to be made, to be built, to be shaped. For Giroux, history as possibility means that tomorrow is not something that necessarily will happen, nor is it a pure repetition of today with its face superficially touched up so it can continue to be the same. Giroux's comprehension of history as possibility recognizes the unquestionable role of subjectivity in the process of knowing. This mode of comprehension, in turn, characterizes his critical and optimistic way of understanding education.

To the extent that I understand history as possibility, I recognize:

1. That subjectivity has to play an important role in the process of transformation;

2. That education becomes relevant to the extent that this role of subjectivity is understood to be a necessary historical and political task; and

3. That education loses meaning if it is not understood, as all practices are, as being subject to limitations. If education could do everything there would be no reason to speak about its limitations. If education could not do anything, there would still be no reason to talk about its limitations.

History as possibility means our refusal to accept dogma as well as our refusal to accept the domestication of time. Men and women make the history that is possible, not the history that they would like to make or the history that sometimes they are told should be made.

It is not possible to deny the force with which Giroux speaks to us, nor the force with which he directs us to a renewed hope, even when his analysis may sadden us. In this new book, Henry Giroux once again challenges us with his critical and brilliant theoretical discussion of trends that constitute the bedrock for both the understanding and the advancement of the present discourse in education.

Introduction:
Teachers as Intellectuals

Critical Educational Theory and the
Language of Critique

Radical pedagogy emerged in full strength as part of the new sociology of education in England and the United States over a decade ago as a critical response to what can be loosely termed the ideology of traditional educational practice.[1] Preoccupied with the imperative to challenge the dominant assumption that schools are the major mechanism for the development of a democratic and egalitarian social order, critical educational theory set itself the task of uncovering how domination and oppression are produced within the various mechanisms of schooling. Rather than accept the notion that schools are vehicles of democracy and social mobility, educational critics make such an assumption problematic. In doing so, their major ideological and political task is to unravel how schools reproduce the logic of capital through the ideological and material forms of privilege and domination that structure the lives of students from various class, gender, and ethnic groupings.

Radical critics, for the most part, agree that educational traditionalists generally refused to interrogate the political nature of public schooling. In fact, traditionalists entirely eluded the issue through the paradoxical attempt of depoliticizing the language of schooling while reproducing and legitimating capitalist ideologies. The most obvious expression of this approach can be seen in the positivist discourse that defined and still defines mainstream educational research and policy and which takes as its most important concerns the mastery of pedagogical techniques and the transmission of knowledge instrumental to the existing society.[2] In the world view of the traditionalists, schools are merely instructional sites. That schools are also cultural and political sites is ignored, as is the notion that they represent areas of accommodation and contestation among differentially empowered cultural and economic groups. From the perspective of critical educational theory, traditionalists suppress important questions regarding the relations among knowledge, power, and domination.

Out of this analysis emerged a new theoretical language and mode of criticism which argues that schools do not provide opportunities in the broad Western humanist tradition for self and social empowerment in the society at large. In opposition to the traditionalist position, leftist critics provide theoretical arguments and empirical evidence to suggest that schools are, in fact, agencies of social, economic, and cultural reproduction.[3] At best, public schooling offers limited individual mobility to members of the working class and other oppressed groups, but it is a powerful instrument for the reproduction of capitalist relations of production and the dominant legitimating ideologies of ruling groups.

Radical critics of education provide a variety of useful models of analysis and research to challenge traditional educational ideology. Against the conservative claim that schools transmit objective knowledge, radical critics developed theories of the hidden curriculum as well as theories of ideology that identify the specific interests underlying different knowledge forms.[4] Rather than viewing school knowledge as objective, as something to be merely transmitted to students, radical theorists argue that school knowledge is a particular representation of dominant culture, a privileged discourse that is constructed through a selective process of emphases and exclusions.[5] Against the claim that schools are only instructional sites, radical critics point to the transmission and reproduction of a dominant culture in schools. Far from being neutral, the dominant culture in the school is characterized by a selective ordering and legitimating of privileged language forms, modes of reasoning, social relations, and lived experiences. In this view, culture is linked to power and to the imposition of a specific set of ruling class codes and experiences.[6] But school culture, it is claimed, functions not only to confirm and privilege students from the dominant classes, but also through exclusion and insult to disconfirm the histories, experiences, and dreams of subordinate groups. Finally, against the claim by traditional educators that schools are apolitical, radical educators illuminate the ways in which the State, through its selective grants, certification policies, and legal powers, influences school practice in the interest of particular dominant ideologies.[7]

Despite its insightful theoretical and political analyses of schooling, radical educational theory suffers from some serious flaws, the most serious being its failure to move beyond the language of critique and domination. That is, radical educators remain mired in a language that links schools primarily to the ideologies and practices of domination or to the narrow parameters of the discourse of political economy. In this view, schools are seen almost exclusively as agencies of social reproduction, producing obedient workers for industrial capital; school knowledge is generally dismissed as a form of bourgeois ideology; and teachers are often portrayed as being trapped in an apparatus of domination that works with all the certainty of a Swiss watch. The tragedy of this position has been that it prevents left educators from developing a programmatic language for either pedagogical or school reform. Within this type of analysis there is little understanding of the contradictions, spaces, and tensions that characterize schooling. There is little possibility for developing a programmatic language either for a critical pedagogy or for institutional and community struggle. Radical educators have focused on the language of domination to such a degree that it undercuts any viable hope for developing a progressive, political educational strategy.

But critical theorists, with few exceptions, have done more than misrepresent the contradictory nature of schools, they have also retreated from the political necessity of challenging the conservative attempt to fashion ideological support for their vision of public education. Consequently, conservatives have adroitly exploited public fears about schools in a manner that has gone almost uncontested by radical educators. Conservatives have not only dominated the debate about the nature and purpose of public schooling, they have also increasingly set the terms around which policy recommendations have been developed and implemented, locally and nationally.

In effect, radical educators have undercut the opportunity both to challenge the conservative attack on schools and the current ways in which schools reproduce deep-seated inequalities and to reconstruct a discourse in which teacher work can be defined through the categories of democracy, empowerment, and possibility. For radical pedagogy to become a viable political project, it has to develop a discourse that combines the language of critique with the language of possibility. In doing so, it has to provide analyses that reveal the opportunities for democratic struggles and reforms within the day-to-day workings of schools. Similarly, it has to provide the theoretical basis for teachers and others to view and experience the nature of teacher work in a critical and potentially transformative way. Two elements of such a discourse that I think are important are the definition of schools as democratic public spheres and the definition of teachers as transformative intellectuals. While these categories are taken up in depth in the rest of the book, I will sketch some of their broader implications and the practices they suggest.

Schooling, the Public Sphere, and Transformative Intellectuals

Any attempt to reformulate the role of educators has to begin with the broader question of how to view the purpose of schooling. I believe that central to a realizable critical pedagogy is the need to view schools as democratic public spheres. This means regarding schools as democratic sites dedicated to forms of self and social empowerment. In these terms, schools are public places where students learn the knowledge and skills necessary to live in an authentic democracy. Instead of defining schools as extensions of the workplace or as front-line institutions in the battle of international markets and foreign competition, schools as democratic public spheres are constructed around forms of critical inquiry that dignify meaningful dialogue and human agency. Students learn the discourse of public association and social responsibility. Such a discourse seeks to recapture the idea of critical democracy as a social movement that supports individual freedom and social justice. Moreover, viewing schools as democratic public spheres provides a rational for defending them along with progressive forms of pedagogy and teacher work as essential institutions and practices in the performance of an important public service. Schools are now defended in a political language as institutions that provide the ideological and material conditions necessary to educate a citizenry in the dynamics of critical literacy and civic courage, and these constitute the basis for functioning as active citizens in a democratic society.

This position owes a great deal to John Dewey's views on democracy, but it goes beyond his position in a number of ways, and these are worth mentioning. I use the term discourse of democracy as both a referent for critique and as ideal grounded in a dialectical notion of the school-society relationship. As a referent for critique, the theory and practice of democracy provides a model for analyzing how schools block the ideological and material dimensions of democracy. For instance, it interrogates the ways in which the discourse of domination manifests itself in forms of knowledge, school organization, teacher ideologies, and teacher-student relationships. Furthermore, inherent in the discourse of democracy is the understanding that schools are contradictory sites; they reproduce the larger society while containing spaces to resist its dominating logic. As an ideal, the discourse of democracy suggest something more programatic and radical. First, it points to the role that teachers and administrators might play as transformative intellectuals who develop counterhegemonic pedagogies that not only empower students by giving them the knowledge and social skills they will need to be able to function in the larger society as critical agents, but also educate them for transformative action. That means educating them to take risks, to struggle for institutional change, and to fight both *against* oppression and *for* democracy outside of schools in other oppositional public spheres and the wider social arena. So, in effect, my view of democracy points to a dual struggle. In the first instance, I accentuate the notion of pedagogical empowerment and in doing so point to the organization, development, and implementation of forms of knowledge and social practices within schools. In the second, I accentuate the notion of pedagogical transformation in which I argue that both teachers and students must be educated to struggle against forms of oppression in the wider society and that schools only represent one important site in such a struggle. This is very different from Dewey's view, because I see democracy as involving not only a pedagogical struggle but also a political and social struggle, one that acknowledges that a critical pedagogy is but one important intervention in the struggle to restructure the ideological and material conditions of the wider society in the interest of creating a truly democratic society.[8]

There is another important and related issue at work in defining schools as democratic public spheres, one that I stress throughout this book. By politicizing the notion of schooling, it becomes possible to illuminate the role that educators and educational researchers play as intellectuals who operate under specific conditions of work and who perform a particular social and political function. The material conditions under which teachers work constitute the basis for either delimiting or empowering their practices as intellectuals. Therefore, teachers as intellectuals will need to reconsider and, possibly, transform the fundamental nature of the conditions under which they work. That is, teachers must be able to shape the ways in which time, space, activity, and knowledge organize everyday life in schools. More specifically, in order to function as intellectuals, teachers must create the ideology and structural conditions necessary for them to write, research, and work with each other in producing curricula and sharing power. In the final analysis, teachers need to develop a discourse and set of assumptions that allow them to function more specifically as transformative intellectuals.[9] As intellectuals, they will combine reflection and action in the interest of empowering students with the skills and knowledge needed to address injustices and to be critical actors committed to developing a world free of oppression and exploitation. Such intellectuals are not merely concerned with promoting individual achievement or advancing students along career ladders, they are concerned with empowering students so they can read the world critically and change it when necessary.

Before I address the specifics of what it means to critically appropriate the concept of transformative intellectual as part of a wider discourse that views radical pedagogy as part of a form of cultural politics, I want to elaborate on some of the concerns that are central to an ontological grounding for what it means to make the pedagogical a form of radical praxis.

There are a number of important concepts that have methodological implications for teachers and researchers who assume the role of a transformative intellectual. The most important referent for such a position is "liberating memory"—the recognition of those instances of public and private suffering whose causes and manifestations require understanding and compassion. Critical educators should begin with those manifestations of suffering that constitute past and immediate conditions of oppression. Uncovering the horror of past suffering and the dignity and solidarity of resistance alerts us to the historical conditions that construct such experiences. This notion of liberating memory does more than recover dangerous instances of the past, it also focuses on the subject of suffering and the reality of those treated as "the other." Then we can begin to understand the reality of human existence and the need for all members of a democratic society to transform existing social conditions so as to eliminate such suffering in the present.[10] Liberating memory points to the role that intellectuals might play as part of a pedagogical web of solidarity designed to keep alive the historical and existential fact of suffering by uncovering and analyzing those forms of historical and popular knowledge that have been suppressed or ignored and through which we once again discover the "ruptural effects of conflict and struggle."[11] Liberating memory represents a declaration, a hope, a discursive reminder that people do not only suffer under the mechanisms of domination, they also resist. Moreover, such resistance is always linked to forms of knowledge and understanding that are the preconditions for saying both a "No" to repression and a "Yes" to the dynamics of struggle and the practical possibilities to which it addresses itself.

There is another important dialectical element that constructs the notion of liberating memory. It "remembers" power as a positive force in the determination of alternatives and counterhegemonic truths. It is a notion of historical remembrance that sustains the memory of social movements that not only resist but also transform in their own interests what it means to develop communities around an alternative horizon of human possibilities. It is, simply, to develop a better way of life.

It is also essential that transformative intellectuals redefine cultural politics with regard to the issue of knowledge, particularly with respect to the construction of classroom pedagogy and student voice. For transformative intellectuals, radical pedagogy as a form of cultural politics has to be understood as a concrete set of practices that produces social forms through which different types of knowledge, sets of experience, and subjectivities are constructed. Put another way, transformative intellectuals need to understand how subjectivities are produced and regulated through historically produced social forms and how these forms carry and embody particular interests.[12] At the core of this position is the need to develop modes of inquiry that not only investigate how experience is shaped, lived, and endured within particular social forms such as schools, but also how certain apparatuses of power produce forms of knowledge that legitimate a particular kind of truth and way of life. Power in this sense has a broader meaning in its connection with knowledge than is generally recognized. Power in this instance, as Foucault points out, not only produces knowledge that distorts reality but also produces a particular version of the "truth."[13] In other words, "Power is not merely mystifying or distorting. Its most dangerous impact is its positive relation to truth, the effects of truth that it produces."[14]

The chapters in this book offer a range of perspectives which have been forged over the past few years. The topics range from literacy to writing classroom objectives to the work of liberation theologians. Yet contained within this wide range are common themes that speak to reconceiving schools as democratic public spheres where both teachers and students work together to forge a new emancipatory vision of community and society. Also in this book are attempts to develop a new language and new categories with which to situate the analysis of schooling. While many of the categories have been selectively appropriated from the sociology of knowledge, theology, cultural studies, and other traditions, they offer educators a unique opportunity for reflecting critically on their own practices and the relationship between schools and the wider society.

I am providing not a recipe so much as I am acknowledging that any discourse, including my own, needs to be engaged critically and selectively so that it can be used within specific contexts by those who see value in it for their own classroom teaching and social struggle. What is at work in this book is a particular way of seeing, a critical discourse that is unfinished, but it is one that may illuminate the specifics of oppression and the possibilities for democratic struggle and renewal.

1

Rethinking the Language of Schooling

By HENRY A. GIROUX

In the current political climate, there is little talk about schools and democracy and a great deal of debate about how schools might become more successful in meeting industrial needs and contributing to economic productivity. Against a landscape of shrinking economic resources, the breakup of liberal and radical public school coalitions, and the erosion of civil rights, the public debate about the nature of schooling has been replaced by the concerns and interests of management experts. That is, amidst the growing failures and disruptions in both American society and in the public schools, a set of concerns and problems has emerged conjured up in terms like "input-output," "predictability," and "cost-effectiveness."

Unfortunately, at a time when we need a different language of analysis to understand the structure and meaning of schooling, Americans have retreated back into the discourse of management and administration, with its focus on issues of efficiency and control. These issues have overshadowed concerns regarding understanding. Similarly, the need to develop at all levels of schooling a radical pedagogy concerned with critical literacy and active citizenship has given way to a conservative pedagogy that emphasizes technique and passivity. The stress is no longer on helping students to "read" the world critically; instead, it is on helping students to "master" the tools of reading. The question of how teachers, administrators, and students produce meaning, and whose interest it serves, is subsumed under the imperative to master the "facts." The script is grim.

These issues raise fundamental questions about how educators and schools contribute to these problems, yet they simultaneously point to the possibility of developing modes of language, thinking, and teaching that may be used to overcome them, or at least help to establish the conditions that may be used to resolve them. I want to pursue this issue by examining a central concern: how can we make schooling meaningful so as to make it critical and how can we make it critical so as to make it emancipatory?

Theory and Language

I want to analyze this question and the ways in which "traditional" views of schooling have responded to it. The precondition for such an analysis is the need for a new theoretical framework and mode of language that will enable teachers, parents, and others to understand both the limits and the enabling possibilities that characterize schools. Currently, traditional language about schooling is anchored in a rather mechanical and limited worldview. Essentially, it is a worldview borrowed primarily from the discourse of behavioristic learning psychology, which focuses on the best way to learn a *given* body of knowledge, and from the logic of scientific management, as reflected in the back-to-basics movement, competency testing, and systems management schemes. The result has been a language that prevents educators from critically examining the ideological assumptions embedded in their own language and the schooling experiences that they help to structure.

Generally speaking, the notion of language is evaluated according to whether it is simple or complex, clear or vague, concrete or abstract. However, this analysis falls prey to a theoretical error; it reduces language to a technical issue, i.e., the issue of clarity. But the real meaning of educational language has to be understood as the product of a specific theoretical framework, via the assumptions that govern it, and, finally, through the social, political, and ideological relations to which it points and which it legitimates. In other words, the issue of clarity often becomes a mask that downplays questions about values and interests while applauding ideas that are well packaged in the language of simplicity. Any educational theory that is to be critical and emancipatory, that is to function in the interests of critical understanding and self-determining action, must generate a discourse that moves beyond the established language of administration and conformity. Such a discourse requires a struggle and a commitment in order to be appropriated and understood. The way language can mystify and hide its own assumptions becomes clear, for instance, in the way educators often label students who respond to alienating and oppressive school experiences with a whole range of resistant behaviors. They call such students deviant rather than resistant, for such a label would raise different questions about the nature of schooling and the reasons for such student behavior.

Generating a New Discourse

Implicit in my analysis is the need to construct a new discourse and mode of analysis about the nature of schooling that would serve a dual purpose. On the one hand, it should analyze and indict the shortcomings and failures inherent in traditional views of schooling. On the other hand, it should reveal new possibilities for thinking about and organizing school experiences. In order to explore the possibilities for reorganization, I want to focus specifically on the following concepts: rationality, problematic, ideology, and cultural capital.

Rationality

The notion of rationality has a dual meaning. First, it refers to the set of assumptions and practices that allows people to understand and shape their own and others' experiences. Second, it refers to the interests that define and qualify how one frames and engages problems confronted in lived experience. For instance, interests exhibited in teacher talk and behavior may be rooted in the need to control, to explain, or to act from principles of justice. Rationality, as a critical construct, can also be applied to classroom materials such as curriculum packages, films. Such materials always embody a set of assumptions about the world, a given subject, and a set of interests. This becomes evident in many of the "teacher proof" instructional materials now flooding the market. These materials promote a deskilling of teachers by separating conception from execution and by reducing the role that teachers play in the actual creation and teaching of such materials. Teacher decisions about what should be taught, how it might meet the intellectual and cultural needs of students, and how it might be evaluated are rendered unimportant in these packages, since they have already predefined and answered such questions. The materials control teachers' decisions, and, as a result, teachers do not need to exercise reasoned judgment. Thus, teachers are reduced to the role of obedient technicians, carrying out the dictates of the curriculum package. Needless to say, teachers may ignore such packages, may use them for different purposes, or may fight their use in the schools. But the real issue is understanding the interests embedded in such curriculum packages and how such interests structure classroom experiences. The language of efficiency and control promotes obedience rather than critique.

Problematic

All modes of rationality contain conceptual structures identified both by the questions raised and questions ignored. These are called problematics. Problematics refer not only to what is included in a worldview, but also, to what is left out and silenced. That which is not said is as important as that which is said. The value of this concept becomes more obvious when one remembers that traditional educational theory has always been wedded to the visible, to the literal, and to what can be seen and operationalized. Educational theory has usually not included a language or mode of analysis that looks beyond the given or the phenomenal. For instance, traditional concerns of educators center around the formal curriculum, and, as a result, the issues that emerge are familiar ones: what subjects are going to be taught? what forms of instruction will be used? what kinds of objectives will be developed? and how can we match the objectives with corresponding forms of evaluation? As important as these concerns are, they dance on the surface of reality. They do not include a focus on the nature and function of the hidden curriculum, that is, those messages and values that are conveyed to students silently through the selection of specific forms of knowledge, the use of specific classroom relations, and the defining characteristics of the school organizational structure. Sexist, racist, and class-specific messages that stalk behind the language of objectives and school discipline are conveniently ignored.

Ideology

Ideology, as I use the term, is a dynamic construct that refers to the ways in which meanings are produced, mediated, and embodied in knowledge forms, social practices, and cultural experiences. In this case, ideology is a set of doctrines as well as a medium through which teachers and educators make sense of their own experiences and those of the world in which they find themselves. As a pedagogical tool, ideology becomes useful for understanding not only how schools sustain and produce meanings, but also how individuals and groups produce, negotiate, modify, or resist them. For instance, an understanding of how ideology works presents teachers with a heuristic tool to examine how their own views about knowledge, human nature, values, and society are mediated through the "common sense" assumptions they use to structure classroom experiences. Assumptions about learning, achievement, teacher-student relations, objectivity, school authority, etc., need to be evaluated critically by educators.

Cultural Capital

Just as a country distributes goods and services, what can be labeled as material capital, it also distributes and legitimates certain forms of knowledge, language practices, values, modes of style, and so forth, or what can be labeled as cultural capital. One must only consider what gets labeled as high status knowledge in the schools and universities and, thus, provide legitimacy to certain forms of knowledge and social practices. Currently, the fine arts, the social science disciplines, and classical languages are not considered as legitimate as those bodies of knowledge found in the natural sciences or those methods of inquiry associated with the areas of business and management. These decisions are arbitrary and are based on certain values and questions of power and control, not to mention a certain view of the nature of society and the future. The concept of cultural capital also represents certain ways of talking, acting, moving, dressing, and socializing that are institutionalized by schools. Schools are not merely instructional sites but also sites where the culture of the dominant society is learned and where students experience the difference between those status and class distinctions that exist in the larger society.

Traditional Schooling

The rationality that dominates traditional views of schooling and curriculum is rooted in the narrow concerns for effectiveness, behavioral objectives, and principles of learning that treat knowledge as something to be consumed and schools as merely instructional sites designed to pass onto students a "common" culture and set of skills that will enable them to operate effectively in the wider society. Steeped in the logic of technical rationality, the problematic of traditional curriculum theory and schooling centers on questions about the most thorough or most efficient ways to learn specific kinds of knowledge, to create moral consensus, and to provide modes of schooling that reproduce the existing society. For instance, traditional educators may ask *how* the school should seek to attain a certain predefined goal, but they rarely ask *why* such a goal might be beneficial to some socioeconomic groups and not to others, or *why* schools, as they are presently organized, tend to block the possibility that specific classes will attain a measure of economic and political autonomy.

The ideology that guides the present rationality of the school is relatively conservative: it is primarily concerned with how-to questions and does not question relationships between knowledge and power or between culture and politics. In other words, questions concerning the role of school as an agency of social and cultural reproduction in a class-divided society are ignored, as are questions that illuminate the intersubjective basis of establishing meaning, knowledge, and what are considered legitimate social relationships. The issue of how teachers, students, and representatives from the wider society generate meaning tends to be obscured in favor of the issue of how people can master someone else's meaning, thus depoliticizing both the notion of school culture and the notion of classroom pedagogy. In my view, this is a limited and sometimes crippling rationality. It ignores the dreams, histories, and visions that people bring to schools. Its central concerns are rooted in a false notion of objectivity and in a discourse that finds its quintessential expression in the attempt to posit universal principles of education that are lodged in the ethos of instrumentalism and a self-serving individualism.

Alternative Theories

Against the theoretical shortcomings that characterize traditional views of schooling and curriculum new theories of educational practice must be developed. Such theories must begin with a continuous and critical questioning of the "taken for granted" in school knowledge and practice. Moreover, an attempt must be made to analyze schools as sites that, while basically reproducing the dominant society, also contain possibilities for educating students to become active, critical citizens (not simply workers). Schools must come to be seen and studied as both instructional and cultural sites.

One of the most important theoretical elements for developing critical modes of schooling centers around the notion of culture. Schools must be seen as institutions marked by the same complex of contradictory cultures that characterize the dominant society. Schools are social sites constituted by a complex of dominant *and* subordinate cultures, each characterized by the power they have to define and legitimate a specific view of reality. Teachers and others interested in education must come to understand how the dominant culture functions at all levels of schooling to disconfirm the cultural experiences of the "excluded majorities." It also means that teachers, parents, and others should fight against the powerlessness of students by affirming their own cultural experiences and histories. For teachers, this means examining their own cultural capital and examining the way in which it either benefits or victimizes students. Thus, the central questions for building a critical pedagogy are the questions of how we help students, particularly from the oppressed classes, recognize that the dominant school culture is not neutral and does not generally serve their needs. At the same time we need to ask how it is that the dominant culture functions to make them, as students, feel powerless. The answer to this lies, in part, in revealing the myths, lies, and injustices at the heart of the dominant school culture and building a critical mode of teaching that engages rather than suppresses history and critical practice. Such an activity calls for a mode of dialogue and critique that unmasks the dominant school culture's attempt to escape from history and that interrogates the assumptions and practices that inform the lived experiences of day-to-day schooling.

Educators and parents will have to come to view knowledge as neither neutral nor objective and, instead, to view it as a social construction embodying particular interests and assumptions. Knowledge must be linked to the issue of power, which suggests that educators and others must raise questions about its truth claims as well as the interests that such knowledge serves. Knowledge, in this case, does not become valuable because it is legitimized by curriculum experts. Its value is linked to the power it has as a mode of critique and social transformation, Knowledge becomes important to the degree that it helps human beings understand not only the assumptions embedded in its form and content, but also the processes whereby knowledge is produced, appropriated, and transformed within specific social and historical settings.

Certainly, a critical view of school knowledge would look different from a traditional view of school knowledge. Critical knowledge would instruct students and teachers alike about their status as a group situated within a society with specific relations of domination and subordination. Critical knowledge would help illuminate how such groups could develop a language and a discourse released from their own partially distorted cultural inheritance. The organizing question here would be: what is it that this society has made of me that I no longer want to be? Put another way, a critical mode of knowledge would illuminate for teachers and students how to appropriate the most radical and affirmative aspects of the dominant and subordinate culture. Finally, such knowledge would have to provide a motivational connection to action itself, it would have to link a critical decoding of history to a vision of the future that not only exploded the myths of the existing society, but also reached into those pockets of desires and needs that harbored a longing for a new society and new forms of social relations, relations free from the pathology of racism, sexism, and class domination.

Teachers and administrators need to address issues concerning the wider functions of schooling. Issues that deal with questions of power, philosophy, social theory, and politics must be opened to scrutiny. Teachers and administrators must be seen as more than technicians. The technocratic, sterile rationality that dominates the wider culture, as well as teacher education, pays little attention to theoretical and ideological issues. Teachers are trained to use forty-seven different models of teaching, administration, or evaluation. Yet, they are not taught to be critical of these models. In short, they are taught a form of conceptual and political illiteracy. Educators should dissuade individuals who reduce teaching to the implementations of methods from entering the teaching profession. Schools need prospective teachers who are both theoreticians and practitioners, who can combine theory, imagination, and techniques. Moreover, public school systems should sever their relations with teacher-training institutions that simply turn out technicians, students who function less as scholars and more as clerks. This move may seem harsh, but it is a small antidote compared to the critical illiteracy and incompetency such teachers often reproduce in our schools.

Instead of mastering and refining the use of methodologies, teachers and administrators should approach education by examining their own perspectives about society, schools, and emancipation. Rather than attempt to escape from their own ideologies and values, educators should confront them critically so as to understand how society has shaped them as individuals, what it is they believe, and how to structure more positively the effects they have upon students and others. Put another way, teachers and administrators, in particular, must attempt to understand how issues of class, gender, and race have left an imprint upon how they think and act. Such a critical interrogation provides the foundation for a democratic school. The democraticization of schooling involves the need for teachers to build alliances with other teachers, and not simply union alliances. Such alliances must develop around new forms of social relations that include both teaching and the organization and administration of school policy. It is important that teachers break through the cellular structure of teaching as it presently exists in most schools. Teachers need to acquire more control over the development of curriculum materials; they need to have more control over how such materials might be taught and evaluated and how alliances over curriculum issues could be established with members of the larger community.

The present structures of most schools isolate teachers and cut off the possibilities for democratic decision making and positive social relations. Relations between school administrators and teaching staff often represent the most disabling aspects of the division of labor, the division between conception and execution. Such a management model is demeaning to teachers and students alike. If we are to take the issue of schooling seriously, schools should be the one site where democratic social relations become a part of one's lived experiences.

Finally, any viable form of schooling needs to be informed by a passion and faith in the necessity of struggling in the interest of creating a better world. These may seem like strange words in a society that has elevated the notion of self-interest to the status of a universal law. And yet our very survival depends on the degree to which the principles of communality, human struggle, and social justice aimed at improving the privileges of all groups eventually prevail. Public schools need to be organized around a vision that celebrates not what is but what could be, a vision that looks beyond the immediate to the future, and a vision that links struggle to a new set of human possibilities. This is a call for public institutions that affirm one's faith in the possibility of people like teachers and administrators taking risks and engaging life so as to enrich it. We must celebrate the critical impulse and lay bare the distinction between reality and the conditions that conceal reality. Such is the task that all educators must face, and I am quite sure that it will not be met by organizing schools around the goals of raising reading and math scores or, for that matter, improving students' SAT scores. These are not minor concerns, but our primary concern is to address the educational issue of what it means to teach students to think critically, to learn how to affirm their own experiences, and to understand the need to struggle individually and collectively for a more just society.

2

Toward a New Sociology of Curriculum

By HENRY A. GIROUX

Anthony Giddens, the English sociologist, once remarked that those who are waiting for a Newton of the social sciences "are not only waiting for a train that won't arrive, they're in the wrong station altogether."[1] Gidden's remark could very well have set the stage for one of the most interesting and urgent debates now taking place in the curriculum field in the United States.

At the heart of this debate is the question of whether the curriculum field can continue to pattern itself after the model of the natural sciences. It is not simply that the field suffers from serious misconceptions regarding its mode of reasoning and methodology. What is at stake is more than a conceptual problem. The real issue centers on whether the field is moribund, both politically and ethically. Is the curriculum field in a state of arrest, incapable of developing either emancipatory intentions or new curricular possibilities?[2]

Debate of this sort is not new. Questions concerning the role that schools and curriculum play in reproducing the values and attitudes necessary for the maintenance of the dominant society have been raised by educators since the turn of the century. What is new is the scope as well

11

as the nature of some of the questions being raised. This should not suggest that a new school or paradigm has appeared in the field. Such an assumption would be both misleading and inaccurate. It would be misleading because those who make up what I will label as the new sociology of curriculum movement represent many critical strands and traditions. It would be inaccurate to call such a movement a paradigm because it would oversimplify its varied members' relatedness and depth of commitment to a new world view, one that speaks to a unifying set of assumptions and guidelines for the development of curriculum theory and practice. Though such a paradigm doesn't exist at the present time, the foundations for such a paradigm can be recognized in some of the broad concerns and related questions voiced by a number of emerging disparate critical traditions.[3]

The singular theme that unites all of these critical traditions is their opposition to what might be called the technocratic rationality that guides traditional curriculum theory and design. This form of rationality has dominated the curriculum field since its inception and can be found in varied forms in the work of Tyler, Taba, Saylor and Alexander, Beauchamp, and others. William F. Pinar claims that between 85 and 95 percent of those who work in the curriculum field share a perspective that is either tied or closely related to the dominant technocratic rationality.[4] Herbert Kliebard has further argued that this form of rationality has evolved in a manner parallel to the scientific management movement of the 1920s, and that early founders of the curriculum movement such as Bobbitt and Charters warmly embraced the principles of scientific management.[5] The school as factory metaphor has a long and extensive history in the curriculum field. Consequently, modes of reasoning, inquiry, and research characteristic of the field have been modeled on assumptions drawn from a model of science and social relations closely tied to the principles of prediction and control.

The new sociology of curriculum critics see their task as more than an attempt to clear up what might be called a conceptual muddle. In the first place, the concepts that underlie the traditional curriculum paradigm serve as guides to action. Secondly, these concepts are inextricably linked to value judgments about standards of morality and questions concerning the nature of freedom and control. More specifically, these assumptions not only represent a set of ideas that educators use to structure their view of curriculum; they also represent a set of material practices embedded in rituals and routines thought of as necessary and natural facts. Thus, they have become forms of objectified history, common-sense assumptions that have been severed from the historical context from which they developed.[6]

The new sociology of curriculum views the basic assumptions embedded in the traditional curriculum paradigm as the basis for both a critique and a limit situation to be overcome in developing new orientations and ways of talking about curriculum. Hence, it is important that we specify what these assumptions are: (a) Theory in the curriculum field should operate in the interest of lawlike propositions that are empirically testable; (b) The natural sciences provide the "proper" model of explanation for the concepts and techniques of curriculum theory, design, and evaluation; (c) Knowledge should be objective and capable of being investigated and described in a neutral fashion; and (d) Statements of value are to be separated from "facts" and "modes of inquiry" that can and ought to be objective.

In the most general sense, the technocratic model of curriculum has been criticized both for its stated claims to the truth and the assumptions implicit in the *kinds* of questions it ignores. Regarding its stated truth claims, critics argue that the traditional model rests on a number of flawed assumptions about the nature and role of theory, knowledge, and science. Moreover, these assumptions have resulted in truncated forms of inquiry that ignore fundamental questions concerning the larger relationship between ideology and school knowledge as well as meaning and social control.[7]

Shortcomings of the Dominant Model

The "new" critics claim that theory in the dominant curriculum model is either ignored altogether or is badly instrumentalized. In other words, theory is important to the degree that it can be rigorously formulated and empirically tested. Its ultimate purpose here is a technocratic one: to reveal lawlike propositions about curriculum design, implementation, and evaluation that can be either factually proven or disproven. Theory is thus reduced to an empirical explanatory framework for social engineering. From this critical perspective, theory appears incapable of stepping outside of its empirical strait jacket in order to raise questions about the nature of truth, the difference between appearance and reality, or the distinction between knowledge and mere opinion. Most importantly, theory in the dominant curriculum paradigm appears unable to provide a rational basis for criticizing the "facts" of the given society. Theory is this case not only ignores its ethical function, it is also stripped of its political function.[8]

Knowledge in the dominant curriculum model is treated primarily as a realm of objective facts. That is, knowledge appears objective in that it is external to the individual and is imposed on him or her. As something external, knowledge is divorced from human meaning and intersubjective exchange. It no longer is seen as something to be questioned, analyzed, and negotiated. Instead, it becomes something to be managed and mastered. In this case, knowledge is removed from the self-formative process of generating one's own set of meanings, a process that involves an interpretive relationship between knower and known. Once the subjective dimension of knowing is lost, the purpose of knowledge becomes one of accumulation and categorization. Questions such as "Why this knowledge?" are superseded by technical questions such as "What is the best way to learn this given body of knowledge?" Within the context of this definition of knowledge, curriculum models are developed that stress "mission specificity," "time on task variables," and "feedback obtained to make adjustments."[9] This view of knowledge is usually accompanied by top-to-bottom classroom social relationships conducive to communiques, not communication.[10] Control, not learning, appears to have a high priority in the traditional curriculum model. What is lost here is the notion that knowledge is not simply "about" an external reality, it is more importantly self-knowledge oriented toward critical understanding and emancipation.

A pivotal force in the traditional curriculum model is the claim to objectivity. Objectivity in this case refers to forms of knowledge and methodological inquiry that are untouched by the untidy world of beliefs and values. While the severance of knowledge and research from value claims may appear to be admirable to some, it hides more than it uncovers. Of course, this is not meant to suggest that challenging the value-neutrality claims of mainstream curriculum theorists is tantamount to supporting the use of bias, prejudice, and superstition in pedagogical inquiry.

Instead, the notion that objectivity is based on the use of normative criteria established by communities of scholars and intellectual workers in any given field is espoused. Intellectual inquiry and research free from values and norms are impossible to achieve. To separate values from facts or social inquiry from ethical considerations is pointless. As Howard Zinn points out, it is like trying to draw a map that illustrates every detail on a chosen piece of terrain.[11] But this is not just a simple matter of intellectual error; it is an ethical failing as well.

The notion that theory, facts, and inquiry can be objectively determined and used falls prey to a set of values that are both conservative and mystifying in their political orientation. As critics such as Paulo Freire have pointed out, schools do not exist in precious isolation from the rest of society. Schools embody collective attitudes that permeate every aspect of their organization.[12] In essence, they are not things, but concrete manifestations of specific rules and social relationships. The nature of their organization is value-based. Similarly, curriculum design, implementation, and evaluation always represent patterns of judgments about the nature of knowledge, classroom social relationships, and the distribution of power. To ignore this is to lose sight of the origins and consequences of the belief system that guides one's behavior in the school setting.

Traditional curriculum represents a firm commitment to a view of rationality that is ahistorical, consensus-oriented, and politically conservative. It supports a passive view of students and appears incapable of examining the ideological presuppositions that tie it to a narrow operational mode of reasoning. Its view of science ignores the competing elements and frames of reference within the scientific community itself.[13] Moreover, it ends up substituting a limited form of scientific methodology based on prediction and control for critical scientific inquiry.

Instead of promoting critical reflection and human understanding, the dominant curriculum model emphasizes the logic of probability as the ultimate definition of truth and meaning. Not only do the concepts that characterize this model appear less than critical, they appear as blank checks that support the status quo. One example of this can be found in the powerful influence of learning psychologists in the field of education with their endless studies on "performance and the interchange between students and teachers."[14] Some critics view this as a strong measure of the political conservatism that dominates the curriculum field. The learning psychology perspective fails to examine the way schools legitimize certain forms of knowledge and cultural interests.[15]

The Challenge

The new sociology of curriculum has mounted a serious challenge against many of the deeply held beliefs and assumptions that characterize traditional curriculum. This challenge is far from uniform and has its roots in continental philosophies as diverse as existentialism, psychoanalysis, Marxism, and phenomenology. The new sociology of curriculum speaks a language that might seem strange when compared to the input-output language of the traditional curriculum model. The new language may be difficult, but it is necessary, because it enables its users to develop new kinds of relationships in the curriculum field and to raise different kinds of questions. This is not a moot point. It would be spurious indeed to dismiss these critics for drawing upon what might appear to be alien forms of language and thought, and some of their detractors have done just that. However, the real point of concern should be whether the language and concepts used are raising profoundly important questions and issues about the curriculum field itself. While it is not possible to present the various factions and issues that make up the new sociology of curriculum movement, the nucleus of some of the more general ideas that run through this perspective can be analyzed briefly.

The new sociology of curriculum group strongly argues that schools are part of a wider societal process and that they must be judged within a specific socioeconomic framework. In addition, the curriculum itself is viewed as a selection from the larger culture. From this perspective the new critics argue for a thorough re-examination of the relationship between curriculum, schools, and society. This re-examination focuses on two broad interrelationships. On the one hand, the focus is on the relationship between schools and the dominant society. The focus here is primarily political and ideological; its emphasis is on highlighting how schools function to reproduce, in both the hidden and formal curricula, the cultural beliefs and economic relationships that support the larger social order. On the other hand, the focus is on how the very texture of day to day classroom relationships generates different meanings, restraints, cultural values, and social relationships. Underlying both of these concerns is a deep seated interest in the relationship between meaning and social control.

A number of these critics have been particularly concerned about how meaning is constructed and acted upon in schools. They support the view that the social construction of the principles that govern the operation of curriculum design, research, and evaluation are often ignored by curriculum specialists and classroom teachers. One consequence has been that many educators often operate out of common-sense assumptions that fail to raise fundamental questions about how teachers perceive their classroom experiences and students. Also ignored are questions about how students perceive and generate meaning in the classroom; similarly, questions concerning how particular classroom materials mediate meanings between teachers and students, schools and the larger society, also go unquestioned. Within this limited view of meaning, prejudices and social myths are relegated to the realm of unquestioned habits of mind and experience.

Given this mode of behavior, there is little room for students to generate their own meanings, to act on their own lived histories, or to develop an attentiveness to critical thought. Learning under such circumstances, it is argued, degenerates into a euphemism for a mode of control that imposes rather than cultivates meaning. This is a crucial point. If teachers do not bracket their own basic assumptions about curriculum and pedagogy, they do more than transmit unquestioned attitudes, norms, and beliefs. They unknowingly may end up endorsing forms of cognitive and dispositional development that strengthen rather than challenge existing forms of institutional oppression. Commonly accepted definitions about work, play, achievement, intelligence, mastery, failure, and learning are socially constructed categories that carry with them the weight of specific interests and norms. To ignore this important notion is to relinquish the possibility for students and teachers alike to shape reality in an image other than the one that is socially prescribed and institutionally legitimated. The failure of curriculum workers to appreciate that there are fundamental interests of knowledge other than prediction, control, and efficiency is not just a matter of misunderstanding, it is a serious ethical and political failing.

Critics such as Michael Apple have gone far beyond stressing the need for a model of curriculum that generates interpretive understanding and purposive learning. These critics have raised the debate over curriculum to a new level of criticism by calling for a view of curriculum that defines it as a study in ideology.[16] In this view, questions concerning the production, distribution, and evaluation of knowledge are directly linked to questions of control and domination in the larger society. This can be more fully understood by examining some of the types of questions that would provide the basis for viewing curriculum from this perspective. These questions would include:

1. What counts as curriculum knowledge?
2. How is such knowledge produced?
3. How is such knowledge transmitted in the classroom?

4. What kinds of classroom social relationships serve to parallel and reproduce the values and norms embodied in the accepted social relations of other dominant social sites?

5. Who has access to legitimate forms of knowledge?

6. Whose interests does this knowledge serve?

7. How are social and political contradictions and tensions mediated through acceptable forms of classroom knowledge and social relationships?

8. How do prevailing methods of evaluation serve to legitimize existing forms of knowledge?

At the core of these questions is the recognition that power, knowledge, ideology, and schooling are linked in everchanging patterns of complexity. The nexus that gives form to these interrelationships is social and political in nature, and it is both a product and process of history. In more concrete terms, curriculum theorists, teachers, and students alike embody certain beliefs and practices, concepts and norms that strongly influence how they perceive and structure their educational experiences. These beliefs and routines are historical and social in nature; moreover, they may be the object of self-reflection, or they may exist unnoticed by the individual they influence. In the latter case, they serve to dominate rather than serve the individual in question.

This approach calls for forms of curriculum that push beyond appreciating that knowledge is a social construction. Also, it stresses the need for examining the constellation of economic, political, and social interests that different forms of knowledge may reflect. To put it another way, curriculum models must develop forms of understanding that relate explanations of social meanings to wider societal parameters in order to be able to judge their claims to the truth.[17]

Significance for the Future

If one purpose of curriculum is to generate possibilities for individual and social emancipation, we will have to develop a new language and new forms of rationality to accomplish such a task. The predicament of the age is no different from the predicament the curriculum field presently faces. And this predicament is as engaging as it is radical: to build the conditions that allow humanity to search for its self-understanding and meaning. The new sociology of curriculum movement provides us with a number of possibilities for developing more flexible and humanizing forms of curriculum.

We must develop a mode of curriculum that cultivates critical theoretical discourse about the quality and purpose of schooling and human life. We need to develop broader perspectives that enrich rather than dominate the field. Critical curriculum theory must be situational. It must analyze the various dimensions of pedagogy as part of the historical and cultural conjunctures in which they occur. And it must do this with the tools that are fashioned from a variety of disciplines. This does not mean that we have to become political scientists or sociologists in order to study curriculum. That is not the case, and it would be inappropriate to do so. Our center of gravity is curriculum, but we need to enrich our focus by drawing upon the concepts and tools that other disciplines offer us.

The foundation for a new mode of curriculum must be as deeply historical as it is critical. In fact, the critical sensibility must be seen as an extension of historical consciousness. The genesis, development, and unfolding of ideas, social relationship, and modes of inquiry and evaluation must be viewed as part of an ongoing development of complex, historically bound social conditions of formations.

The new mode of curriculum must be deeply personal, but only in the sense that it recognizes individual uniqueness and needs as part of a specific social reality. We must not confuse self-indulgence with critical pedagogy. Individual and social needs have to be linked and mediated through a critical perspective tied to notions of emancipation. Curriculum models must address themselves to the concrete personal experiences of specific cultural groups and populations. Curriculum educators must be able to recognize the relevance and importance of accepting and using multiple languages and forms of cultural capital (systems of meaning, tastes, ways of viewing the world, style, and so on). At the same time, educators must acknowledge that the call for cultural pluralism is empty unless it is recognized that the relationship between different cultural groups is mediated through the dominant cultural system. Thus, our task is to unravel these relationships for different cultural groups to emancipate them from the imposed kinds of definitions and emotional pain that minorities of class and color have a history of in this country.

A new mode of curriculum must abandon the ideological pretense of being value-free. To acknowledge that the choices we make concerning all facets of curriculum and pedagogy are value-laden is to liberate ourselves from imposing our own values on others. To admit as such means that we can begin with the notion that reality should never be taken as a given, but instead, has to be questioned and analyzed. In other words, knowledge has to be made problematic and has to be situated in classroom social relationships that allow for debate and communications.

Finally, a new mode of curriculum rationality will have to subordinate technical interests to ethical considerations. The questions of means must be subordinated to questions that speak to the ethical consequences of our pursuits. Although these suggestions represent a broad theoretical sweep, they do provide a starting point for developing new modes of curriculum inquiry. Also, the somewhat disparate traditions of the new sociology of curriculum have helped to translate some of the larger abstract issues surrounding the purpose and meaning of schooling into concrete curriculum problems and avenues for further study and research.

I began this chapter by pointing out that the traditional model of curriculum was moribund, politically and ethically. I want to go back to that statement and clarify it, lest it be confused with a form of un-warranted optimism. The dominant technocratic curriculum paradigm may be aging, but it is far from a historical relic. The struggle to replace it with principles and assumptions consistent with the vision of the new sociology of curriculum movement will be difficult indeed. But one thing is certain. The struggle for a new mode of curriculum rationality cannot be approached as a technical task only. It must be seen as a social struggle deeply committed to what Herbert Marcuse has aptly termed "the eman-cipation of sensibility, reason, and imagination in all spheres of subjec-tivity and objectivity."[18] The new sociology of curriculum has helped to make this struggle just a bit easier. The rest is up to us.

3

Social Education in the Classroom: The Dynamics of the Hidden Curriculum

By HENRY A. GIROUX and ANTHONY N. PENNA

The belief that schooling can be defined as the sum of its official course offerings is a naive one. Yet such an implicit belief served as the theme of the social studies curriculum development reform movement of the 1960s and early 1970s. Developers believed that if they changed the curriculum of the nation's schools, the schools' ills would be remedied.[1] In recent years, however, numerous reasons have been offered to explain the seeming inability of the reform movement to penetrate the traditional patterns of instruction in the schools. Inadequate teacher preparation and curriculum materials which overestimated the perceived capabilities of students represent the more familiar, albeit uncritical, explanations offered by educators. Now, some of them lend uncritical support for the back-to-basics movement in social studies education, assuming once again that new curriculum materials will provide an answer to the question of how to bring about change in social studies education. Attend to the cognitive needs and capabilities of students, they argue, and the failures of the recent reform movement will be overcome.[2]

Unfortunately, such recommendations are based heavily on structural-functional educational models of curriculum theory[3] which fail to perceive the purpose of social education beyond its limited explicit instructional outcomes. Further, there is a failure to recognize the complex, intimate relationship between the institution of the school and the nation's economic and political institutions. Once the relationship between schooling and the larger society is recognized, questions about the nature and meaning of the schooling experience can be viewed from a theoretical perspective capable of illuminating the often ignored relationship between school knowledge and social control. By viewing schools within the context of the larger society, social studies developers can begin to focus on the tacit teaching that goes on in schools and help to uncover the ideological messages embedded in both the content of the formal curriculum and the social relations of the classroom encounter.

It is only recently that some educators have begun to raise questions which point to the need for a thorough study of the interconnections between ideology, instruction, and curriculum.[4] For instance, Michael Apple argues that we need to

> examine critically not just "how a student acquires more knowledge" (the dominant question in our efficiency minded field) but "why and how particular aspects of the collective culture are presented in school as objective, factual knowledge." How concretely may official knowledge represent ideological configurations of the dominant interests in a society? How do schools legitimate these limited and partial standards of knowing as unquestioned truths? These questions must be asked of at least three areas of school life: (1) How the basic day-to-day regularities of schools contribute to students learning these ideologies; (2) how the specific forms of curricular knowledge reflect these configurations; and (3) how these ideologies are reflected in the fundamental perspectives educators themselves employ to order, guide, and give meaning to their own activity.[5]

If educators such as Apple, Bourdieu, and Bernstein are correct, and we think they are, then social studies developers will have to build their pedagogical models upon a theoretical framework which situates schools within a sociopolitical context. As such, the main assertion of this chapter is that social studies developers will have to comprehend the school as an agent of socialization. Furthermore, they will have to identify those structural properties at the core of the schooling process which link it to comparable properties in the workplace and other sociopolitical spheres.

In brief, they will have to approach their task systemically rather than in the traditional fragmented fashion which assumes incorrectly that the classroom can become a vehicle for helping each student to develop his/her full potential as a critical thinker and responsible participant in the democratic process by changing only the content and methodology of the school's official social studies curricula.

We believe that two major tasks for social studies educators are to identify those social processes which work against the ethical and political purpose of schooling in a democratic society and to construct new elements which provide the underpinning for new social studies programs. Initially, developers will have to understand the contradictions between the official curriculum, namely the explicit cognitive and affective goals of formal instruction, and the "hidden curriculum,"[6]—the unstated norms, values, and beliefs that are transmitted to students through the underlying structure of meaning and in both the formal content the social relations of school and classroom life.[7] Even more they will have to recognize the function of a hidden curriculum and its capacity for undermining the goals of social education.

Social studies developers will have to shift their attention from a technical, ahistorical, view of schooling to a sociopolitical perspective which focuses on the relationship between schooling and the idea of justice. The goals of social education should be redefined and understood as an extension of ethics directed toward "the arena of excellence and responsibility where by acting together, men (and women) can become truly free."[8] Thus, social studies developers will have to answer anew the question: "What is learned in school?" Fortunately, a few educators writing out of a number of different theoretical traditions have already taken up the challenge.

Traditions in Educational Theory

Three different traditions in educational theory have helped to illuminate the socializing role of schools and the meaning and stucture of the hidden curriculum. They are (1) a structural-functional view of schooling: (2) a phenomenological view characteristic of the new sociology of education; and (3) a radical critical view, often associated with the neo-Marxist analysis of educational theory and practice. Each of these views share distinctly different theoretical assumptions concerning the meaning of knowledge, classroom social relationships, and the political and cultural nature of schooling. While we have based our analysis of the hidden curriculum on assumptions and insights drawn from all three traditions, we believe that the structural-functional and pheonomenological approaches suffer from serious deficiencies. The neo-Marxist position, it seems to us, provides the most insightful and comprehensive model for a more progressive approach for understanding the nature of schooling and developing an emancipatory program for social education. Before examining the specific contributions that these three traditions have made to the notion of the hidden curriculum and the socializing role of schools, a general overview of some of their basic assumptions will be provided.

The structural-functionalist approach has as one of its primary interests how social norms and values are transmitted within the context of the schools. Relying primarily upon a positivist sociological model, this approach has highlighted how schools socialize students to accept unquestionably a set of beliefs, rules, and dispositions as fundamental to the functioning of the larger society. For the structural-functionalists, the school provides a valuable service in training students to uphold commitments and to learn skills required by society.[9] The value of this approach is threefold: (1) it makes clear that schools do not exist in precious isolation, removed from the interests of the larger society; (2) it spells out specific norms and structural properties of the hidden curriculum; and (3) it raises questions about the specifically historical character of meaning and social control in schools.[10]

While insightful in many respects, the structural-functional model is marred by a number of theoretical shortcomings which characterize its basic assumptions. Rejecting the notion that growth develops from conflict, it stresses consensus and stability rather than movement. As a result, it downplays the notions of social conflict and competing socioeconomic interests. Moreover, it represents an apolitical posture that sees as unproblematic the basic beliefs, values, and structural socioeconomic arrangements characteristic of American society.[11] Consequently, the structural-functionalist position defines students in reductionist behavioral terms as products of socialization. By defining students as passive recipients, conflict is explained mainly as a function of faulty socialization, the causes of which usually lie in institutions outside of the classroom or school or in the individual as deviant. Thus the school appears to exist happily beyond the imperatives and influence of class and power. Similarly, knowledge is appreciated for its instrumental market value. Finally, in the structural-functional model, students accept social conformity and lose the ability to make meaning for themselves.

The social-phenomenological approach to educational theory, often called the new sociology, moves far beyond the structural-functionalist position in its approach to the study of schooling. The new sociology focuses critically on a number of assumptions about classroom interactions and social encounters. For the new sociologists, any valid theory of socialization has to be seen as "a theory of the construction of social reality, if not of a particular historical social order."[12] They posit a model of socialization in which meaning is made interactively. That is, meaning is "given" by situations but also created by students as they interact in classrooms. Moreover, the social construction of meaning by both teachers and students raises anew questions about the objective nature of knowledge itself. For the new sociologists, the principles governing the organization, distribution, and evaluation of knowledge are not absolute and objective; instead, they are sociohistorical constructs forged by active human beings creating rather than simply existing in the world.

In this approach, the view of students as actors with a fixed identity is replaced by a more dynamic model of student behavior. The new sociologists focus on the participation of students in defining and redefining their worlds. Thus the focus of classroom studies with the rise of the new sociology has shifted from an exclusive emphasis on institutional behavior to a focus on students' interactions with language, social relations, and categories of meaning. The proponents of the new sociology have provided a new dimension to the study of the relationship between socialization and the school curriculum.[13] (Young, 1971; Keddie, 1973; Jenks, 1977; Eggleston, 1977). The new sociology raises to a new level of discussion the relationship between the distribution of power and knowledge. It requires social studies curriculum developers to make problematic many of the truisms that characterized the selection, organization, and distribution of knowledge and pedagogical styles inherent in curriculum development. In one sense, the new sociology has stripped the school curriculum of its innocence.

But the new sociology is not without its flaws, flaws that undermine its ability to resolve the very problems it identified. The most thoughtful critique lodged against the new sociology is that it represents a form of subjective idealism.[14] Allegedly, at its core the new sociology lacks an adequate theory of social change and consciousness. While it helps educators to uncover the ways in which knowledge is defined and imposed, it fails to provide criteria for measuring the value of different forms of classroom knowledge. By endorsing the value and relevance of students' intentionality, the new sociology has succumbed to a notion of cultural relativity. It lacks a theoretical construct to explain the role ideology plays in the construction of knowledge by students. It fails to account for the fact that the way students perceive the external world does not always correspond to the actual structure and content of that world. Subjective perceptions are dialectically related to the social world and do not simply mirror it. To ignore this, as the new sociology proponents have, is to fall prey to a distorted subjectivism. Sharp and Greene have captured this position cogently.

> The social world is more than the mere constellations of meaning. Although we can accept that the knowing subject acts in the world on the basis of his understanding, that there is always a subjective factor which enters into knowledge of the world, it does not follow from this that the world possesses the character which the knowing subject bestows upon it, that the objects which we know in the social world are mere subjective creations capable of being differently constituted in an infinite variety of ways. The phenomenologist appears to be putting forward what we could argue is an extreme form of subjective idealism. Where the external objective world is merely a constitution of the creative consciousness, the subject-object dualism disappears in the triumph of the constituting subject.[15]

In the final analysis, the new sociology fails in spite of its desire for radical change and fundamental egalitarianism. Its failure lies in its inability to illuminate how social and political structures mask reality and promote ideological hegemony.[16] Thus, this position not only fails to explain how different varieties of classroom meanings, knowledge, and experiences arise, it also fails to explain how they are able to sustain themselves. By focusing exclusively on the micro-level of schooling, on studies of classroom interaction, the new sociology falls short of illustrating how sociopolitical arrangements influence and constrain individual and collective efforts to construct knowledge and meaning. These arrangements probably play an important role in influencing the very texture of classroom life.

A third position is a neo-Marxist approach to socialization and social change. While this position is not without its own flaws, its value lies in being able to move beyond the apolitical view of the functionalist position as well as the subjective idealism of the new sociology. At the core of the neo-Marxist approach is a recognition of the relationship between economic and cultural reproduction. Inherent in this perspective is an intersection of theory, ideology, and social practice. Schools are viewed as agents of ideological control which reproduce and maintain dominant beliefs, values and norms. This is not meant to suggest that schools are merely factories which process students and mirror the interests of the larger society; such a perspective is clearly mechanistic and reductionist.[17] The neo-Marxist position points out that schools in corresponding ways are linked to the principles and processes governing the workplace. The cutting edge of this perspective is its insistence on connecting macro forces in the larger society to micro analysis such as classroom studies.

The neo-Marxist approach more clearly than the other two approaches identified in this chapter illuminates how social reproduction is linked to classroom social relationships and how the construction of knowledge is related to the notion of false consciousness. While stressing the importance of a student's subjective role in constituting meaning for himself, neo-Marxists are equally concerned with the ways in which social and economic conditions constrain and distort social construction of meaning, particularly as mediated through the hidden curriculum. Not only do classroom studies have to be linked to the study of the larger society, they have to be connected to a notion of justice, one that is capable of articulating how certain unjust social structures can be identified and replaced.

School Knowledge and Classroom Relations

While the neo-Marxist perspective provides an important focus on the ideological nature of the process of schooling and the larger social order, it has done little to explicate in specific terms the kinds of knowledge and classroom social relationships that have been used to reproduce the reified consciousness that maintains the cultural and economic interests of a stratified society. This is where the structural functionalists and new sociology adherents have made valuable contributions to the study of curriculum and social education. By drawing on the insights within a new Marxist framework, we can begin to answer the fundamental question of "What is learned in schools?"

In response to the question, Robert Dreeben points out that the student learns more than simply instructional knowledge and skills, and that the traditional view of schooling as being "primarily cognitive in nature is at best only partially tenable."[18] Stephen Arons reinforces this view by calling school "a social environment from which a child may learn much more than what is in the formal curriculum."[19] Implicit in this analysis of the school and classroom as a socializing agent is an important pedagogical premise—any curriculum designed to introduce positive changes in classrooms will fail, unless such a proposal is rooted in an understanding of those sociopolitical forces that strongly influence the very texture of day-to-day classroom pedagogical practices.

Since it is not entirely clear to social studies educators that schools are indeed sociopolitical institutions, a case must first be made to validate the position that schools are inextricably linked to other social agencies and institutions within American society. Ralph Tyler highlights the social function of schools by pointing out that all educational philosophies are essentially an outgrowth of one of two possible theoretical perspectives. He claims that a statement of educational philosophy can be built upon one of the following questions: "Should the schools develop young people to fit into present society as it is, or does the school have a revolutionary mission to develop young people who will seek to improve the society?"[20]

Tyler's point about educational philosopy is important for a number of reasons. First, it reinforces the notion that schools have a sociopolitical function and cannot exist independently of the society in which they operate. Second, Tyler recognizes that underlying every educational program designed to intervene in the structure of the schools there lies a theoretical frame of reference. Paulo Freire, the Brazilian educator, argues both points in his claim that,

> There is no such thing as a neutral educational process. Education either functions as an instrument which is used to facilitate the integration of the younger generation into the logic of the present system and bring about conformity to it, or, it becomes the "practice of freedom"—the means by which men and women deal critically and creatively with reality and discover how to participate in the transformation of their world.[21]

Whether they realize it or not, social studies educators work in the service of one of the two positions outlined by Tyler and Freire.

An examination of schooling and its sociological ties to the family and the workplace can illuminate the social and political functions of schools. While a number of sociologists convincingly point out that schools no longer assume the role of a surrogate family, they do perform a socializing function that the social structure of the family cannot satisfy. For instance, comparing the functions of the family to those of the school. Robert Dreeben argues that the structural properties of the family, while satisfying specific affective needs of children, cannot adequately socialize them to function in the adult world. According to him, schooling demands the formation of social relationships that are more time-bounded, more diverse, less dependent, and less emotive than those of the family. Unlike the family, schools separate performance from emotional expression and perform what is considered their most explicit purpose, "imparting the skills, information, and beliefs each child will eventually need as an adult member of society."[22]

Dreeben argues that schools do more than provide instruction. They provide norms, or principles of conduct, which are learned through the varied social experiences in schools that influence students' lives. Though he ignores the political nature of these social experiences, he does mention four important norms that students learn: independence, achievement, universalism, and specificity.

Worth noting is Dreeben's failure to mention in specific ideological terms the cultural values that support and give meaning to these norms. Two examples will suffice. Independence is defined as "handling tasks with which under different circumstances, one can rightfully expect the help of others."[23] Achievement is defined so as to assure pupils of the gratification of "winning and losing," and while not stated by Dreeben, justifies extrinsic rewards and the notion that someone must always come in last.

That students learn more than cognitive skills is illuminated further in Bernstein's analysis which brings into sharp focus some of the features of the political nature of schooling. His analysis argues that students learn values and norms that would produce "good" industrial workers. Students internalize values which stress a respect for authority, punctuality, cleanliness, docility, and conformity. What the students learn from the formally sanctioned content of the curriculum is much less important than what they learn from the ideological assumptions embedded in the school's three message systems: the system of curriculum; the system of classroom pedagogical styles; and the system of evaluation.[24] In describing what students learn from the school's hidden curriculum, Stanley Aronowitz provides a capsule view of the socializing process that operate within these "message" systems:

> Indeed, the child learns in school. . . . The child learns that the teacher is the authoritative person in the classroom, but that she is subordinate to a principal. Thus the structure of society can be learned through understanding the hierarchy of power within the structure of the school. Similarly, the working-class child learns its role in society. On one side, school impresses students as a whole with their powerlessness since they are without the knowledge required to become citizens and workers. On the other, the hierarchy of occupations and classes is reproduced by the hierarchy of grade levels and tracks within grades. Promotion to successive grades is the reward for having mastered the approved political and social behavior as well as the prescribed 'cognitive' material. But within grades, particularly in large urban schools, further distinctions among students are made on the basis of imputed intelligence and that in turn is determined by the probable ability of children to succeed in terms of standards set by the educational system.[25]

Writers such as Dreeben and Aronowitz have helped to make it clear that the school functions as an agency of socialization within a network of larger institutions. Yet, with few exceptions, the political role of the school and how that role affects educational objectives, methods, content, and organizational structures has not been adequately illuminated by social studies educators.[26]

While commenting on the consequences of ignoring the political nature of education, Jerome Bruner candidly indicates that educators can no longer strike a fictional posture of neutrality and objectivity.

> A theory of instruction is a political theory in the power sense that it derives from consensus concerning the distribution of power within the society—who shall be educated and to fulfill what roles? In the very same sense, pedagogical theory must surely derive from a conception of economics, for where there is a division of labor within the society and an exchange of goods and services for wealth and prestige, then how people are educated and in what number and with what constraints on the use of resources are all relevant issues. The psychologist or educator who formulates pedagogical theory without regard to the political, economic, and social setting of the educational process courts triviality and merits being ignored in the community and in the classroom.[27]

As mentioned previously, a serious approach to social studies educational change would have to begin with an examination of the contradictions that exist between the school's hidden curriculum and official curriculum. Any approach to social studies curriculum development that ignores the existence of the hidden curriculum runs the risk of not only being incomplete, but also insignificant. For the heart of the school's function is not to be found simply in the daily dispensing of information by teachers, but also "in the social relations of the educational encounter."[28]

School Curriculum Organization

But before any study of classroom social relations is put forth, it must be made clear that the *content* of what is taught in social studies classes plays a vital role in the political socialization of students. For instance, a number of studies have pointed out that what counts as "objective" knowledge in social studies textbooks, in fact, often represents a one-sided and theoretically distorted view of the subject under study.[29] Knowledge is often accepted as truth legitimizing a specific view of the world that is either questionable or patently false. The selection, organization, and distribution of social studies knowledge is hidden from the realm of ideology.[30] In addition to its overt and covert messages, the way knowledge is selected and organized represents *a priori* assumptions by the educator about its value and legitimacy. In the final analysis, these are ideological considerations that structure the students' perception of the world. If the fragile ideological nature of these considerations is not made clear to students, then they will learn more about social conformity than critical inquiry. To break through the "hidden curriculum" of knowledge, social studies educators much help students understand that knowledge is not only variable and linked to human interest but also must be examined in regards to its claims to validity. Popkewitz has succinctly focused in on this issue for social studies educators with his claim.

> Constructing curriculum requires that educators give attention to the social disciplines as a human product whose meanings are transmitted in social processes. Instruction should give serious attention to the conflicting views of the world these crafts generate, the social location and the social contexts of inquiry. To plan for children's study of ideas, educators are compelled to inquire into the nature and character of the discourse found in history, sociology, or anthropology. What problems does each deal with? What modes of thought exist? What are its paradigmatic tasks? What limitations are placed on the knowledge of their findings? Instruction should be concerned with the different per-

spectives of phenomena that are within each discipline and how these men and women come to know what they know.[31]

Moreover, it follows that equal weight must be given in any analysis of the hidden curriculum to the organizational structures that influence and govern teacher-student interactions within the classroom. For these suggest an ideological character that is no less compelling than curriculum content in the socialization process at work in the classroom encounter. Though distinctly apolitical in nature, Philip Jackson's work represents one of the more sophisticated attempts to analyze the social processes that give shape to another dimension of the hidden curriculum. Unlike the official curriculum, with its stated cognitive and affective objectives, the hidden curriculum in this case is rooted in those organizational aspects of classroom life which are not commonly perceived by either students or teachers. According to Jackson, elements of the hidden curriculum are shaped by three key analytical concepts: crowds, praise, and power.[32]

In short, working in classrooms means learning to live in crowds. Coupled with the prevailing values of the educational system, this has profound implications for the social education established in the schools. Equally significant is the fact that schools are evaluative settings, and what a student learns is not only how to be evaluated, but how to evaluate himself and others as well. Finally, schools are marked by a basic, concrete division between the powerful (teachers) and the powerless (students). As Jackson points out, what this means "in three major ways, then—as members of crowds, as potential recipients of praise or reproof, and as pawns of institutional authorities—students are confronted with aspects of reality that at least during their childhood years are relatively confined to the hours spent in the classroom."[33]

In more specific terms, especially those that highlight student-teacher interactions, Jackson's analysis of the hidden curriculum proves to be particularly instructive. Learning to live in crowds affects students in a number of important ways. Students have to learn constantly to wait to use resources, with the ultimate outcome being that they learn to postpone or give up desires. In spite of continual interruptions in the classroom, students have to learn to be quiet. Though students work in groups with other people whom they eventually get to know, they have to learn how to be isolated in a crowd. For Jackson, the quintessential virtue learned by students under these conditions is patience (i.e., not a patience rooted in mediated restraint, but one that is rooted in an unwarranted submission to authority). "They must also, to some extent, learn to suffer in silence. They are expected to bear with equanimity, in other words, the continued delay, denial and interruption of their personal wishes and desires."[34]

Praise and power in the classroom are inextricably connected to one another. While students may find themselves in a position occasionally in which they can evaluate each other, the unquestioned source of praise and reproof is the teacher. Though the administration of positive and negative sanctions is the teacher's most visible symbol of power, the real significance of his or her role lies in the network of social relationships and values that are reproduced with the use of that authority. The nature of the hidden curriculum is nowhere more clearly revealed than in the system of evaluation. The potential effect of evaluation comes into sharp focus where one recognizes that what is taught and evaluated in the classroom is both academic and nonacademic, and includes in the latter institutional adjustment and specific personal qualities.

In fact, some notable studies have been made that support the above hypothesis. Bowles and Gintis, after reviewing a number of studies that link personality traits, attitudes, and behavioral attributes to school grades, reached the following conclusions:

> Students are rewarded for exhibiting discipline, subordinacy, intellectually as opposed to emotionally oriented behavior, and hard work independent from intrinsic task motivation. Moreover, these traits are rewarded independently of any effect of 'proper demeanor' on scholastic achievement.[35]

In addition, they point out that students who are rated high in citizenship (i.e., conformity to the social order of the school), also rated "significantly below average on measures of creativity and mental flexibility."[36] Viewed from the student's perspective, the classroom becomes a miniature workplace in which time, space, content, and structure are fixed by others. Rewards are extrinsic, and all social interaction between teachers and students are mediated by hierarchically organized structures. The underlying message learned in this context points less to schools helping students to think critically about the world in which they live, than it does to schools acting as agents of social control.

Teachers obviously play a vital role in maintaining the structure of schools and transmitting the values needed to support the larger social order.[37] Lortie's study of teachers indicates that they generally are unable to offset the conservative pedagogical influences accepted by them during their pre-college and college schooling. He also claims that "recruitment resources foster a conservative outlook among entrants . . . they appeal strongly to young people who are favorably disposed toward the existing system of schools."[38] Lortie also found that one of the most severe shortcomings of teachers was their subjective, idiosyncratic approach to teaching. Lacking a thoughtout theoretical framework from which to develop a methodology and content, teachers lacked significant criteria to shape, guide, or evaluate their own work. But more importantly, they pass their distrust of theory on to their students and help in perpetuating intellectual passivity.

As mentioned before, at the heart of the social educational encounter is a hidden curriculum whose values shape and influence practically every aspect of the student's educational experience. But this should not suggest that the hidden curriculum is so powerful that there is little hope for educational reform. Instead, the hidden curriculum should be seen as *providing* a possible direction for focusing educational change. For instance, while social studies developers alone cannot eliminate the hidden curriculum, they can identify its organizational structure and the political assumptions upon which it rests. By doing so, they can develop a pedagogy, curriculum materials, and classroom structural properties which offset the most undemocratic features of the traditional hidden curriculum. In doing so, a first but significant step will be made to help teachers and students reach beyond the classroom experience and tentatively move toward changing those institutional arrangements.

Democratic Conditions and Collective Action

Before changes in social education and in social studies development can be undertaken, however, social studies educators will have to develop very specific classroom processes designed to promote values and beliefs which encourage democratic, critical modes of student-teacher participation and interaction. That the traditional hidden curriculum of schooling is inimical to the stated aims of the official curriculum no longer escapes astute social analysis.[39] Instead of preparing students to enter the society with skills that will allow them to reflect critically upon and intervene in the world in order to change it, schools are conservative forces which, for the most part, socialize students to conform to the status quo. The structure, organization, and content of contemporary schooling equip students with the personality needs desired in the bureaucratically structured, hierarchically organized work force. As Philip Jackson has pointed out:

> So far as their power structure is concerned, classrooms are not too dissimilar from factories and offices, those ubiquitous organizations in which so many of our adult life is spent. Thus, schools might really be called a preparation for life, but not in the usual sense in which educators employ that term.[40]

The remaining section of this paper will identify an alternative set of values and classroom social processes. In our view, these alternatives represent a basis for formulating a collectivist and democratic social education stripped of egoistic individualism and alienating social relationships. These values and processes should be used by social studies educators in developing a content and pedagogy which link theory and practice and restore to students and teachers an awareness of the social and personal importance of active participation and critical thinking. While the values will be enumerated at the outset, the classroom processes will be illuminated through an analysis of the specific features that in our judgment should characterize social education.

The values and social processes which provide the theoretical underpinning for social education include developing in students a respect for moral commitment, group solidarity and social responsibility. In addition, a nonauthoritarian individualism should be fostered, one that maintains a balance with group cooperation and social awareness. Every effort should be made to give students an awareness of the necessity of developing choices of their own, and to act on those choices with an understanding of situational constraints. The educational process itself will be open to examination in relation to its links to the larger society.

Students should experience social studies as an apprenticeship in the milieu of social action, or as Freire[41] has stated, students should be taught the practice of thinking about practice. One way of doing this is to view and evaluate each learning experience, whenever possible, with respect to its connections with the larger social-economic totality. Moreover, it is important that students not only think about both the content and practice of critical communication but recognize as well the importance of translating the outcome of these experiences into concrete action. For example, it is folly in our view to engage students in topics of political and social inequality in the classroom and in the larger political world and to ignore the realities and pernicious effects of economic and income inequality. Even when linkage to the larger reality is made, a failure to address and to implement the practical will not provide students with the learning implied in Freire's appeal. In other words, it is important that social studies educators provide students with the opportunity to grasp the dynamic dialectic between critical consciousness and social action. There is a need then to integrate critical awareness, social processes, and social practice in such a way that what is made clear to students is not simply how the forces of social control work but also how they can be overcome. Students should be able to recognize the truth value of Marx's eleventh thesis on Feuerbach. The philosophers have only interpreted the world in various ways; the point is, to change it."[42]

Many liberal social studies educators accept these values and social processes and attempt to develop content-based curriculum which translates them into practice. But, in effect, liberals strip these values and social processes of their radical content by situating them within the framework of social adjustment rather than social and political emancipation. The liberal philosophic stance with its emphasis on progress through social melioration, the value of meritocracy and the professional expert, and the viability of a mass education system dedicated *to serving* the needs of the industrial order fails to penetrate and utilize the radical cutting edge of the values and social processes we support. Elizabeth Cagan captures the contradiction between liberal thought and radical values and social practices in her comment:

> While liberal reformers intend to use education to promote equality, community, and humanistic social interaction, they do not confront those aspects of the schools which pull in the opposite direction. Their blindness to these contradictions may stem from their class position: as middle-class reformers they are unwilling to advocate the kind of egalitarianism which is necessary for a true human community. Reforms in pedagogical technique have been instituted, but the . . . [hidden curriculum] remain(s) in effect. This hidden curriculum promotes competitiveness, individualism, and authoritarianism.[43]

The social processes of most classrooms militate against students developing a sense of community. As in the larger societal order, competition and individual striving are at the core of American schooling. In ideological terms, collectivity and social solidarity represent powerful structural threats to the ethos of capitalism. This ethos is built not only upon the atomization and division of labor but also on the fragmentation of consciousness and social relationships.[44] Whatever virtues about collectivity that are brought to the public's attention exist solely in form and not in substance. Both in and out of schools, self-interest represents the criterion for acting on and entering into social relationships. The structure of schooling reproduces the ethos of privatization and the moral posture of selfishness at almost every level of the formal and hidden curricula. Whether gently supporting the philosophy of "do your own thing" or maintaining pedagogical structures which undermine collective action, the message coming from most classrooms is one that enshrines the self at the expense of the group. The hidden message is one that supports alienation.[45]

The classroom scenario that fosters this unbridled individualism is a familiar one. Students traditionally sit in rows staring at the back of each others' heads and at the teacher who faces them in symbolic, authoritarian fashion, or in a large semi-circle with teacher and student space rigidly prescribed. Events in the classroom are governed by a rigid time schedule imposed by a system of bells and reinforced by cues from teachers while the class is in session. Instruction and, hopefully, some formal learning usually begin and end because it is the correct predetermined time, not because a cognitive process has been stimulated into action.

Implementation

A number of social processes help to undermine the authoritarian effects of the hidden curriculum in the classroom. Our terminology will be familiar to all social studies developers. Liberals among them will espouse the immediate instructional goals, but only reconstructionists will accept the long range implications of these processes for life in classrooms, schools, and larger social/political institutions.

The pedagogical foundation for democratic processes in the classroom can be established by eliminating the pernicious practice of "tracking" students. This tradition in schools of grouping students according to "abilities" and perceived performance is of dubious instructional value. The justification for this practice is based on traditional genetic theories which have been systematically refuted on intellectual and ethical grounds.[46] A more heterogeneous class provides a better opportunity for flexibility to be manifested. For instance, in the heterogeneous class setting, students who qualitatively perform faster than other students could be given the opportunity to function as peers acting as individual or group leaders for other students. In such a situation, students can act collectively in the process of learning and teaching. As such, knowledge becomes the vehicle for dialogue and analysis as well as the basis for new classroom social relationship. Moreover, not only are more progressive social relationships developed in this context, but traditional notions of learning and achievement are now made problematic. It must be stressed that social education should be based on a notion of achievement that is at odds with traditional genetic theories of intelligence which serve as the theoretical base to support tracking.

With the elimination of tracking, power is further diffused in a classroom so individuals in both peer and group-leadership roles are able to assume leadership positions formerly reserved for the teacher alone. In other words, with the breakdown of rigid, hierarchical roles and rules, which Basil Bernstein has called "strong framing," both students and teachers can explore democratic relationships rarely developed in the traditional classroom.[47] These new relationships will also allow teachers to set the groundwork for breaking down the cellular structure exposed by Dan Lortie. The cellular structure refers to the failure of teachers to mutually adapt their task and actions. Most teachers do not share pedagogical strategies; and thus they lack any cohesiveness in their professional interpersonal relationships.[48] By sharing their power and roles, teachers will be in a better position to break through the provincialism and narrow socialization that prevents them from sharing and examining their theory and practice of pedagogy with both students and colleagues.

Another important change that such courses should perpetuate centers around the issue of authority and grades. Extrinsic rewards should be minimized whenever possible, and students should be given the opportunity to experience roles that will enable them to direct the learning process, independently of the behavior usually associated with an emphasis on grades as rewards. Social relationships in the traditional classroom are based upon power relations inextricably linked to the teacher's allotment and distribution of grades. Grades become in many cases the ultimate discipline instruments by which the teacher imposes his desired values, behavior patterns and beliefs upon students.[49] Dialogical grading eliminates this pernicious practice since it allows students to gain some control over the distribution of grades and thereby weakens the traditional correspondence between grades and authority. We refer to such grading as dialogical because it involves a dialogue between students and teachers over the criteria, function, and consequences of the system of evaluation. The use of the term is in fact an extension of Freire's emphasis on the role of dialogue in clarifying and democratizing social relationships.[50]

While opportunities for dialogue with teachers and peers should be encouraged, they are not conducive to large group settings. In small groups, students should evaluate and test the logic in each other's work. The importance of group work to social education rests on a number of crucial assumptions. Group work represents one of the most effective ways to demystify the traditional, manipulative role of the teacher; moreover, it provides students with social contexts which stress social responsibility and group solidarity.

Group interaction provides students with the experiences that they need in order to realize that they can learn from one another. Only by diffusing authority along horizontal lines will students be able to share and appreciate the importance of learning collectively. Crucial to such a process is the element of dialogue. Through group dialogue, the norms of cooperation and sociability offset the traditional hidden curriculum's emphasis on competition and excessive individualism. In addition, the process of group instruction provides students with the opportunity for experiencing, rather than simply hearing about, the dynamics of participatory democracy.

In short, developing an awareness that is nurtured in a shared task to democratize classroom relationships is imperative for students if they are to overcome the lack of community reminiscent of the traditional classroom and the larger social order. The group encounter provides the social basis for the development of such a consciousness. Under such conditions, social relations of education marked by dominance, subordination, and an uncritical respect for authority can be effectively minimized.

Social relations marked by reciprocity and communality are not the only by-products of the group component. Another important feature centers around giving students the opportunity to serve an apprenticeship in teaching. By evaluating each other's work, acting as peer-leaders, participating in and leading discussions, students learn that teaching is not based on intuitive and imitative pedagogical approaches. Instead, by establishing a close working relationship with teachers and peers, students are given the chance to understand that an analytical, codified body of experience is the central element in any pedagogy. This helps both students and teachers to recognize that behind any pedagogy are values, beliefs, and assumptions informed by a particular world-view. Most students see teaching in terms of individual personalities rather than the result of a thought out set of socially constructed pedagogical axioms.[51] By using this course of action, both students and teachers are provided with a "particular" framework for teaching that highlights the theoretical underpinnings of classroom pedagogy.

The concept of time in schools restricts the development of healthy social and intellectual relationships among students and teachers. Reminiscent of life in factories with its production schedules and hierarchial work relationships, the daily routine of most classrooms acts as a brake upon participation and democratic processes. Modified self-pacing is a classroom process that is more compatible with the view that aptitude is the amount of time required by the students to develop a critical comprehension and resolution of the task under study.

It is imperative that students be given the opportunity to work alone and in groups at a comfortable learning pace so as to be able to quickly develop a learning style that enables them to move beyond the fragmented and atheoretical pedagogies that now characterize American education.[52] The flexible use of a mode of self-paced learning should eliminate these practices.

Self-pacing is important for other reasons. The delay and denial characteristic of most conventional classrooms can be offset by freeing teachers and students to respond to each other almost immediately. Students need not wait to get feedback and communication about their work. This militates against students giving up or postponing their desire to learn or to share and analyze what they have learned with other students. Modified self-pacing allows students to work alone or with other students at a comfortable pace, within reasonable bounds mutually agreed upon by teachers and students. Under this format, the clock ceases to shape the pace and character of the class, and the tyranny of a rigid time schedule gives way to a schedule governed by reciprocal exchanges. Moreover, since students have a measure of control over their work, grades, and time, this eliminates pitting students against one another and reinforces the notion that learning is essentially a shared phenomenon.

In political terms, the self-pacing and peer-leader features challenge the idea that the teacher is the indispensible expert, alone qualified to define and distribute knowledge.[53] Moreover, with the use of peers and modified self-pacing, democratic classroom relationships are developed and the one-dimensionality of traditional classroom social relationships gives way to the possiblity of infinitely richer classroom social encounters. These classroom social encounters are reciprocally humanizing and are mediated through an emancipatory conceptual framework.

The peer-leader and self-paced features represent two social processes that significantly offset some of the organizational and structural properties of the traditional classroom. In most traditional classrooms, students work in an isolated and independent fashion. This is usually rationalized by educators on the grounds that it fosters independence. In part, this is true, but it fosters a type of independence that precludes the development of social relationships among age peers and adults that promote opportunities to share and work in an interdependent fashion. Moreover, its function appears to be more ideological than rational, and represents a strong pedagogical component in upholding the division of labor characteristic of the larger society. In any case, the traditional notion of independence does not strike a balance between developing one's specific talents and sharing tasks with other students. The self-paced and peer features smoothly reconcile this contradiction. Students not only are given ample opportunity to explore their talents and interests at a pace they can control, they also can share their interests with other people. They get help from both the classroom leaders and from their peers.

Conclusion

This chapter provides the groundwork for a new thrust in the task of identifying the dynamics and ideological assumptions underlying specific patterns of socialization in social studies classrooms. By identifying the social processes of classroom and school life which make these patterns operative and highlighting the normative nature of social studies knowledge, it attempts to clarify the dichotomy between the goals of social studies developers and the process of schooling. In our judgement, the recognition of this dichotomy between the official and hidden curriculum will compel social studies educators to develop a new theoretical perspective about the dynamics of educational change, one that penetrates the functional relationships that exist between the institutions of the schools, the workplace and the political world. In so doing, they will begin to uncover those social processes in all sociopolitical institutions including the classroom which militate against the creation of a democratic, social education. Further enumeration and elucidation of those processes as well as the search for interconnections among them will become the necessary prerequisites for educators planning to intervene into the educational process.

The message is a clear one. Social studies educators will run the risk of repeated failure unless they develop a structural foundation that will counter the social processes and values of the hidden curriculum. If social solidarity, individual growth, and dedication to social action are to emerge from social education, the hidden curriculum will have to be either eliminated or minimized. There is little room in social education for tracking and social sorting, hierarchical social relationships, the correspondence between evaluation and power, and the fragmented and isolated interpersonal dynamics of the classroom encounter, all of which characterize the hidden curriculum. These classroom processes will have to be replaced by democratic social processes and values which take into consideration the reciprocal interaction of goals, pedagogy, content, and structure.

This task will not be an easy one; the changes to be made will be difficult and often frustrating but nonetheless necessary. Educational reformers can no longer operate within the limited confines of traditional educational theory and practice. It should be clear that social education is normative and political in essence, and at its best can be both emancipatory and reflective. By stepping outside the traditional parameters of educational theory and practice, we can view schooling as inextricably linked to a web of larger socioeconomic and political arrangements. And by analyzing the nature of the relationship between schools and the dominant society in political and normative terms we can counter a hidden curriculum defined through the ideology of traditional classroom social processes. If social education is in Kant's words to be used to educate students for a better society, social studies educators will even have to go further than democratizing their schools and classrooms. They will have to do more than help develop changes in student consciousness; they will have to help implement the rationale for reconstructing a new social order whose institutional arrangements, in the final analysis, will provide the basis for a truly humanizing education.

4

Overcoming Behavioral and Humanistic Objectives

By HENRY A. GIROUX

A heated debate has been waged among educators over the issue of developing course objectives. The intensity and nature of the debate has been brought into focus for most middle and secondary school teachers as they have watched their school systems swing in pendulum-like fashion from the "open-ended" humanistic objective movement of the sixties to the "demonstrate it with certainty" behavioral movement of the seventies. In retrospect, both movements have shed some light on the problematic complexity of course design, implementation, and evaluation. But in the final analysis, neither movement has provided a theoretical model for developing course objectives which adequately balances a need for certainty and exactness with other modes of learning and valuing.

The purpose of this is to examine the shortcomings of the two major "schools"[1] that presently dominate the educational establishment's thinking about developing course objectives. Moreover, this proposes a new pedagogical approach which allows educators to develop course objectives that illuminate the relationship between classroom methodology and content and their respective valuation underpinnings. It is believed that through an examination of the latter relationship, the complex interplay between schools and the larger social order will be highlighted. Hopefully this will persuade educators to question many of the "common sense" and unexamined assumptions that shape the design and evaluation of their courses. In addition, this chapter shifts the center of gravity in the current debate over course objectives away from an either/or perspective on the validity of the different schools of objectives and provides a new focus that will help educators to determine what types of objectives are most suitable for developing different sets of interlocking pedagogical goals.

At first glance, it appears that both the humanistic and behavioral objectives schools exist on vastly different pedagogical planets, with little or no room for dialogue over their respective differences. Instead of looking beyond the categorical parameters of their major assumptions, both schools appear encrusted in what amounts to a self-serving, uncritical acceptance of their guiding theoretical tenets.[2] In part, the contrast between both schools is fortified by major criticisms that illuminate their respective limitations as well as their different approaches to developing classroom objectives. For instance, it has been noted by many critics that while the need for exactness and certainty among supporters of the behavioral objectives school is understandable, its concern with trivial knowledge, its overly cognitive emphasis, and its denial of the value of personal meaning are disturbing.[3] On the other hand, supporters of the humanistic objectives school often find themselves developing courses that lack certainty and clarity of direction. Such courses usually are built around fuzzy and tentative statements of purpose, the value of which usually remains a mystery to teachers and students alike.[4]

The clearly antagonistic position of both schools has forced many educators looking for a viable approach to developing course objectives to fall into an either/or position, a watered-down choice that ends up reproducing the very problem that it was supposed to have solved. Good sense appears to dictate that a qualitatively different position could develop if each school began an earnest dialogue with one another, a dialogue which would point to a synthesis of their respective positions. While the latter approach seems feasible, it falls flat when a distinction is made between common sense and good sense. What is needed is not so much a dialogue between the two schools as is a willingness for each school to reflect critically on the shortcomings of its own approach. Forthcoming from such an approach should be less a dialogue than a metamorphosis to a new position, one which bypasses dialogue for self-criticism and theoretical freshness. The starting point for such an approach might be to look at the commonalities that both schools share, commonalities that appear to prevent them from moving beyond the limiting pedagogical assumptions that identify their uniquely different positions.

Both schools share the following commonalities: a truncated notion of the function of schooling; a tacit advocacy of a view which denies the importance of theoretical models and theoretical conflict; and an inability to give due weight to a student's cultural capital as a starting point for learning activities. In addition, both schools have failed to examine the latent functions of schooling even though such functions affect the objectives of the formal curriculum.[5] The net result has been a theoretical impasse among those educators who identify with either a humanistic or behavioral position.

Each of the above commonalities will be examined briefly below. More importantly, these commonalities will be analyzed, not only for the questions they pose, but also for the direction to which they point in helping teachers to construct a more encompassing and flexible model and language in the development and implementation of course objectives.

Teaching students how to read, write, and comprehend the conceptual framework of a given course has often been defined by educators as a technical task.[6] "Technical," as it is used here, refers to the definition applied in the "strict sciences." Technical refers to a form of rationality whose dominant interest lies in models that promote certainty and technical control; the term also suggests an emphasis on efficiency and how-to-do techniques that ignore the more important questions of ends. For instance, often ignored are questions such as: "Why are we doing what we are doing?" Or, "Why is this knowledge being learned?" "Why is this type of pedagogical style being used to transmit information in the classroom?" "Why this form of evaluation?" While the behaviorists have generally avoided the questions of ends, the humanists have limited questions concerning ends to the immediacy of the classroom setting and have ignored "helping students bent on surpassing what is merely 'given', on breaking through the everyday experiences."[7]

Neither the humanists nor the behaviorists have addressed themselves adequately to the barriers that prevent human understanding and dialogue concerning the relationship between socially constructed knowledge and the normative dimensions of classroom interaction. Under such circumstances, questions concerning the connection between classroom knowledge and the socially constructed categories used to legitimate that knowledge are ignored. Young has stated the problem well in claiming that educators in the United States have hardly considered "the content of education, either in terms of how the education system might influence publicly available meanings or with how contemporary definitions of cultures have consequences for the organization of knowledge in the school system."[8] Consequently, the role of schools as social mechanisms for selecting, preserving, and passing on competencies of a highly ideological and valuative nature has been obscured.

It is worth stressing that the knowledge passed on to students in schools is selected from a larger universe of knowledge. The problem this poses for educators, one that has been overlooked by both the humanistic and behavioral objectives schools, has been stated clearly by Apple:

> We need to examine critically not just "how a student acquires more knowledge" (the dominant question in our efficiency minded field) but "why and how particular aspects of the collective culture are presented in school as objective, factual knowledge." How, *concretely*, may official knowledge represent ideological configurations of the dominant interests in a society? How do schools legitimate these limited and partial standards of knowing as unquestioned truths? These questions must be asked of at least three areas of school life: (1) how the basic day-to-day regularities of schools contribute to [students learning] these ideologies; (2) how the specific forms of curricular knowledge reflect these configurations; and (3) how these ideologies are reflected in the fundamental perspectives educators themselves employ to order, guide, and give meaning to their own activity.[9]

Thus, the reduction of teaching objectives to a concern with either style, i.e., "deep subjectivity," or content by both schools has resulted in the failure to develop an adequate theoretical model capable of generating course objectives that link content with classroom social relations in such a way as to avoid either the "feel more, think less" syndrome or the "learn more and suffer" approach.

Both schools have ignored the importance of developing course objectives that stress the importance of theory, particularly the relationship between theory and facts. The crucial relationship between theory and facts is important for students to understand for a number of reasons. The most obvious is that theory represents the conceptual framework which mediates between human beings and the objective nature of the larger social reality. Most importantly, theoretical frameworks, whether conscious or not, operate as a set of filters through which people view information, select facts, study social reality, define problems, and eventually develop tentative solutions to those problems. Simply put, it is theory that permits students, teachers, and other educators to see what they are seeing. What is not so obvious is that theory does more than structure one's selection of the facts that shape one's world. Theory also plays a vital role in reproducing a reality that includes tacit common sense assumptions about what society and history are all about.[10] The point here is that theory is responsible for creating facts as well as selecting them, and all too often the fragile ideological assumptions upon which these facts are constructed are highly questionable. Theory, in the most general sense, is crucial to almost every stage of thinking. Not only because it helps us order and select data, but because it also provides the conceptual tools by which to question the data itself. If students are taught to recognize that theoretical frameworks and facts are an inseparable part of what we call knowledge, the first step will be made to help them assess their own theoretical framework as well as to move beyond the mystifying and limiting task of treating information through the use of simple classifications, descriptions, and generalizations. Most importantly, knowledge for the student is conceived, in this case, as more than a "neutral picturing of fact."[11]

If different theoretical models generate different ways of defining knowledge, then it should be clear that knowledge is not the end of thinking, but is the mediating link between students and teachers. As a mediating link, knowledge should be treated as problematic, and thus, as an object of inquiry. This is not to suggest that all knowledge and theoretical models should be given equal weight. The latter approach is precisely the pitfall into which many members of the humanistic objectives school fall.[12] Once objectives are developed which allow students to understand that there is a link between facts and values, then the question of how information is selected, arranged, and sequenced to construct and interpret a view of reality takes on an axiomatic dimension. In other words, the relationship between theory and facts can be seen as more than a cognitive operation, a technical task stripped of ideology and values. The latter relationship has to be viewed as being an ideological process central to the question of how one's belief and value system is used in the shaping of one's world.

Another commonality shared by the humanistic and behavioral objectives schools centers around the notion of cultural capital. Cultural capital refers to the cognitive, linguistic, and dispositional attributes that different students bring to schools. Both the humanistic and behaviorist schools have failed to analyze the importance of the relationship between classroom objectives and cultural capital. The recent works of Bourdieu and Bernstein suggest that crucial to the development of progressive classroom social relationships is the opening of channels of communication which allow students to use those forms of linguistic and cultural capital through which they give meaning to their everyday experiences.[13] If students are subjected in the classroom to a language as well as a set of beliefs and values whose implicit message is that they are culturally illiterate, students will learn very little about critical thinking, and a great deal about what Freire has called the "culture of silence."[14]

A new approach to the development of course objectives must go beyond the limitations of the humanistic and behavioral objectives schools. The starting point for such a task is to view educational knowledge as a study in ideology, one that raises questions about the so-called shared assumptions embodied in the content, implementation, and evaluation of course design. The latter task suggests using new terms to develop and classify objectives that serve to illuminate the link between socially constructed knowledge and classroom learning. The model that is about to be presented for developing course objectives is built around two concepts labeled macro-objectives and micro-objectives. After defining and explaining the latter concepts, I will comment on the latent function of schooling, one of the most important commonalities that has prevented the humanistic and behaviorist schools from moving beyond the limitations of their respective positions.

Macro-objectives are designed to provide the theoretical building blocks that will enable students to make connections between the methods, content, and structure of a course and its significance to the larger social reality. In effect, what these objectives do is act as mediating concepts between the students' classroom experiences, cognitive as well as noncognitive, and their lives outside the classroom. Utilizing such concepts, students should be able to analyze course content, values, and norms in relation to the ends they are designed to serve or might serve. In general terms, macro-objectives include the following: differentiating between directive and productive knowledge, making the hidden curriculum explicit, and helping students develop a critical, political consciousness.

Micro-objectives generally represent the traditional course objectives. They are usually limited by the specificity or narrowness of their purpose, which is shaped by the uniqueness of the course they are designed to serve. In other words, micro-objectives consist of those imposed conceptions that make up the core of a given subject and define its path of inquiry. In varying combinations, most courses include many of the following micro-objectives: the acquisition of selected knowledge, the development of specialized learning skills, the development of specific inquiry skills. The strengths and weaknesses of these micro-objectives have been analyzed many times by other educators; what is under question is not the validity of these specific objectives so much as their relationship as a set of limited objectives to a broader set of objectives, the macro-objectives. Consequently, it is the macro-objectives, rather than the micro-objectives, that warrant analysis.

The importance of the relationship between macro- and micro-objectives arises out of the necessity to make clear to students what the connections are between the course objectives and the norms, values, and structural relationships rooted in the dynamics of the established society. Macro-objectives serve specifically as mediating concepts that illuminate the meaning and significance micro-objectives might have with respect to the socio-political structures that exists outside of the classroom. In short, macro-objectives are designed to provide a paradigm which will enable students to question the purpose and value of micro-objectives, not only as they apply to a given course, but also as they apply to the society at large. One such important macro-objective centers around helping students to differentiate between the notions of directive and productive knowledge.

Productive knowledge is primarily concerned with means; the application of this type of knowledge results in the reproduction of material goods and services. Thus productive knowledge is instrumental in the sense of innovating new methods in technology and science. Directive knowledge is a mode of inquiry designed to answer questions that productive knowledge cannot answer; it is concerned with speculative questions centering around the relationship of means to ends. Directive knowledge is a philosophical mode of inquiry in which students question the purpose of what they are learning. It is knowledge that questions now productive knowledge is to be used. Directive knowledge formulates the most important questions in improving the quality of life because it asks "For what end?"

The importance of this macro-objective cannot be overstated. If knowledge is reduced to the mere organization, classification, and computation of data, then its purpose is not questioned and it can be used to serve ends established by someone else. Under such circumstances, students, as well as teachers, are denied the opportunity to examine knowledge critically, and social and political conformity end up masquerading as "acceptable" pedagogy. If students are to recognize the importance of the socio-political application of knowledge, they will have to learn to approach it from the discerning perspective of both the productive and directive standpoints. This perspective applies not only to course content, but also to methodology and structure as well. The social theorist, Max Horkheimer, forcefully recognized the importance of this perspective when he pointed out that the nature of truth cannot be discovered through a methodology that ignores the question of ends.[15]

In addition to Horkheimer, philosophers from Plato to Gramsci have rightly claimed that knowledge should play an emancipatory role by providing students with a unity, logic, and sense of direction that will allow them to consider all of the implications of what they are taught, whether in or out of school. By using the directive-productive classification, students will be able to recognize that knowledge has a social function which extends it beyond the goal of mastering a given academic subject. As a result, the interrelation between knowledge and social action becomes possible for students. Fromm defined the interrelation between knowledge and social action in the following way.

> The interrelation between concern and knowledge has often been expressed, and rightly so, in terms of the interrelation between theory and practice. As Marx once wrote, one must not only interpret the world, but one must change it. Indeed, interpretation without intention of change is empty; change without interpretation is blind. Interpretation and change, theory and practice, are not two separate factors which can be combined; they are interrelated in such a way that knowledge becomes fertilized by practice and practice is guided by knowledge; theory and practice both change their nature once they cease to be separate.[16]

If Fromm is taken seriously, the concern with knowledge becomes viable in pedagogical terms only when such knowledge is tested with an explicit end in mind. Far from being deterministic, the importance of this position is that it makes clear the need for educators to develop objectives that would help students to analyze the complex interplay and social tensions that arise between questions concerning means and ends. Such an analysis would enable students to approach their lives when faced with the problem of action by asking themselves: "What is the moral justification for this action?" The directive-productive perspective provides one possible approach to this issue.

An equally important macro-objective centers around making the traditional hidden curriculum explicit. The hidden curriculum here refers to those unstated norms, values, and beliefs that are transmitted to students through the underlying structure of a given class. An extensive amount of research suggests that what students learn in school is shaped more by the hidden curriculum, the underlying pattern of social relationships in both the classroom and the larger school, than by the formal curriculum.[17] In addition, the hidden curriculum often acts at cross-purposes with the stated goals of the formal curriculum, and rather than promote effective learning, it vitiates such learning. Under such conditions, subordination, conformity, and discipline replace the development of critical thinking and productive social relationships as the primary characteristics of the schooling experience.[18] While the hidden curriculum cannot be entirely eliminated, its structural properties can be identified and modified to create conditions that facilitate developing pedagogical methods and content that help to make students active subjects in the classroom rather than simply recipient objects. By making both students and teachers aware of the hidden curriculum as it has traditionally operated, both groups can develop an understanding of its components and effects and work to form new insights about it. Once the hidden curriculum becomes obvious, students and teachers will be more sensitive to recognizing and altering its worst effects and can work to build new structures, methods, and social relationships in which underlying classroom norms and values will work so as to promote learning rather than adjustment.

A third macro-objective centers around helping students develop a critical, political consciousness. Support for this position has a long history, and can be found in the writings of the ancient Greeks. For the ancient Greeks, the ultimate test of the educational system was the moral and political quality of the students that it produced. Iglitzin, commenting on the Greek notion of politics and education, claims that "the Greek conception of political thought centered around the notion that the concepts of education, virtue and political participation are all inextricably related. Thus, education in the Greek sense must include the joys and responsibilities of full civic participation."[19] The development of a macro-objective that seeks to perpetuate a critical, political consciousness among students rests on an assumption shared by Kant who said that youth "ought to be educated not for the present, but for a better future condition of the human race, that is, for the idea of humanity."[20] The political implications of Kant's remark should be clear. The point is, this objective does not mean stressing political content in the most literal sense of the term, but suggests providing students with a methodology that allows them to look beyond their private lives to an understanding of the political, social, and economic foundations of the larger society. Political in this sense means having the cognitive and intellectual tools that allow active participation in such a society.

One approach to this macro-objective points to teaching students the meaning and importance of the notion of frame of reference. By being made aware that everybody has a frame of reference, operating either consciously or unconsciously, students will have the opportunity to develop a theoretical framework in which they can order their experiences and recognize the social basis of their perceptions. Markovic, the outstanding Yugoslavian philosopher, directly links the growth of a critical, political consciousness to the development of a frame of reference, i.e., worldview:

> World view helps to bring to consciousness what one is in the habit of doing unconsciously. If the theory is valid it increases our knowledge about ourselves and our doing, it enables us to control our own powers, to reflect about them critically and rationally, and to improve our future ways of acting. If it is true that we follow certain rules whenever our activity is well organized and directed toward some goal, then ignorance of these rules is a specific form of alienation.[21]

The importance of students becoming conscious of their own frame of reference takes on an added significance when that frame of reference is informed by a mode of reasoning that helps them to link the personal to the social; in other words, an epistemology that helps them to recognize the social, thus political nature of thinking and acting. The assumption behind this position is that knowledge is a political-social phenomenon that can be most meaningfully studied by examining the network of connections in which it is embedded. This position represents using a methodology that stresses the connection between values and facts as well as perceiving knowledge by attempting to understand its causal links, i.e., the network or relations that give it meaning.

If students are to develop a political consciousness, it must become clear to them that schooling is a political process, not only because it contains a political message or deals with political topics on occasion, but also because it is produced and situated in a complex of social and political relations from which it cannot be abstracted. Consequently, students must be given the opportunity both to understand the political nature of the schooling process and to use it as a micro-cosmic model in which they can apply the criticism and analysis that will prove beneficial once they leave the school and enter the larger society. From this point of view, this macro-objective should help to generate in students a desire to combine analytical and reflective thinking with various forms of class-room social interaction. Reflecting on the Deweyite origin of such an aim, Kohlberg has pointed out that "this means that the classroom, itself, must be seen as an arena in which the social and political process takes place in microcosm.[22]

In conclusion, macro-objectives provide a classificatory scheme designed to help students and teachers move beyond notions of learning limited by the parameters of a given subject or course. More importantly, the macro- micro-objectives distinction allows educators to use diverse objectives in order to explore the relationship between students' classroom experiences and sociopolitical forces that shape the dominant culture. For instance, the macro-micro model would permit teachers who do not wholeheartedly susbcribe to the behaviorist position on objectives to select behavioral objectives as micro-objectives while being able to use other types of objectives as macro-objectives. The flexibility of this approach not only makes it easier to assess the effectiveness of different types of educational objectives, it also insures that any course design will be based on an approach that links different forms of learning with socially contructed norms and values. Educators must move beyond the theoretical schizophrenia that presently characterizes the objectives movement. Only then will they move closer to developing course objectives designed to foster educational experiences for their students that will illuminate the political richness and social complexity of the interplay between what is learned in school and the experience of everday life.

5

Writing and Critical Thinking in the Social Studies

By HENRY A. GIROUX

> General, a man is quite expendable. He can fly and he can kill. But he has one defect: He can think.
>
> —Bertolt Brecht.

In a recent speech on writing, before the National Council of Teachers of English, novelist Jerzy Kosinski claimed that students were "not verbal; they could not describe what they read, they could not describe their own emotions." Kosinski elaborated his point by claiming that the prevailing American culture deadens individual awareness and thinking. Implicit in Kosinski's charge is the assumption that there is a relationship between writing and thinking. More specifically, poor writing reflects poor thinking, and what teachers often view as simply an "error" in writing, in fact, is a reflection of an error in thinking itself.

The purpose of this chapter is to examine traditional theoretical assumptions about the pedagogy of both writing and critical thinking. In addition, this chapter attempts to show, not only that the pedagogy of writing and critical thinking are linked dialectically, but also to illustrate how a pedagogy of writing can be used as a learning vehicle to help students learn and think critically about any given social studies subject.

Traditional Approaches to Writing

The history of the last few decades indicates that traditional approaches to the pedagogy of writing do not work.[1] Part of this failure can be connected to what Van Nostrand calls the primitive state of the art of teaching writing. As Van Nostrand and others have pointed out, traditional writing instruction has been dominated by a number of powerful but misleading assumptions that have reduced the teaching of writing to a largely procedural, parochial, and namely, technocratic pedagogy.[2]

One assumption is that writing has to be taught exclusively by English teachers. The evidence is quite clear on this point. At all levels of education, instruction in writing exists either exclusively within the domain of English departments or such instruction is carried out primarily by English teachers. Moreover, most of the research and publications about instruction in writing are written exclusively for people in English departments. Further assumptions follow from the monopolization of the pedagogy of writing by English teachers. The more important include: (1) a great deal is known about the pedagogy of writing; (2) English teachers, by virtue of their training, are in a privileged position to teach writing; and (3) writing instruction is a skill marginally connected to the learning of other subjects.

All of the above assumptions need to be questioned, but it has been only recently that these assumptions have been challenged and replaced with a more accurate understanding of what constitutes writing in both general and specific terms. Moreover, it has been only within the last decade that revisionist definitions of writing have been linked to comparable learning strategies.[3] But before proceeding to define the latter new approaches to the instruction of writing, I want to illuminate some of the traditional ideas about writing by examining three prevailing "schools" that continue to capitalize upon and reproduce misguided notions about the nature and pedagogy of writing.

The three major schools that presently dominate the teaching of writing are what I define as (1) the "technocratic school," (2) the "mimetic school," and (3) the "romantic school." It should be noted that there are other schools of instruction that, in some cases, represent new and progressive approaches to writing, but they are few in number and are not characteristic of the field. Moreover, it is crucial to stress that the three schools under examination represent tendencies rather than fixed, theoretical positions.

The technocratic school is the most influential as well as the best known of the three schools. This school's approach is purely formalistic and is characterized by a strict emphasis on rules, exhortations about what to do or not to do as one writes. Writing in this case is viewed as a craft, a matter of technique that begins by stressing grammar and ends by emphasizing the coordination and development of larger syntactical structures. The single, most important theoretical assumption that guides the technocratic approach is that writing is an artifact, the learning of a series of skills that range from simple grammatical encodings to complicated syntactical constructions. The devotees of this group range from hardcore users of traditional English grammar and composition texts to "avant garde" advocates of the many texts on transformational grammar.

At the heart of the technocratic approach is a failure to ground the pedagogy of writing in a conceptual framework that allows students to make connections between what Vygotsky has called inner speech and elaborated written speech.[4] Such connections involve a link between the subjective perceptions that students internalize and their objectification of those experiences for a given audience. In short, the technocratic school has failed to understand a powerful dimension of the writing process, a dimension in which writing functions both as a structured medium for generating knowledge as well as a means for constructing logical thought. What the technocratic school fails to perceive is that writing is a process, a unique mode of learning that corresponds to powerful learning strategies that examine the complex relationship among the reader, the subject, and the writer. Consequently, writing as a form of praxis, a way of structuring consciousness, is viewed simply as a technical skill, reduced to a simplistic, crude instrumentalism divorced from content, ideation, and normative underpinnings.

Fortunately, within the last few years, a great deal of research has been done which indicates that the teaching of formal grammar has either no effect on the improvement of writing or has a negative effect.[5] Unfortunately, while the latter research serves to undermine core assumptions of the technocratic school, the latter's popularity remains intact, especially with the recent growth of the back-to-basics movement in education. Even more distressing is research which indicates that while there are some instructional manuals in writing which give lip service to the connection between writing and thinking, most of these manuals "are about tidying up and transcribing thought, not thinking".[6]

The mimetic school offers a much different, but no less misleading, perspective on both the process and pedagogy of writing. Rather than starting from the bottom up by teaching grammar and syntax, supporters of this camp begin at the top by having students read the works of "reputable" authors ranging from Plato to Norman Mailer. The mimetic school assumes that students learn how to write by reading books that serve as models of good writing. Unfortunately, it remains to be explained just how this approach works. It appears to operate off a version of the "osmotic" principle. Thus, if students read enough Hemingway, Vidal, and others, they will learn how to write as a result of a process of assimilation.

At a conference on teaching writing held at the Graduate Center of the City University of New York, Susan Sontag and Francine du Plessix Gray reiterated the value of the mimetic approach to writing. Sontag argued that students should be taught how to think before they write; one way of learning how to think as well as learning how to write would be to imitate good writers "who can be assigned in small doses—a paragraph or a page—and then imitated by the students."[7] Francine du Plessix Gray echoed Sontag's suggestion by calling upon teachers to give students close readings of "Orwell, Agee, and Walt Whitman's prose."[8] This approach may familiarize students with significant works of literature, but its value as a writing technique is severely limited. The decline in writing ability in recent years is just as notable among English literature majors as it is among students from other disciplines.[9]

Though Sontag and others see a connection between thinking and writing, the transition from the former to the latter cannot be made through an act of fate. Reading the work of reputable authors neither guarantees that one will be able to think any better, nor that one will be able to write any better. Ironically, the mimetic approach seems to reinforce the latter point with its rather casual argument that there are good writers and there are bad writers, and given the proper conditions, the good writers will bloom. In popular terms, this translates into the Calvinist notion that "some folks have it and some folks don't." Of course, on a more subtle level this position also rejects the need for a pedagogy of writing. Writing in this case is not pedagogically based, it is biologically based. One does not teach writing, one simply provides a place for the students to write.

A third approach to writing, the romantic school, rests on the premise that there is a causal relationship between making students "feel good" and improving students' writing abilities. Writing in this case is viewed as the product of a catalytic discharge of joyful emotion. The proponents of this school draw heavily upon a loose collection of thinkers such as Carl Rogers, Abraham Maslow, and Gordon Alport whose roots are in the personal, existential counseling tradition. Known as the post-Freudian group, its proponents reject the pessimism of the early post-1945 existentialists and stress an optimistic belief in the worthiness of the individual's capacity to grow and realize self-fulfillment. Unfortunately, supporters of the post-Freudian position in the English field, such as Sidney B. Simon and George E. Newell accept at face value the theoretical assumptions on which the position is based. For the sake of clarity, it is necessary to provide a brief analysis of some of the more important assumptions of the post-Freudian position.[10]

For the post-Freudians, the individual seems to exist in a land of free-floating, interpersonal relations, held back from self-fulfillment only by the limits of individual will and the personal release of frustration. What the post-Freudians ignore are the external realities that mediate between the individual's desires and the fulfillment of those desires. Similarly, they fail to realize that success is not simply a matter of will, magically breezing through the paper barricades of the real world; in reality, "success" represents an ability to deal concretely with the sociopolitical forces that generate doubt, conflict, anguish, and the possibility of making mistakes. The point here is that happiness and human will alone are rendered meaningless when they are not examined through a theoretical perspective that situates and analyzes them within concrete sociohistorical circumstances. Sensitivity towards one's feelings is no excuse for an indifference toward the more distant social forces that define the immediate, the immediate in this sense being the classroom and the day-to-day social relationships of the educational encounter.[11]

The basic problem with the romantic school is that it overemphasizes the importance of the "inner self." An overemphasis of the student's need to recognize the "inner self" ignores the objective nature of a pedagogy of writing that has its own laws, laws that have to be taught and cannot be understood intuitively by students who are given the opportunity to revel expressively in the assertion of "positive" feelings. The latter critique is not meant to undermine the importance of the affective dimension as a motivational factor in the teaching of writing. The affective mode is necessary, but at the same time, it is incomplete. It takes a leap of faith to claim that there is a one-to-one correspondence between students "feeling good" and their being able to write well. "Feeling good" is no substitute for a systematic approach to learning a sound and developed pedagogy of writing, one that helps students to understand what happens as they write. When the interpersonal dimension becomes such a substitute, it appears to translate itself into the converse of its stated objective and ends up as "feel more and think less."[12]

All of these schools of pedagogy share a common flaw, one that has had considerable influence over preventing the development of a new approach to the theory and practice of writing. Each of these camps fails to examine the question of what happens when one writes. Thus, the notion of writing as both an interdisciplinary process and as an epistemology capable of teaching students how to think critically and rationally about a subject cannot be ignored.

Epistemologically, writing must be viewed as a dialectical process rather than an instrumental skill. As an instrumental skill, writing is limited to a static concern with traditional rhetorical categories such as argument, exposition, narration, and grammar usage. Such categories fail, as Britton has pointed out, to provide an understanding of what the writing process is all about.[13] A dialectical approach would examine the writing process as a series of relationships between the writer and the subject, between the writer and the reader, and between the subject matter and the reader. In general terms, such an approach to writing would mean considering writing in its broadest relationship to the learning and communicating processes. In this case, learning how to write would not mean learning how to develop an instrumental delivery system, but as Dr. Carlos Baker has said, would mean learning how to think.[14] Writing in this case is an epistemology, a mode of learning.

More precisely put, the notion of writing as a mode of learning has to be distinguished from the general notion of communication. As in writing, when we speak we learn more about what we want to say by simply saying it. We learn as we speak. The same is true of writing, we learn as we write. The correlation seems obvious and natural; yet it is both misleading and incorrect. Though both forms of communication involve learning more about a given subject, the laws governing oral communication are much different from those governing written communication. In oral communication, the relationship between speaker and listener is grounded in a number of existential stimuli such as facial expressions, pitch and intonation, emotional intensity, and in some cases, tactile cues such as touching. In addition, if the listener is confused, one can stop the speaker and ask for clarifications. Written communication lacks such luxuries. The writer's relationship to the reader is much more tenuous and is held together by the writer's promise to provide the reader with important and interesting information. And not unlike a good work of art, good writing demands an integration of form and content, the quality of which will hold the reader's attention. Unfortunately, what often happens is that the writer promises one thing to the reader and ends up delivering something else. Van Nostrand has stated the problem well.

> The essential relationship between writer and reader is a contract: a unilateral contract that the writer makes. The writer implies a promise to convey something of value, some kind of information, in return for the reader's attention. But the writer tends to violate this contract simply by writing. The reader expects what is promised, but gets something else instead, which is a record of the writer's attempts to state some elusive relationship, often including false starts, unlikely assertions, muddled references to antecedents, transposed word groups, and ambiguous metaphors. These are all normal signs of the writer's normal learning process. To the reader, however, they are detours around what was promised.[15]

Differentiating between written and oral communication has marked the first step for a growing number of scholars like Emig, Freire, Van Nostrand, and Vygotsky in redefining what constitutes the pedagogy of writing. Discarding the notion of writing as a drill in the mastery of techniques, the latter group has made significant advances in developing theoretically informed strategies in which writing is defined as an active relationship that mediates between the subject and the world. More specifically, such a relationship has important implications about both the form and content of learning, especially with respect to the concept of critical thinking. It is through an examination of what constitutes critical thinking that the implications for a new approach to writing will be explored.

Toward a Pedagogy Of Critical Thinking

For the sake of clarification, I want to stress that it is not my purpose to provide an in-depth treatment of what constitutes critical thinking. Such a task remains for another time. In the account that follows, I simply want to suggest a few theoretical components that I think constitute a good starting point for a pedagogy of critical thinking. In addition, it will serve as an introduction for the next section in which the application of a specific writing model to an American history course will be illustrated as a nexus that integrates writing and critical thinking. While the immediate focus of the next section will be on subject matter drawn from the discipline of history, the underlying concepts and suggestions can be applied to other social studies subjects.

I want to begin by commenting in general terms on the problems that continue to shape social studies teaching. These problems are important, I believe, because they reflect a pedagogical misunderstanding on the part of educators over what constitutes critical thinking in both general and specific terms. First, most of what students acquire in school is a systematic exposure of selected aspects of human history and culture. Yet, the normative nature of the material selected is presented as both unproblematic and value free. In the name of objectivity, a large part of our social studies curricula universalizes dominant norms, values, and perspectives that represent interpretive and normative perspectives on social reality.[16] The latter approach to social studies might be aptly characterized as the pedagogy of the "immaculate perception." Second, the pedagogy of the "immaculate perception" represents an approach to learning that not only sanctions dominant categories of knowledge and values, but also reinforces a theoretical and undialectical approach to structuring one's perception of the world. Students are not taught to look at curricula knowledge, the facts, within a wider context of learning. Moreover, the relationship between theory and "facts" is often ignored, thus making it all too difficult for students to develop a conceptual apparatus for investigating the ideological and epistemological nature of what constitutes a "fact" in the first place. Lastly, the pedagogy of the "immaculate perception" both creates and reproduces classroom social relationships that are not only boring for most students but also, more importantly, mystifying. Rather than developing actively critical thinkers, such a pedagogy produces students who are either afraid or unable to think critically.[17]

Before examining the nature of critical thinking, a short comment should be made about the source of the pedagogical ills that are gnawing at North American schools and the social studies field in particular. If the social studies field, particularly at the secondary education level, is in part characterized by a pedagogy that inveighs against critical thinking, who in the final analysis is responsible for such a default? Any conclusive answer to such a question would have to begin with the recognition that it is too simple-minded a response to lay the blame exclusively on either teachers or students. Such a perspective ignores that the essence of schooling lies in its relationship to the larger socioeconomic reality, particularly the institutions of work. Schools appear to have little to do with the Kantian notion that they should function to educate students for a "better future condition of the human race, that is for the idea of humanity."[18] The real business of schools appears to be to socialize students into accepting and reproducing the existing society.[19] While teachers cannot be blamed in the long run for many of the ills that plague North American education, they can examine the common-sense assumptions behind their approaches to teaching. This means they would have to reshape and restructure their pedagogy in accordance with the categorical dictum once voiced by Nietzsche, "A great truth wants to be criticized, not idolized."[20] This leads us directly to the thorny issue of defining the concept of critical thinking in both theoretical and programmatic terms.

Traditional views on the nature of critical thinking have failed to support Nietzsche's call for a critical search for the truth. This is true, not only because textbooks and pedagogical approaches in the social studies have objectified prevailing norms, beliefs, and attitudes, but also because of the very way in which critical thinking has been defined. The most powerful, yet limited, definition of critical thinking comes out of the positivist tradition in the applied sciences and suffers from what I call the Internal Consistency position.[21] According to the adherents of the Internal Consistency position, critical thinking refers primarily to teaching students how to analyze and develop reading and writing assignments from the perspective of formal, logical patterns of consistency. In this case, the student is taught to examine the logical development of a theme, "advance organizers," systematic argument, the validity of evidence, and how to determine whether a conclusion flows from the data under study. While all of the latter learning skills are important, their limitations as a whole lie in what is excluded, and it is with respect to what is missing that the ideology of such an approach is revealed.

At the core of what we call critical thinking, there are two major assumptions that are missing. First, there is a relationship between theory and facts; second, knowledge cannot be separated from human interests, norms, and values. Despite a seeming oversimplification, it is within the context of these two assumptions that further assumptions can be developed, and a theoretical, programmatic groundwork can be created for a pedagogical approach to teaching students how to think critically.

Alvin Gouldner has stressed the importance of acknowledging the relationship between theory and facts, a relationship that raises fundamental questions about the fragile nature of knowledge. "[Critical thinking] . . . is here construed as the capacity to make problematic what had hitherto been treated as given; to bring into reflection what before had only been used . . . to examine critically the life we lead. This view of rationality situates it in the capacity to think about our thinking."[22] Translated pedagogically, this means that facts, issues, and events in any social studies should be presented problematically to students. Knowledge in this case demands constant searching, invention, and reinvention. Knowledge is not the end of thinking, as Paulo Freire claims, but rather the mediating link between students and teachers. The latter suggests not only a very different approach to classroom social relationships as compared to those that have prevailed traditionally, but it also suggests that a great deal of time should be spent teaching students about the notion of frame of reference and its use as a theoretical/conceptual interpretive tool. By looking at similar information through different frames of reference, students can *begin* to treat knowledge as problematic, and thus, as an object of inquiry.

The connection between theory and facts throws into high relief another fundamental component of a critical thinking pedagogy: the relationships between facts and values. How information is selected, arranged, and sequenced to construct a picture of contemporary or historical reality is more than a cognitive operation; it is also a process intimately connected to the beliefs and values that guide one's life. Implicit in the reordering of knowledge are ideological assumptions about how one views the world, assumptions that constitute a distinction between the essential and the nonessential, the important and the nonimportant. The point here is that any concept of frame of reference has to be presented to students as more than an epistemological framework, it also has to include an axiomatic dimension. Moreover, to separate facts from values is to run the risk of teaching students how to deal with means divorced from the question of ends.

Related to the two major assumptions about critical thinking is a procedural issue that centers around what might be called the contextualization of information. Students need to learn how to be able to move outside of their own frame of reference so that they can question the legitimacy of a given fact, concept, or issue. They also have to learn how to perceive the very essence of what they are examining by placing it critically within a system of relationships that give it meaning. In other words, students must be taught to think dialectically rather than in an isolated and compartmentalized fashion. Fredric Jameson, while pointing out the limitations of an undialectical approach to thinking, presents a fitting comment on the need for a more dialectical approach to the latter. "[t]he antispeculative bias of that tradition, its emphasis on the individual fact or item at the expense of the network of relationships in which the item may be embedded, continue to encourage submission to what is by preventing its followers from making connections, and in particular, from drawing the otherwise unavoidable conclusions on the political level."[23]

In addition to the contextualization of information, the form and content of classroom social relations have to be considered in any pedagogy that concerns itself with critical thinking. Any pedagogy of critical thinking that ignores the social relations of the classroom runs the risk of being mystifying and incomplete. Sartre has captured the latter point with his comment that knowledge is a form of praxis.[24] In other words, knowledge is not studied for its own sake but is seen as a mediation between the individual and the larger social reality. Within the context of such a pedagogy, students become subjects in the act of learning. Under such circumstances, students must be able to examine the content and the structure of the classroom relationships that provide the boundaries for their own learning. The important point here is that if educational knowledge is to be a study in ideology, the question of what constitutes legitimate knowledge must be undertaken amidst classroom social relations that encourage such an approach. Any approach to critical thinking, regardless of how progressive it might be, will vitiate its own possibilities if it operates out of a web of classroom social relationships that are authoritatively hierarchical and promote passivity, docility, and silence. Social relations in the classroom that glorify the teacher as the expert, the dispenser of knowledge, end up crippling student imagination and creativity; in addition, such approaches teach students more about the legitimacy of passivity, than about the need to examine critically the lives they lead.[25]

Crucial to the development of progressive classroom social relationships is the opening of channels of communication in which students use the linguistic and cultural capital they bring to the classroom. If students are subjected to a language as well as a belief and value setting whose implicit message suggests that they are culturally illiterate, students will learn very little about critical thinking, and a great deal about what Paulo Freire has called the "culture of silence."[26]

Bourdieu and others have unveiled the essence of the "culture of silence" pedagogy by pointing out that classroom knowledge, far from being the "outcome of negotiated meanings between students and teachers," is often the imposition of a literacy and cultural style "that is specific to the language socialization of the privileged classes."[27] In short, if knowledge is to be used by students to give meaning to their existence, educators will have to use the students' values, beliefs, and knowledge as an important part of the learning process before, as Maxine Greene points out, "a leap to the theoretical" can be attempted.[28]

In conclusion, the task for linking writing, learning, and critical thinking means redefining the pedagogy of both writing and critical thinking. The final section of this chapter will illustrate how a writing model can be used as a learning vehicle to help students think critically about what constitutes knowledge, in general terms, and more specifically, what constitutes the meaning of history.

A Writing-History Model

The initial response of many social studies teachers to the suggestion that they rely upon writing as a learning vehicle to teach a social studies subject might be, "Writing is a separate subject, and I have a hard enough time simply teaching in my field." The response is a fair one, given the attitude towards writing that has dominated the social studies field, but it is misguided. Writing is more than a subject, it is a process that can be used to teach students a subject by allowing them to assume the same role as the writer who authors the books and texts that are used as learning sources. In other words, social studies teachers can provide students with a writing model that helps them learn a subject by mastering the same fundamental writing and thinking processes used by writers themselves. From this point on, future references will be made specifically to a writing model adapted to a text designed to teach episodes in an American history course.[29] The model presented is not limited to the teaching of American history; it can be applied with slight modifications to any other social studies course.

Central to a sound pedagogy of history is that the writing of history entails a process. The historian defines a principle that relates the details of any event or series of events. Once a principle of relationship is established in terms of cause and effect, the historian can begin to make choices. These choices involve selecting evidence, making assertions that incorporate evidence, and presenting assertions in a sequence. This process clarifies the relationship among the events that the historian has perceived. Thus, making choices among pieces of information results in the record that we call history. This process generates the meaning of history itself. It follows, therefore, that the writing of history engenders a critical ability to understand history. The latter represents not only a sound learning principle for a budding professional historian, but it also provides the pedagogical groundwork for teaching students how to write, learn, and restructure their views of history.

A viable approach to an integrated pedagogy of writing and history should begin by developing a methodology designed to teach students something about the nature of history. This could be done by showing students how to read history by first showing them how history is written. Specifically, such an approach would enable students to read parts of published histories of actual events, to compose limited histories of those events, and then, to compare their own writings with written history. Central to this pedagogical approach is that a distinction should be made between how to write history and merely reproducing it. Students should not be put through the task of completing assignments which demand that they do no more than copy from other historical sources. Instead, an approach should be used in which students would go through the process of making the same kinds of choices that every historian makes. Consequently, students should be taught to judge any history for what it is—an author's attempt to explain the significance of what happened and why it happened.

Fundamental to the methodology to be analyzed is a description of the writing concepts involved in the writer-historian's learning process, as well as a description of the strategies to be used in juxtaposing and communicating these concepts. The writing concepts to be used in the pedagogical approach presented in Figure 1 include the following: frame of reference, gathering information, developing an organizing idea, and using evidence. Figure 1 illustrates one way in which these concepts can be organized. All of these concepts should be presented to the students as problematic. Thus each of the underlying assumptions, meanings, and relationships that these concepts have for the different historians who use them should be analyzed and questioned by students. This brings us to one of the more important learning assumptions in a writing-critical thinking model: making an issue problematic.

The problematic nature of a subject, such as the passing of American

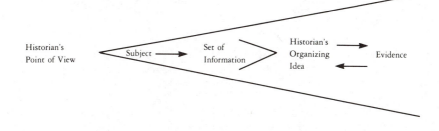

Figure 1. Writing concepts.

immigration laws, might first be presented to students in the following manner. A chapter on "American Immigration" could begin as a section that introduces the issue as a specific historical dilemma that every historian who writes about the subject has to face. The dilemma could take the form of a specific question. In this case, the question is, "Were the restriction laws limiting immigration to the United States justified?" Students will then be placed in the position of being able to explore, through discussion and dialogue, what the interpretive dimensions of history suggest about the relationship between historical knowledge and human interests. Of course, at this point discussions should step outside of the above issue, and data from the students' own lives could be examined as questions to be looked at from a variety of perspectives.

The next step should be used to help students to understand what has previously been referred to in this article as the dialectical approach to thinking. In this case, the student should be presented with a number of overviews on the passing of the restrictive immigration laws. The point to be discussed and made clear is that the laws themselves cannot be understood fully unless examined within a broader historical context. It is the contextualization of an event and its importance to learning that is at stake in this section. To further bring home this point, a leap should then be made to other issues more closely related to the students' lives and experiences; these issues can then be explained.

Once the overview approach has been concluded, the more systematic concept of frame of reference can be presented. The latter can be introduced by relating it to a writing concept known as "organizing idea." To make the point more concrete, students are provided with an analysis of how two historians who had access to the same information on American immigration policy developed different organizing ideas in order to relate that information. The student is then presented with the following comment on two specific historians:

> In his book, *American Immigration,* Maldwyn Allen Jones has an organizing idea that criticizes the passage of the restriction laws by claiming that immigrants provided valuable skills and labor in developing America's cities and industries.
>
> In a different book, *Immigration,* Henry Pratt Fairchild uses an organizing idea that justifies the passage of the restriction laws. Fairchild claims that immigrants displaced native workers from jobs by lowering wages and intensifying unemployment.
>
> You can see that Jones and Fairchild have different organizing ideas. In order to understand why these two historians have different organizing ideas, you should know about another writing concept called Frame of Reference.[30]

The concept of frame of reference is explained to the student; its relationship to the notion of organizing idea is then illuminated through the use of the following example which is taken from Giroux, Karras, and Capizano.[31]

> This example shows how two different frames of reference, when applied to the *same* event and the *same* set of facts or information, can produce two *different* organizing ideas.
>
> *Jones' Frame of Reference might be*
> Immigrants made positive contributions to America's growth.
>
> *. . . and this subject: The Restrictive Immigration Laws;*
> *and this set of information:*
> - birth rate decline dwindling among Americans in 1830s
> - rise of industrialism
> - settlement of West
> - influx of skilled immigrant labor
>
> *and this Organizing Idea:*
> Immigrants played a positive role in the growth of America's cities and industry by providing valuable skills and labor.
>
> *Fairchild's Frame of Reference might be*
> Immigrants represented a negative force in American history.

. . . and this subject: The Restrictive Immigration Laws;
and this set of information:
- birth rate decline dwindling among Americans in 1830s
- rise of industrialism
- settlement of West
- influx of skilled immigrant labor

and this Organizing Idea:
Immigrants displaced native workers from jobs by lowering wages
and intensifying unemployment.

At this point in the lesson, it might be useful to use a modified version
of Freire's approach to literacy in order to allow students not only to work
together, but also to help them further understand the frame of reference
and organizing ideas concepts.[32] A picture or set of pictures that deal
with controversial issues in the students' community can be shown to the
class. From the picture, the students should isolate a number of important
pieces of information. They should then be asked to write a five-paragraph
essay incorporating the five pieces of information. Once they finish the
essay, they should number the paragraphs, and on a separate piece of
paper they can write down one organizing idea for each paragraph, five
organizing ideas in all. Once they finish, they can be placed in groups
to discuss both the meaning and the sequencing of the ideas. Both the
meaning and the ordering of their ideas become problematic through this
exercise.

The next part of the lesson centers around two comparative readings
on the immigration laws; the readings represent different historical accounts written by historians with different frames of reference. If the
reading level of these historical sources is too difficult, each historical
account should be broken down into paragraphs and each paragraph should
be preceded by the subject of the paragraph as well as a list of synonyms
for potentially difficult words. The student then reads the paragraphs and
writes an organizing idea in the form of an assertion for each paragraph,
using the stated subject of the paragraph as the subject for the organizing
idea. Through this exercise, students are given the opportunity to familiarize themselves further with the concept of organizing idea by analyzing two sets of organizing ideas, each set related to a different frame
of reference. The following is an example of the introductory paragraphs
from two different readings on American immigration:[33]

Reading 1 from "Conditions in America
as Affected by Immigration"

1. New Class of Immigrants

prevailing—present
incentive—attraction

Into this favored section of the earth's surface have been introduced
ever increasing numbers of the lower classes of foreign nations. What
has been their effect upon the *prevailing* standard of living? As a major
premise, it will be granted that the standard of living of the working
classes of the United States has been and still is superior to that of the
nations which have furnished the bulk of the immigrants. Common
observation and general testimony establish this beyond the need of
proof. Particularly at the present time, if this were not so, very few of
our immigrants would come, for, as we have seen, this is the great
incentive which draws them. It is significant, however, that the bulk of
immigration has been recruited from more and more backward races of
Europe as the decades have succeeded each other.

ORGANIZING IDEA:

Reading 2 from "Economic Affects of Immigration"

1. Mistaken Beliefs about Jobs

persistent—to continue in spite of interference
recurrent—happening over and over again
misconception—mistaken belief

One of the most *persistent* and *recurrent* economic fallacies in popular
thought is the notion that immigrants take away the jobs of native
Americans. This rests on the *misconception* that only a fixed number of
jobs exist in any economy and that any newcomer threatens the job of
any old resident. Such a theory, sometimes referred to as the "lump of
labor fallacy," has been repeatedly refuted by competent economists.

ORGANIZING IDEA:

Once the comparative readings section is finished, students are given
the opportunity to demonstrate a working knowledge of both the historical
content of the lesson as well as the writing axioms under study. One
example of such a writing assignment is presented below.[34] In this assignment students are given a frame of reference and a set of information.

They are then asked to add three to five new pieces of information taken from either the overview sections or from other historical sources. Students are then asked to write an organizing idea and to construct a paragraph using at least four pieces of information taken from the completed set.

Writing Assignment 1

I. Frame of Reference:
Immigration has contributed positively to the growth and stability of the United States.

II. Set of Information:
- immigrants from northern Europe
- settled in cities
- political machines
- growth of Catholic Church
- mass migrations from southeastern Europe

III. Add three to five pieces of information to this list:
1. _____
2. _____
3. _____
4. _____
5. _____

IV. State your organizing idea:
1. _____
_____

V. Write a paragraph using at least four pieces of information:
1. Paragraph:
_____
_____

Once a student finishes the writing assignment, I have found it useful to have him or her meet with three to five other students so they can read and evaluate each other's papers. It is important that some criteria for evaluating the written assignmnents be made very clear to the students. For instance, in the above groups students are told when reading each other's papers to make sure that (1) the additional three to five pieces of information are relevant to the topic at hand; (2) the organizing idea matches the given frame of reference; (3) the paragraph contains all of the chosen pieces of information; and (4) the information in the paragraph is held together adequately around the stated organizing idea. The precise criteria make it easier for the students to evaluate the papers and also help them to deal somewhat objectively with the criticism they hand out as well as receive. Once the group is able to focus clearly on what it is they are looking for in the written assignments, they seem much more capable of looking dispassionately at their own as well as other's mistakes.

With respect to evaluating this type of lesson, it is important that the student play a significant role in the evaluation process. If classroom social relationships are to be compatible with a pedagogy designed to further critical thinking, students must be given the responsibility to evaluate and correct their own mistakes. Using this approach, unsatisfactory performance is treated as a vehicle to promote a learning experience, one which can be shared by other students. For instance, students can evaluate and grade each other's group papers and maintain the group until every member receives a passing grade. Moreover, at the end of the lesson, students can play a significant role in providing input for progress checks that would measure both historical content as well as the mastery of the writing axioms under study. At the end of one lesson, a class suggested that both the historical content and the writing axioms could be evaluated through a progress check based on the model used in the first group writing assignment. Using the latter model, students would be given the opportunity to demonstrate their knowledge of writing concepts such as frame of reference, organizing idea, and organizing information. By writing a paragraph or a series of paragraphs, students were given the opportunity to exhibit, not only an understanding of the writing concepts, but also the chance *to demonstrate* a rationale for using them.

The task of teaching students how to write and think critically is not an easy one for social studies teachers. With respect to writing, it means rejecting conventional views of writing as either a craft, a biological disposition, or an exercise in feeling good. What must be demonstrated is that writing is an interdisciplinary process based on axioms of learning behavior. Recognizing these axioms, students should be able to use their writing as a pedagogical tool to think more critically about the subject matter under study. This leads us to a second point.

Neither classrooms nor students exist in precious isolation abstracted from the larger society in which we live. Pedagogical techniques used to teach writing and critical thinking become meaningless if they don't incorporate the "cultural capital" that structures students' lives. More specifically, if students are to analyze social studies subjects from a critical perspective, such an analysis must be steeped in pedagogical structures that promote productive communication and dialogue. The latter point is important because it is only in the absence of oppressive, hierarchical classroom social relations that students and teachers will be able to communicate, without fear and intimidation, within the context of their own language and culture. Moreover, with the development of democratized classroom social relations, students will be given the opportunity to step outside of their own language and culture by learning how to examine the basic assumptions that shape their lives through frames of reference different from their own. As Freire claims, students who see knowledge as problematic perform a "reflection" which translates into a critical "reading" of reality. This marks the first step in developing a pedagogy which generates the "will to write and create."[35]

The properties of writing and critical thinking outlined in this article have enormous potential for the teaching of social studies, not only because they help to teach students the fundamentally important relationships between writing and thinking, but also because they help students to reshape and restructure their views of any given social studies subject. Any subject loses its appeal and its legitimacy when it is viewed as a subject written by "experts," accessible to students only from a distance. By using the pedagogical model presented in this article, students have a chance to get "inside" a subject and to think critically so that they may provide their own interpretations of the material. What does all of this mean in the long run? Again, Freire has captured the sentiment well.

> For only as men [*sic*]grasp the themes [of their times] can they intervene in reality instead of remaining mere onlookers. And only by developing a permanently critical attitude can men overcome a posture of adjustment. . . .[36]

6

Mass Culture and the Rise of the New Illiteracy: Implications for Reading

By HENRY A. GIROUX

Secure yourselves Knowledge, you who are frozen!
You who are starving, grab hold of the book: It's a Weapon.
You must take over the leadership.

—Bertolt Brecht

In this era of capitalism, Americans appear to be faced with a major paradox about the relationship between technology, culture, and emancipation. On the one hand, the increasing development of science and technology provides the possibility of freeing humans from dehumanizing and back-breaking labor. In turn, this freedom offers humanity new opportunities for the development of, and access to, a culture that promotes a more critical and qualitatively discriminatory sensibility in all modes of communication and experience. On the other hand, the development of technology and science, constructed according to the laws of capitalist rationality, has ushered in forms of domination and control that appear to thwart rather than extend the possibilities of human emancipation.[1]

It is within the parameters of this paradox that an examination of the value and function of reading in a multimedia society can be analyzed. The necessity for such a perspective rests with the intricate, though often overlooked, linkages that exist between the various modes of communication and the existing socio-political forces that dominate this society. To speak of one without the other represents not only a conceptual problem but a political failing as well. In broad general terms, this means that any understanding of the relationship between the electronic media and the print culture becomes muddled unless such a relationship is situated within the specific social and historical context in which it is found. To place one's analysis in such a context is to oppose mainstream social theorists who have failed to study the dynamics of the print and visual modes of communication within the larger critical concepts of history, mass culture, and ideology.[2] Their failure to do so is, in fact, indicative of the more serious ideological failure to recognize the changing dialectical qualities and functions that both electronic media and print culture have had historically and continue to have today.[3] Historically, the relationship between changes in society and changes in communication has been dictated less by the nature of the developing technology of communication than by the dominant ideology and existing social formations of the given society. For instance, in contrast to the United States today, reading aloud and in public was commonplace during the late Middle Ages, as it is in contemporary China. Similarly, unlike most countries in the West, there are no copyright laws in Cuba because the government believes that books should be used to diffuse culture and not be used for commercial purposes.[4] This indicates that the interaction between social and technical changes is a complex one in which the shape and use of a mode of communication is determined by forces other than those of the existing technology. In addition, there are profound questions lurking behind the varied functions that print and visual modes of communication have in different social and historical contexts. Who controls the different modes of communication, and in whose interests do they operate? More succinctly put, do the modes of communication operate in the interest of oppression or liberation? Unfortunately, these are questions that mainstream social theorists have chosen to ignore.[5] One way of approaching these questions is through what I have termed the dialectic of use and potential in technology.

Underlying the dialectic of oppression and liberation that is inherent in all forms of communication is the fundamental distinction between the use that is made of a particular mode of communication, such as television, and the potential use it may have in a given society. To focus on the contradiction between use and potential represents one viable way of analyzing the changing relationship between visual and print cultures in this society. Not to do so is to fall prey to either a brand of technological fatalism or a brand of technological utopianism.[6] In both cases, technology is abstracted from its socio-historical roots, removed from the imperatives of class and power, and defined within the conceptual strait-jacket of technological determinism.

A more critical approach would attempt to lay bare "some of the concrete and complex linkages between cultural creation and distribution and economic and social forms."[7] This requires that we redefine culture in political terms, and look at the way visual and print cultures operate as mechanisms of social and cultural reproduction. But the concept of social and cultural reproduction must first be explained before we can analyze its mechanisms in detail. The notion of reproduction clarifies the relationship between culture and society so as to suggest the subordinacy of culture to the dominant society. This is an important point for two reasons. First, mainstream anthropologists have traditionally depoliticized the notion of culture by making it synonymous with "a peoples' way of life."[8] Consequently, they have made it difficult to study the important relationship between society and culture, particularly the relationship between ideology and social control. Second, the locus of domination in the advanced industrial countries has undergone a significant change and we need a politicized notion of culture to examine that change. A more fruitful analysis than that of mainstream social scientists can be found in the work of the Italian social theorist, Antonio Gramsci, as well as in the more recent work of the Frankfurt School and their followers.[9]

Cultural Hegemony

From the perspective of Gramsci and others, the locus of domination in the advanced industrial countries of the West has shifted from a reliance upon force (police, army, etc.) to the use of a cultural apparatus which promotes consensus through the reproduction and distribution of dominant systems of beliefs and attitudes. Gramsci called this form of control ideological hegemony, a form of control that not only manipulated consciousness but also saturated the daily routines and practices that guided everyday behavior. The Frankfurt School carried this analysis much further and pointed to the increasing development of technology to reproduce the dominant culture and maintain existing socioeconomic arrangements. More recently, the work of Pierre Bourdieu and Basil Bernstein has demonstrated that the dominant society not only distributes materials and goods but also reproduces and distributes cultural capital, i.e., those systems of meanings, taste, dispositions, attitudes and norms that are directly and indirectly defined by the dominant society as socially legitimate.[10] From this perspective, the reproduction of a society is intimately tied to the production and distribution of its cultural messages. As such, the cultural apparatus for reproducing the dominant culture and communicating it to the pblic becomes an important political issue. In effect, culture is now viewed not only as an ideological expression of the dominant society, but also refers to the form and structure of the technology that communicates the messages that "lay the psychological and moral foundations for the economic and political system."[11]

As an ideological expression of the dominant society, the dominant culture is deeply tied to the ethos of consumerism and positivism. As the culture became industrialized in the early part of the twentieth century, it reached into new forms of communication to spread its message. The production of goods was now paralleled by the evergrowing reproduction of consciousness. Moreover, as twentieth century capitalism gave rise to mass advertising and its attendant gospel of unending consumerism, all spheres of social existence were now informed, though far from entirely controlled, by the newly charged rationality of advanced industrial capitalism. Mass marketing, for example, drastically changed the realms of work and leisure and, as Stuart Ewen has pointed out, set the stage for control over daily life.

> During the 1920s the stage was set by which the expanding diversity of corporate organization might do cultural battle with a population which was in need of, and demanding, social change. The stage was in the theatre of daily life, and it was within the intimacies of that reality—productive, cultural, social, psychological—that a corporate pièce-de-théâtre was being scripted.[12]

While industrialized culture was radically transforming daily life, scientific management was altering traditional patterns of work. Craft production gave way to a fragmented work process in which conception was separated from both the execution and experience of work. One result was a work process that reduced labor to a series of preordained and lifeless gestures.[13]

Accompanying these changes in the workplace and the realm of leisure was a form of technocratic legitimation based on a positivist view of science and technology. This form of rationality defined itself through the alleged unalterable and productive effects that the developing forces of technology and science were having on the foundations of twentieth century progress. Whereas progress in the United States in the eighteenth and nineteenth centuries was linked to the development of moral self-improvement and self-discipline in the interest of building a better society, progress in the twentieth century was stripped of its concern with improving the human condition and became dedicated to material and technical growth.[14] What was once considered humanly possible, an issue involving values and human ends, was now reduced to what was technically possible. The application of scientific methodology to new forms of technology appeared as a social force generated by its own laws, laws governed by a rationality that appeared to exist above and beyond human control.

As a mode of legitimation, this form of technocratic rationality has become the prevailing cultural hegemony. As the prevailing consciousness, it celebrates the continued enlargement of the comforts of life and the productivity of labor through increasing submission of the public to laws that govern the technical mastery of both human beings and nature. The price for increased productivity is the continued refinement and administration of not simply the forces of production but the constitutive nature of consciousness itself.

The Culture Industry

Hans Enzensberger (1974) has claimed that the electronic media, operating in the service of this technocratic rationality, have become the major force in what he calls the industrialization of the mind. He points out that the mind industry transcends particularistic discussion of the print and visual cultures. He writes that "Hardly anyone seems to be aware of the phenomenon as a whole: the industrialization of the human mind. This is a process which cannot be understood by a mere examination of its machinery."[15] Moreover:

> The mind industry's main business and concern is not to sell its product, it is to "sell" the existing order. To perpetuate the pattern of man's domination by man, no matter who runs the society, and by whatever means. Its main task is to expand and train our consciousness—in order to exploit it.[16]

More recent critics have gone much further than Enzensberger and claim that the massified culture industry at the present time in the United States represents an assault on the capacity of human beings to even think in critical terms or, for that matter, to engage in meaningful social discourse.[17] Aronowitz refers to this phenomenon as the "new illiteracy" and claims that not only critical thinking but the substance of democracy itself is at stake. He speaks eloquently to this issue:

> The new situation raises the issue of the competence of people to effectively communicate ideational content. The issue is the capacity for conceptual thought itself. . . . Since critical thinking is the fundamental precondition for an autonomous and self-motivated public or citizenry, its decline would threaten the future of democratic social, cultural, and political forms.[18]

These critics view visual culture in particular as playing a significant and important role in reducing collective thought and imagination to strictly technical dimensions. Yet none of these critics supports the Orwellian nightmare of a monolithic consciousness industry that runs without contradictions or resistance. Such a position is vulgar and overly deterministic. Moreover, it fails to acknowledge that the electronic media, as well as print culture, are not a causal agent as much as a mediating force in the reproduction of consciousness.[19] The technology of the consciousness industry cannot *produce* culture; it can only reproduce and distribute it. Concomitantly, the consciousness industry is not the only agency of socialization. In other words, mass culture in its various forms generates contradictions as well as consensus, though not with equal weight. In both objective and subjective terms, the technology of the mass culture industry creates pockets of resistance fueled by its own contradictions. For instance, it constantly generates expectations and needs that it cannot ultimately satisfy, yet it contains within its technology the possibility of real communication among people—i.e., people could become transmitters as well as receivers of information.

Print versus Visual

The important question that remains is whether a distinction should be made between print and visual cultures regarding their possibilities as a force for liberation or domination at this moment in history. For reasons outlined below, I think the answer is a resounding yes.

It is fairly obvious that each culture has its own centre of gravity, providing a different experience as well as a different form of access to knowledge. But it is not so obvious what this means when analyzed in sociopolitical terms. For example, in ideal-essence terms, print and visual cultures should complement each other, but at the present historical juncture, they don't. The visual culture, particularly television, is the most dominant form of communication because its technology offers much greater possibilities for manipulation and social control. This becomes particularly apparent when it is compared to the technology of reading.

While it is true that, historically, reading created a class-specific audience because of the technical and critical skills needed to use it, the same cannot be said of the visual culture, which has all but eliminated any reliance upon a class-specific audience to use its technology or to understand its messages. To put it another way, the visual culture has eliminated the need for any specific public to use the kind of critical and discriminating skills that are necessary to approach a mode of communication. The very notion of "mass culture" suggests not only the importance of quantity but also the reduction of thought and experience to the level of mere spectatorship. The disease in this case is powerlessness, and the cure is a form of manufactured escapism. Of course, the print culture lends itself to the manipulation of consciousness as well, and in an important sense all modes of communication can be manipulatory. The real question is how possible it is to turn everyone into a manipulator of the technology of mass communication. A number of critics have pointed out that the development of print culture helped to produce a mass bourgeois public sphere that nurtured the discussion of current events, newspapers, and books.[20] This is a crucial point, because the technology of the print media necessitates a form of rationality that contains room for critical thinking and analysis. For instance, print culture is a medium that demands attentiveness. It is not as obtrusive as the visual culture; it lacks the "tactile" qualities of the latter. As a result, one has to approach it with intentionality; this form of intentionality becomes clear when we consider that the written word is governed by the logic of conciseness, clarity, and cogency. It has to be that way, at least in principle, because the printed word "freezes" information. When reading, one has more time to stop and reflect on what has been written. It is possible with the written word to assess more rigorously the validity and truth value of an argument. The form of print technology itself retains a check on the overly blatant manipulation of the written message. In other words, there is a tension in print technology between its form and content. The critical eye that reading ideally demands puts a check on the manipulation of the message.

There are other considerations regarding print technology that make it emancipatory at the present time. It is inexpensive to produce and consume. Consequently, through the plethora of books, newspapers, and magazines that flood the market, one has access to a great number of views and positions on any subject. The American left has been accused of relying too heavily upon print technology.[21] The critique is revealing not because it belies a certain amount of elitism on the part of the left, but because it indicates that reading technology provides a greater opportunity for transmitting one's views than any other form of communication. The left simply does not have access to the visual culture. Television, radio, and film production are centrally controlled by the ruling interests. Moreover, these modes of communication are much too important to the corporate interests to be democratized. The visual media are presently demagogue of one-way communication. And part of the reason for this lies in their power to influence people, a characteristic as endemic to their technology as it is to the social relations that determine their one-sided use. The power of that influence can, in part, be measured by the following figures: "96 percent of American households own at least one television, . . . the average television is on over six hours a day, and . . . ten percent of American households own at least three televisions."[22]

Theodore Adorno (1978) has written that "whoever speaks of culture speaks about administration as well, whether this is his intention or not."[23] Aronowitz illuminates Adorno's remarks by claiming that *visual culture* is industrializing the mind by colonizing the realm of leisure.[24] Again, it is worth pointing out that such a position does not overlook the dialectical interplay between the visual culture and the public at large. People respond to visual culture with different attitudes and needs. The issue is that the visual culture has grown so large and is so centralized, penetrating the "private space" of individuals to such a degree that, in many cases, it reduces cognition and human experience to a mere shadow of technique and the consumer culture.

The visual culture is presently accessible predominantly as a one-way mode of communication. In addition, as a motor force in shaping experience, it has some powerful advantages over print culture. The visual culture, especially television, is situated in "tactile" stimuli such as imagery and sound which, in different combinations and forms, closely simulate face-to-face reality. The power of the visual culture to restrict thought patterns derives not only from the messages and myths it distributes (a topic too well known to be discussed here) but from the techniques that it uses.

The dominant technique that characterizes the visual culture has its roots in the division of labor that it emulates in the larger society. Fragmentation and immediacy of information are the order of the day. Rapid camera work and sharp editing create the immediate effect of appealing to the emotions while, at the same time, short-circuiting critical reflection.[25] Since it is impossible for the viewer, unless he has a videotape machine, to slow down or reobserve the rapid diffusion of images, he has little opportunity to distance himself from the content of the visual production and reflect on its meaning. Furthermore, the images are not only presented with machine-gun speed; they usually lack a particular unity, as in news presentations, or they lack a larger context—i.e., they are unfocalized. In this context, the image subsumes reality, and the fact becomes the arbiter of the truth. The French situationists refer to the enshrinement of the image as the "spectacle." As Norman Fruchter describes it:

> The spectacle is the continuously produced and therefore continuously evolving pseudo-reality, predominantly visual, which each individual encounters, inhabits and accepts as public and official reality, thereby denying as much as possible the daily private reality of exploration, suffering and inauthenticity he or she experiences.[26]

The enshrinement of the image, the spectacle, finds some of its manifestations in the star system, the identification of the aesthetic with "entertainment," and the glorification of sensational and violent themes. Between the glut of stylistic and over-dramatized images of reality, the visual media, especially television, soothe the public with their display of "objectivity" and their concern with the "facts." The objectivity of the visual media appears guaranteed in the brute presence of the camera, with its ability either to focus immediately on a given event or to capture every gesture and movement in its dramatic rendering of reality. Fredric Jameson describes this position well when he writes:

We are made secure in the illusion that the camera is witnessing everything exactly as it happened and that what it sees is all there is. The camera is absolute presence and absolute truth: thus, the aesthetic of representation collapses the density of the historical event, and flattens it back into fiction.[27]

Amidst the fragmentation of images and the overflow of information, the intrusion of the "fact" appears like a reliable trustworthy tool to sort out the confusion and uncertainty. As Gitlin point out in his analysis of television and the culture of positivism:

Television contributes powerfully to a fetishism of facts. . . . Since history is bewildering, complex, and outside popular control, the raw muscular fact takes on an inordinate importance. . . . The facts themselves seem to explain, to reassure, or to alarm, all in a managed way. Facts demand attention, they get into the stream of discussion, they seem legitimate and trustworthy, they guide—and all along they seem to be leaving the choice to the consumer, the audience.[28]

While the visual media are not the only force in promoting social and cultural reproduction, they may be the most powerful. Aronowitz points to studies that suggest a growing tendency among students to view things literally rather than conceptually; these studies have also pointed to the growing inability of students to think dialectically, to see things in a wider context, or to make connections between seemingly unrelated objects or events. He and others have also complained about students being tied to the "factuality" of the world, and appearing to have a great deal of difficulty in using concepts which may controvert appearances.[29]

The response of some critics to the developing power and sophistication of the visual media has been to celebrate the virtues of the electronic media in general while, at the same time, calling for a moratorium on reading and print.[30] These critics point to the virtues and possibilities in two-way communication inherent in the electronic media, and suggest that the age of print is a dying cultural relic. They also point out that the visual culture is not going to go away, and they urge their readers to grapple with it. This is a noble but misguided position. The electronic media are in the hands of the corporate trust, and it would take a redistribution of power and wealth to place them at the public's disposal.[31] This is an important task, but it must be preceded by a change in the collective consciousness and accompanied by the development of an ongoing political struggle. Moreover, it underestimates the power of the visual media to define the use of their own technology. In other words, even with the growing accessibility of such means of electronic communication as cameras, video systems, as well as nonvisual electronic media such as CB radios, the public views these modes of communication as important only for leisure activities.[32]

Redefinition of Literacy

If the visual culture within the context of the present society threatens self reflection and critical thought, we are going to have to redefine our notions of literacy and rely heavily upon the print culture to teach people the rudiments of critical thinking and social action. The point here is that we must move beyond the positivistic notion of literacy that characterizes the social sciences today.[33] Instead of formulating literacy in terms of the mastery of techniques, we must broaden its meaning to include the ability to read critically, both within and outside one's experiences, and with conceptual power. This means that literacy would enable people to decode critically their personal and social worlds and thereby further their ability to challenge the myths and beliefs that structure their perceptions and experiences. Literacy, as Freire never tires of telling us, must be linked to a theory of knowledge, one that is consistent with an emancipatory political perspective and one that gives the fullest expression to illuminating the power of social relationships in the act of knowing. This is crucial because it suggests not only that one should learn how to read messages critically but also that critical analysis can only take place when knowledge serves as a subject of investigation, as a mediating force between people.[34]

True literacy involves dialogue and social relationships free from top-to-bottom authoritarian structures. At the present historical juncture, reading provides the opportunity for the development of progressive approaches to literary as both a mode of critical consciousness and a fundamental springboard for social action. Print culture is accessible and cheap, and its materials can be produced and manufactured by the public. Reading in groups, as well as reading alone, affords the "private" space and distance that the electronic and visual cultures seldom provide. Print technology contains the immediate promise of turning people into social agents who can manipulate and use the book, newspaper, and other forms of print communication to their own advantage. It contains the promise of emancipation. Moreover, print culture allows for the development of methods of conceptualization and social organization that might eliminate the present role of the electronic and the visual media as an oppressive force. This is the concept that gives Brecht's exhortation—"You who are starving, grab hold of the book: It's a weapon."[35]—more urgency today than it did when he wrote it over three decades ago.

7

Critical Pedagogy, Cultural Politics, and the Discourse of Experience

By HENRY A. GIROUX

Writing about the act of studying, the Brazilian educator Paulo Freire argues that "studying is a difficult task that requires a systematic critical attitude and intellectual discipline acquired only through practice."[1] He further argues that underlying the nature of this practice are two important pedagogical assumptions. First, the reader should assume the role of a subject in the act of studying. Second, the act of studying is not merely a relationship with the immediacy of the text; on the contrary, it is in the broader sense an attitude toward the world. He is worth quoting at length on these issues:

> Studying a text calls for an analysis of the study of the one who, through studying wrote it. It requires an understanding of the sociological-historical conditioning of knowledge. And it requires an investigation of the content under study and of other dimensions of knowledge. Studying is a form of reinventing, re-creating, rewriting, and this is a subject's, not an object's task. Further, with this approach a reader cannot separate herself or himself from the text because she or he would

be renouncing a critical attitude toward the text. . . . Because the act of study is an attitude toward the world, the act of study cannot be reduced to the relationship of reader to book or reader to text. In fact, a [text] reflects its author's confrontation with the world. It expresses this confrontation. . . . One who studies should never stop being curious about other people and reality. There are those who ask, those who try to find answers and those who keep on searching.[2]

Freire's comments are an important place to begin this chapter because they make suggestive and problematic the issue of how to theorize and develop a pedagogy that embodies forms of experience in which teachers and students display a sense of critical agency and empowerment. Freire's emphasis on the notion of agency, in this case, is particularly important because it conjures up images both of critique and of possibility. In the first instance, there is an implied demand to understand how experience in schools is accomplished in a manner that actively silences the possibility for critical learning and for critical agency. In the second instance, Freire distinctly employs a language and a challenge for organizing pedagogical experiences within social forms and practices that speak to developing more critical, open, explorative, and collective modes of learning.

I will argue that for such a challenge to be met critical educators need to develop a discourse that can be used to interrogate schools as ideological and material embodiments of a complex web of relations of culture and power, on the one hand, and as socially constructed sites of contestation actively involved in the production of lived experiences on the other. Underlying such an approach would be an attempt to define how pedagogical practice represents a particular politics of experience, that is, a cultural field where knowledge, discourse, and power intersect so as to produce historically specific practices of moral and social regulation.[3] Similarly, this problematic points to the need to interrogate how human experiences are produced, contested, and legitimated within the dynamics of everyday classroom life. The theoretical importance of this type of interrogation is directly linked to the need for critical educators to fashion a discourse in which a more comprehensive politics of culture and experience can be developed. At issue here is the recognition that schools are historical and structural embodiments of forms and culture that are ideological in the sense that they signify reality in ways that are often actively contested and experienced differently by various individuals and groups. That is, schools are anything but ideologically innocent; nor are they simply reproductive of dominant social relations and interests. Yet they do exercise forms of political and moral regulation intimately connected with technologies of power that "produce asymmetries in the abilities of individuals and groups to define and realize their needs."[4] More specifically, schools establish the conditions under which some individuals and groups define the terms by which others live, resist, affirm, and participate in the construction of their own identities and subjectivities.

Within this theoretical perspective, I will argue that power has to be understood as a concrete set of practices that produce social forms through which different sets of experience and modes of subjectivities are constructed.[5] Discourse in this equation is both constitutive of and a product of power. It functions to produce and legitimate configurations of time, space, and narrative which position teachers and students so as to privilege particular renderings of ideology, behavior, and the representation of everyday life. Discourse as a technology of power is given concrete expression in forms of knowledge that constitute the formal curricula as well as in the classroom social relations that "impale" themselves on both the body and the mind.[6] Needless to say, these pedagogical practices and forms are "read" in different ways by both teachers and students.[7] But nonetheless within these socially constructed sets of pedagogical practices are forces that actively work to produce subjectivities that consciously and unconsciously display a particular "sense" of the world.

In this case, the problem to be analyzed has a dual focus. First, I want to interrogate those forms of educational discourse and practices that produce real injustices and inequities through a particular structuring of pedagogical experiences. Second, I want to move beyond the language of critique and in doing so analyze the possibility for constructing forms of pedagogical practice that allow for teachers and students to assume the thoughtful, critical role of transformative intellectuals. In each instance, I will look at the ways in which schools both embody and reflect social antagonisms through the social relations that are constructed around particular pedagogical views of culture, knowledge, and experience.

Education and the Discourse of Management and Control

Schools should teach you to realize yourself, but they don't. They teach you to be a book. It's easy to become a book, but to become yourself you've got to be given various choices and be helped to look at the choices. You've got to learn that, otherwise you're not prepared for the outside world.[8]

The high school student who gave this reply provides both an important reading of his own school experience and an indication that the pedagogical discourse and practices that shaped it were not successful. But to argue that such a pedagogy was not successful demands further elaboration as to how such a discourse and practice characterize themselves, what assumptions inform them, and what particular interests underlie their view of culture, knowledge, and the teacher-student relations they support.

The set of pedagogical practices I am about to analyze are informed by a discourse that I want to label as the discourse of management and control. Inherent in this discourse is a view of culture and knowledge in which both are often treated as part of a storehouse of artifacts constituted as canon. While this discourse has a number of characteristic expressions, its most recent theoretical defense can be found in Adler's *The Paideia Proposal*. Adler calls for the schools to implement a core course of subjects in all twelve years of public schooling. His appeal is to forms of pedagogy that enable students to master skills and specific forms of understanding with respect to predetermined forms of knowledge. In this view, knowledge appears beyond the reach of critical interrogation except at the level of immediate application. In other words, there is no mention of how such knowledge gets chosen, whose interests it represents, or why students might be interested in learning it. In fact, students in this perspective are constituted as a unitary body removed from the ideological and material differences that construct their subjectivities, interests, and concerns in diverse and multiple ways. I would argue that the concept of difference in this instance becomes the negative apparition of the "other." This is particularly clear in Adler's case since he dismisses the diverse social and cultural difference among students with the simplistic and reductionistic comment that "Despite their manifold individual differences the children are all the same in their human nature."[9] In this discourse a predetermined and hierarchically arranged body of knowledge is taken as the cultural currency to be dispensed to all children regardless of their differences and interests. Equally important is the fact that the acquisition of such knowledge becomes the structuring principle around which the school curriculum is organized and particular classroom social relations legitimated. In this case, it is an appeal to school knowledge exclusively that constitutes the measure and worth of what defines the learning experience. That is, the value of both teacher and student experience is premised on the transmission and inculcation of what can be termed "positive knowledge." Consequently, it is in the distribution, management, measurement, and legitimation of such knowledge that this type of pedagogy invests its energies. Cusick, in his ethnographic study of three urban secondary schools, comments on the problematic nature of legitimating and organizing schools' practices around the notion of "positive knowledge."

> By positive knowledge I mean that which is generally accepted as having an empirical or traditional base. . . . The assumption that the acquisition of positive knowledge can be made interesting and appealing in part underlies the laws that compel everyone to attend school, at least until their mid teens. . . . The conventional assumption would have it that the curriculum of a school exists as a body of knowledge, agreed upon by staff and approved by the general community and by district authorities who have some expertise, and that it reflects the best thinking about what young people need to succeed in our society. But I did not find that.[10]

What Cusick did find was that school knowledge organized in these terms was not compelling enough to interest many of the students he observed. Moreover, educators locked into this perspective responded to student disinterest, violence, and resistance by shifting their concerns from actually teaching positive knowledge to maintaining order and control, or as they put it, "keeping the lid on." Cusick is worth quoting at length:

> Not only did the administrators spend their time on those matters [administration and control], they also tended to evaluate other elements, such as the performance of teachers, according to their ability to maintain order. They tended to arrange other elements of the school according to how they contributed or failed to contribute to the maintenance of order. The oustanding example of that was the implementation in both urban schools of the five-by-five day, wherein the students were brought in early in the morning, given five periods of instruction with a few minutes in between and a fifteen-minute mid-morning break, and released before one o'clock. There were no free periods, study halls, cafeteria sessions, or assemblies. No occasions were allowed in which violence could occur. The importance of maintaining order in those public secondary schools could not be underestimated.[11]

Within this discourse student experience is reduced to the immediacy of its performance and exists as something to be measured, administered, registered, and controlled. Its distinctiveness, its disjunctions, its lived quality are all dissolved in an ideology of control and management. A major problem with this perspective is that the celebration of such knowledge does not guarantee that students will have any interest in the pedagogical practices it produces, especially since such knowledge appears to have little connection to the everyday experiences of the students themselves. Moreover, teachers who structure classroom experiences out of this discourse generally face enormous problems in the public schools, especially those in the urban centers. Boredom and/or disruption appear to be its primary products. To some extent, of course, teachers who rely upon classroom practices that exhibit a disrespect for both students and critical learning are themselves victims of specific labor conditions that virtually make it impossible for them to assume the position of a critical educator. At the same time, the conditions of labor under which teachers work are mutually determined by dominant interests and discourses that provide the ideological legitimation for promoting hegemonic classroom practices. The following quote may exaggerate the logic of management and control at work in this discourse, but it certainly lays bare its ideology. There is a certain touch of irony in this example in that the author is a writing instructor advocating the virtues of docility to his student readers:

> Docility means "teachableness" and is simply the quality of being willing to follow simple instructions and to have confidence in the instructor, who has been through all the learning—and perhaps much teaching—before and just might know what he [sic] is doing . . . [You] even without any talent, by patiently, docilely, and seriously following a step by step method can produce a good theme.[12]

This type of discourse not only wages symbolic violence against students in that it devalues the cultural capital they possess as a significant basis for school knowledge and inquiry, it also tends to position teachers within pedagogical models that legitimate their role as "clerks" of the empire. Unfortunately, the technocratic interests that embody the notion of teachers as clerks is part of a long tradition of management models of pedagogy and administration that have dominated American public education.[13] More recent expressions of this logic include a variety of accountability models, management by objectives, teacher-proof curriculum materials, and state-mandated certification requirements. Underlying all of these approaches to administration and teacher work is a set of principles at odds with the notion that teachers should be involved collectively in producing curricular materials suited to the cultural and social contexts in which they teach. Questions regarding cultural specificity, teacher judgment, and how student experiences and histories relate to the learning process itself are ignored. It is possible to go even further and say that the latter issues represent a mode of teacher autonomy and control that are a hindrance to school administrators who believe that excellence is a quality to be displayed primarily in higher reading, math, and college board scores. This becomes more obvious in light of a major assumption underlying the discourse of management and control: that the behavior of teachers needs to be controlled and made consistent and predictable across different schools and student populations. It is important to note that the outcome for school systems that adopt this ideology is not merely the development of authoritarian form of school control and more standardized and manageable forms of pedagogy. This type of school policy also makes for good public relations in that school administrators can provide technical solutions to the complex social, political, and economic problems that plague their schools, while simultaneously invoking the principles of accountability as an indicator of success. The message to the public is clear: if the problem can be measured it can be solved. But mainstream educational discourse is not all of one piece: there is another position within mainstream educational discourse that does not ignore the relationship between knowledge and learning, on the one hand, and student experience on the other. It is to this position that I will now turn.

Education and the Discourse of Relevance

The discourse of relevance in educational theory and practice has a long association with various tenets of what has been loosely called progressive education in the United States. From Dewey to the Free School Movement to the 1960s and '70s to the present emphasis on multiculturalism, there has been a concern with taking the needs and cultural experiences of students as a starting point from which to develop relevant forms of pedagogy.[14] Since it is impossible to analyze in this essay all of the theoretical twists and turns this movement has taken, I want to focus exclusively on some of its dominant ideological tendencies along with the way in which its discourses structure the experiences of both students and teachers.

In its most common-sense form the educational discourse of relevance privileges a notion of experience in which experience is either equated with "fulfilling the needs of kids" or with developing cordial relations with students so as to be able to maintain order and control in the school. In many respects these two discourses represent different sides of the same educational ideology. In the discourse of "need fulfillment," the concept of need represents an *absence* of a particular set of experiences. In most cases, what educators believe are missing are either the culturally specific experiences that enrich the students lives or the fundamental skills they "need" to get jobs once they leave public school. Underlying this view of experience is the logic of cultural deprivation theory, which defines education in terms of cultural enrichment, remediation, and basics.

Within this discourse, there is little recognition that what is legitimated as privileged experience often represents the endorsement of a particular way of life that signifies its superiority with a "revenge" on those who do not share its attributes. More specifically, the experience of the student as other in cast within a discourse that often labels that experience as deviant, underprivileged, or uncultured. Consequently, not only do students bear the sole responsibility for school failure, but there is also little or no theoretical room for interrogating the ways in which administrators and teachers actually create and sustain the problems they attribute to the students in question. This uncritical view of students, particularly of those from subordinate groups, is mirrored in a refusal by the discourse of relevance to examine critically how it provides and legitimates forms of experience that embody the logic of domination. One glaring example of this was brought home to me by a secondary school teacher in one of my graduate courses who constantly referred to her working-class students as "low life." In this case, she had no sense of how her language actively constructed her relations with these students, though I am sure the message was not lost on them. One type of practice that emerges from this discourse often places teachers in the position of blaming students for their perceived problems while simultaneously humiliating them in an effort to get them to participate in class. The following quote captures this approach:

> The teacher after taking attendance for fifteen minutes, wrote a few phrases on the board: "Adam and Eve," "spontaneous generation," and "evolution," and told the students that: "For the next forty minutes you are to write an essay on how you think the world started, and here are three possibilities which you know, we discussed last week. I did

this with my college prep class and they like it. . . . It will do you good. Teach you to think for a change, which is something you don't do often."[15]

When students refuse to acquiesce to this type of humiliating discourse, teachers and school administrators generally face problems of order and control. One response is the discourse of cordial relations. The classic instance of dealing with students in this discourse is to try to keep them happy by either indulging their personal interests through appropriately developed modes of low status knowledge or by developing good rapport with them.[16] Defined within a logic that views them as the other, students now become objects of inquiry in the interest of being understood so as to be more easily controlled. The knowledge, for example, used by teachers with these students is often drawn from cultural forms identified with class-, race-, and gender-specific interests. But relevance, in this instance, has little to do with emancipatory concerns. Instead, it translates into pedagogical practices that attempt to appropriate forms of student and popular culture in the interests of "keeping the lid on." Furthermore, it provides a legitimating ideology for forms of class-, race-, and gender-specific forms of tracking. The tracking at issue here is developed in its most subtle form through an endless series of school electives that appear to legitimate the cultures of subordinated groups while actually incorporating them in a trivial pedagogical fashion. Thus, working-class girls are advised by guidance teachers to take "Girl Talk" while middle-class students have no doubts about the importance of taking classes in literary criticism. In the name of relevance and order, working-class boys are encouraged to select industrial arts while their middle-class counterparts take courses in advanced chemistry. These practices and social forms along with the divergent interests and pedagogies they produce have been analyzed extensively elsewhere and need not be repeated here.[17]

In its more theoretically argued forms, the discourse of relevance translates into what I will call the discourse of integration, a transition signaled by a more liberal view of student experience and culture. Within this discourse, student experience is defined either through the individualizing psychology of "child centeredness" or the logic of normative pluralism. Understood as part of natural unfolding process, student experience is not tied to the imperatives of rigid disciplinary authority but to the exercise of self-control and self-regulation. The focus of analysis in this discourse is the child as a unitary subject, and the pedagogical practices emphasized are structured around the goal of encouraging healthy expression and harmonious social relations.

Central to the discourse of integration is a problematic that equates freedom with the bestowal of love and what Carl Rogers calls "unconditional positive regard" and "emphatic understanding."[18] This pedagogical canon positions teachers within a set of social relations that strongly emphasizes self-directed learning, links knowledge to the personal experiences of students, and attempts to help students to interact with one another in a positive and harmonious fashion. How student experiences get developed within this discourse is, of course, directly related to the larger question of how they are constructed and understood within the multiple discourses that embody and reproduce the social and cultural relations that characterize the large society. While this issue is generally ignored in the language of child centeredness, it is appropriated as a central concern in another version of the discourse of integration, which employs what can be called the pedagogy of normative pluralism.

In the pedagogy of normative pluralism the analysis and meaning of experience shifts from a concern with the individual child to the student as part of a specific cultural group. Accordingly, the naming and understanding of experience proceed through a range of social categories that situates the individual child within a network of diverse cultural connections. Of central theoretical importance is the way in which the concept of culture is defined and interrogated in this perspective. In anthropological terms, culture is viewed as the ways in which human beings make sense of their lives, feelings, beliefs, thoughts, and the wider society.[19] Within this discourse, the notion of difference is stripped of its otherness and accommodated to the logic of a "polite civic humanism."[20] That is, difference no longer symbolizes the threat of disruption. On the contrary, it now signals an invitation for diverse cultural groups to join hands under the democratic banner of an integrative pluralism. It is worth pointing out that the relation between difference and pluralism is central to this perspective; it serves to legitimate the idea that in spite of differences manifested around race, ethnicity, language, values, and life styles there is an underlying equality among different cultural groups that disavows privileging any one of them. Thus, the notion of difference is subsumed within a discourse and set of practices that promote harmony, equality, and respect within and between diverse cultural groups.

This is not to suggest that conflict is ignored in this approach, nor am I suggesting that the social and political antagonisms that characterize the relationship between different cultural groups and the larger society are denied. On the contrary, such problems generally are recognized but they are seen as issues to be discussed and overcome in the interest of creating a "happy and co-operative class," which will play a fundamental role in bringing about a "happy and cooperative world."[21] Within this context, cultural representations of difference as conflict and tension only become pedagogically workable within the lanaguage of unity and co-operation. Consequently, the concept of difference turns into its opposite, for difference now becomes meaningful as something to be resolved within *relevant* forms of exchange and class discussions. Lost here is a respect for the autonomy of different cultural logics and any understanding of how such logics operate within asymmetrical relations of power and domination. In other words, the equality that is associated with different forms of culture as lived and embodied experiences serves to displace political considerations regarding the ways in which dominant and subordinate groups are produced, mediated, and expressed within concrete social practices both in and outside of schools.

The pedagogical practices developed out of this notion of difference and cultural diversity are suffused with the language of positive thinking. This becomes clear in the curriculum projects developed around these practices. These practices generally structure curriculum problems so as to include references to the conflicts and tensions that exist among different groups. But rather than educating students to the ways in which different groups struggle within relations of power and domination as these are played out in the larger social arena, these approaches subordinate issues of struggle and power to the task of developing pedagogical goals that foster a mutual respect and understanding among various cultural groups. The apologetic nature of this discourse, one that quietly ignores the complexity and sweat of social change, is evident in the kinds of educational objectives that structure its classroom practices. The following are characteristic:

> It is important for students in a multicultural setting, as well as a more homogeneous setting, to develop a multicultural perspective. The development of competencies to function comfortably in a multicultural settings should lead to (1) increased self-awareness and self respect, (2) a greater self respect for cultural groups different from students' own, (3) the extension of cultural pluralism and equity in the United States, and (4) fewer intergroup conflicts caused by ignorance and misunderstanding.[22]

In its more theoretically sophisticated versions, the pedagogy of normative pluralism recognizes the existence of racial, gender, ethnic, and other types of conflict among different groups but is more ideologically honest about why they should not be emphasized in the curriculum. Appealing to the interests of a common culture, this position calls for a pedagogical emphasis on the common interests and ideals that characterize the nation. As one of its spokespersons, Nathan Glazer, puts it, the choice of what is taught "must be guided . . . by our conception of a desirable society, of the relationship between what we select to teach and the ability of people to achieve such a society and live together in it."[23] What is troubling in this position is that it lacks any sense of culture as a terrain of struggle; moreover, it does not pay any attention to the relationship between knowledge and power. In fact, underlying Glazer's statement is a facile egalitarianism that assumes but does not demonstrate that all groups can actively participate in the development of such a society. The structured silence that underlies his unitary "our" suggests an unwillingness to either indict or interrogate existing structures of domination while appealing to a fictitious harmony. It is a harmony that is nothing more than an imagery in the discourse of those who do not have to suffer the injustices experienced by subordinated groups. In short, the pedagogy of normative pluralism falls prey to a perspective that idealizes the future while stripping the present of its deeply rooted contradictions and tensions. This is not merely the discourse of harmony; it is also a set of interests that refuses to posit the relations between culture and power as a moral question demanding emancipatory political action.

I have already registered some criticisms concerning some of the assumptions that inform the discourse of relevance and integration, but I want to elaborate on these before I analyze how a critical pedagogy can be fashioned out of a theory of cultural politics.[24]

The discourse of relevance and integration falls prey to a deeply ingrained ideological tendency in American education, as well as the mainstream social sciences, to separate culture from the relations of power. Culture in this view becomes the object of sociological inquiry and is analyzed primarily as an artifact that embodies and expresses the traditions and values of diverse groups. There is no attempt in this view to understand culture as the shared and lived principles of life, characteristic of different groups and classes as these emerge within asymmetrical relations of power and fields of struggle. In essence, culture as a particular relation between dominant and subordinate groups, expressed in the form of lived antagonistic relations that embody produce particular forms of meaning and action, remains unexplored in the discourse of relevance and integration. Actually, this discourse excludes the concept of dominant and subordinate culture altogether, and by doing so fails to recognize the importance of wider political and social forces as these affect all aspects of school organization and everyday classroom life.

By refusing to acknowledge the relations between culture and power, the discourse of relevance and integration fails to understand how schools themselves are implicated in reproducing dominating discourses and social practices. In this view it is assumed that schools can analyze problems faced by different cultural groups and out of such analyses students will develop a sense of understanding and mutual respect that will in some way influence the wider society. But schools do more than influence society; they are also shaped by it. That is, schools are inextricably linked to a larger set of political and cultural processes, and they not only reflect the antagonisms embodied in such processes but also embody and reproduce them. The question generally ignored in this discourse is how do schools actually work to produce class, race, and gender differentiations along with the fundamental antagonisms that structure them. In other words, in what ways are the wider forms of political, economic, social, and ideological domination and subordination invested in the language, texts, and social practices of the schools as well as in the experiences of the teachers and students themselves? Similarly, how is power within schools expressed as a set of relations that privilege some groups while disconfirming others? The important point here is that the discourse of relevance and integration not only lacks an adequate theory of domination and the role that schools play in such a process, but it also lacks a critical understanding of how experience is *named, constructed,* and *legitimated* in schools. Understood in these terms, such a discourse fails to analyze how the social relations that students and teachers bring to the classroom get expressed and mediated. Simon poses the question in a way that illuminates the complexity of the problem overlooked in this discourse:

> Our concern as educators is to develop a way of thinking about the construction and definition of subjectivity within the concrete social forms of our everyday existence in a way that grasps schooling as a cultural and political site that [embodies] a project of regulation and transformation. As educators we are required to take a position on the acceptability of such forms. We also recognize that while schooling is productive it is not so in isolation, but in complex relations with other

forms organized in other states. . . . In working to reconstruct aspects of schooling [educators should attempt] to understand how it becomes implicated in the production of subjectivities [and] recognize [how] existing social forms legitimate and produce real inequities which serve the interest of some over others and that a transformative pedagogy is oppositional in intent and threatening to some in its practice.[25]

Simon rightly argues that schools are sites of contestation and struggle and that, as sites of cultural production, they embody representations and practices that construct as well as block the possibilities for human agency among students. This becomes clear by recognizing that one of the most important elements at work in the construction of experience and subjectivity in schools is language. In this case, language intersects with power in the way a particular linguistic form is used in schools to legitimate and structure the ideologies and modes of life of specific groups. Language, in this case, is intimately related to power and functions to both position and constitute the way that teachers and students define, mediate, and understand their relation to each other and the larger society. Another major criticism of the discourse of relevance and integration is that it depoliticizes the notion of language by defining it primarily in technical terms (mastery), or in terms that argue for its communicative value in developing dialogue and transmitting information. In other words, language is privileged as a medium for verbal exchanges and presenting knowledge, and, as such, is abstracted from its constitutive role as an instrument and site of struggle over different meanings, practices, and readings of the world. Within this discourse, there is no sense of how language practices can be used to actively silence some students, or how the privileging of particular forms of language can work to disconfirm the traditions, practices, and values that subordinate language practices embody and reflect. Similarly, there is the failure to develop the important pedagogical task of having teachers learn forms of language literacy, in which one has a critical understanding of the structure of language as well as the theoretical skills needed to help students develop a language in which they can both validate and critically engage their own experiences and cultural milieux.[26]

It is not surprising that within this discourse questions of cultural difference are generally reduced to a single emphasis on the transmission of curriculum. The learning and understanding of school knowledge become the sole media through which problems are identified and resolved. Lost here are the ways in which power is invested in institutional and ideological forces that bear down on and shape social practices of schooling in a manner not evident through an analysis of curriculum texts in their isolated moment of classroom usage. There is no clear understanding, for example, of how social relations operate in schools through the organization of time, space, and resources, or the way in which different groups experience these relations via their economic, political, and social locations outside of schools. But this discourse not only fails to understand schooling as a cultural process that is inextricably linked to the inescapable presence of wider social forces; it also appears incapable of recognizing how forms of resistance might emerge in schools.[27]

A further theoretical limitation of the discourse of relevance and integration is that it fails to analyze how the school as an agent of social and cultural control is mediated and contested by those whose interests it does not serve. In part this is due to a functionalist view of schooling, one in which schools are unproblematically seen as serving the needs of the dominant society while not questioning either the nature of that society or the effects it has on the daily practices of schooling itself. The theoretical price paid for this type of functionalism is high. One consequence is that schools apparently are removed from the tensions and antagonisms that characterize the wider society. As a result, it becomes impossible to understand schools as sites actively involved in ongoing struggles over power and meaning. Furthermore, there is no theoretical room in this discourse to understand why subordinate groups may actively resist and deny the dominant culture as it is embodied in various aspects of daily classroom life.

Critical Pedagogy and the Discourse of Cultural Politics

I now want to shift theoretical gears and return to the assumption, implicit in Paulo Freire's statement at the beginning of this chapter, that learning involves a subject in the act of studying and that the act of studying is constructed out of a broader relationship with the world. I want to begin by making a bold move. I want to argue that for a critical pedagogy to be developed as a form of cultural politics, it is imperative that both teachers and students be viewed as transformative intellectuals.[28] The category of transformative intellectual is helpful in a number of ways.

First, it signifies a form of labor in which thinking and acting are inextricably related, and, as such, offers a counter-ideology to instrumental and management pedagogies that separate conception from execution and ignore the specificity of experiences and subjective forms that shape both teacher and student behavior. Second, the concept of transformative intellectual calls into play the political and normative interests that underlie the social functions which structure and are expressed in teacher and student work. In other words, it serves as a critical referent for educators to make problematic the interests that are inscribed in the institutional forms and everyday practices that are subjectively experienced and reproduced in schools. Finally, viewing teachers and students as intellectuals further demands a critical discourse that analyzes how cultural forms bear down on schools and how such forms are experienced subjectively. This means that critical educators need to understand how lived and material forms of culture are subject to political organization, that is, how they are produced and regulated.

In effect, I am arguing for a pedagogy of cultural politics that is developed around a critically affirmative language that allows educators as transformative intellectuals to understand how subjectivities are produced within those social forms in which people move but which are often only partially understood.[29] Such a pedagogy makes problematic how teachers and students sustain, resist, or accommodate those languages, ideologies, social processes, and myths that position them within existing relations of power and dependency. Moreover, it points to the need to develop a theory of politics and culture that analyzes power as an active process—one that is produced as part of a continually shifting balance of resources and practices in the struggle for privileging specific ways of naming, organizing, and experiencing social reality. Power, in this case, becomes a form of cultural production, linking agency and structure through the ways in which public and private representations are concretely organized and structured within schools. Furthermore, power is understood as an embodied and fractured set of experiences that are lived and suffered by individuals and groups within specific contexts and settings. Within this perspective, the concept of experience is linked to the broader issue of how subjectivities are inscribed within cultural processes that develop with regard to the dynamics of production, transformation, and struggle. Understood in these terms, a pedagogy of cultural politics presents a twofold set of tasks for critical educators. First, they need to analyze how cultural production is organized within asymmetrical relations of power in schools. Second, they need to construct political strategies for participating in social struggles designed to fight for schools as democratic public spheres.

In order to make these tasks realizable, it is necessary to assess the political limits and pedagogical potentialities of the different but related instances of cultural production that constitute the various processes of schooling. It is important to note that I am calling these social processes instances of cultural production rather than using the dominant left concept of reproduction.[30] The latter, I believe, points adequately to the various economic and political ideologies and interests that get reconstituted within the relations of schooling, but it lacks an understanding of how such interests are mediated, worked on, and subjectively produced, regardless of the interests that finally emerge.

A critical pedagogy that assumes the form of a cultural politics needs to examine how cultural processes are produced and transformed within three particular, though related, fields of discourse. These are: *the discourse of production, the discourse of text analysis,* and *the discourse of lived cultures.* Each of these discourses has a history of theoretical development in various models of left analysis, and each has been subjected to intense discussion and criticism, which need not be repeated here.[31] What I want to do is to look at these discourses in terms of the potentialities they exhibit in their interconnections, particularly as they point to a new set of categories for developing forms of educational practices that empower teachers and students around emancipatory interests.

Education and the Discourses of Production, Text Analysis, and Lived Cultures

The discourse of production in educational theory has focused on the ways in which the structural forces outside the immediacy of school life construct the objective conditions within which schools function. Within this discourse are illuminating analyses of the state, the workplace, foundations, publishing companies, and other political interests that directly or indirectly influence school policy. Moreover, schools are understood within a network of larger connections that allow analyses of them as historical and social constructions, embodiments of social forms that always bear a relationship to the wider society. At its best, the discourse of production alerts us to the need to understand the importance of ideological and material structures as particular sets of practices and interests that legitimate specific public representations and ways of life. It is inconceivable to analyze the process of schooling without understanding how these wider forms of production are constructed, manifested, and contested both in and out of schools. An obvious example of this is to analyze the ways in which state policy embodies and promotes particular practices that legitimate and privilege some forms of knowledge over others or some groups over others. Equally significant would be an analysis of how dominant modes of discourse in educational practice are constructed, sustained, and circulated outside of schools. For instance, critical educators need to do more than identify the language and values of corporate ideologies as they are manifested in school curricula; they also need to deconstruct the processes through which they are produced and circulated. Another important aspect of the discourse of production is that it points to the way in which labor is objectively constructed; that is, it provides an analysis of the conditions under which people work and the political importance of these conditions in either limiting or enabling what educators can do. This issue is especially important for analyzing the critical possibilities that exist for public school teachers and students within specific conditions of labor to act and be treated as intellectuals. Quite simply, if teachers and students are subject to conditions of overcrowding, lack of time to work collectively in a creative fashion, or to rules and regulations that disempower them, the technical and social conditions of labor have to be understood and addressed as part of the discourse of reform and struggle.

At the same time, the discourse of production has to be supplemented with analyses of textual forms. In this case, it is necessary to enlist a discourse that can critically interrogate cultural forms as they are produced and used within specific classrooms. What is significant about this type of discourse is that it provides teachers and students with the critical tools necessary to analyze those socially constructed representations and interests that organize and emphasize particular readings of curricula materials. This is a particularly important mode of analysis because it argues against the idea that the means of representation in texts are merely neutral conveyors of ideas.

It points to the need for careful systematic analyses of the way in which material is used and ordered in school curricula and how its "signifiers" register particular ideological pressures and tendencies. At its best, such a discourse allows teachers and students to deconstruct meanings that are silently built into the structuring principles of the various systems of meaning that organize everyday life in schools. In effect, it adds a new theoretical twist to analyzing how the hidden curriculum works in schools.

This type of textual criticism can be used. for example, to analyze how the technical conventions or images within various forms such as narrative, mode of address, and ideological reference attempt to construct a limited range of positions from which they are to be read. Richard Johnson says:

> The legitimate object of an identification of "positions" is the pressures or tendencies on the reader, the theoretical problematic which produces subjective forms, the directions in which they move in their force — once inhabited. . . . If we add to this, the argument that certain kinds of text ("realism") naturalise the means by which positioning is achieved, we have a dual insight of great force. The particular promise is to render processes hitherto unconsciously suffered (and enjoyed) open to explicit analysis.[32]

Coupled with traditional forms of ideology critique of the subject content of school materials, the discourse of text analysis provides a valuable insight into how subjectivities and cultural forms work within schools. The value of this kind of work has been exhibited in analysis of the structured principles used in the construction of prepackaged curriculum materials, where it has been argued that such principles utilize a mode of address that positions teachers merely as implementers of knowledge.[33] Such a positioning clearly is at odds with treating both teachers and students as intellectuals. In a brilliant display of this approach Judith Williamson has provided an extensive study of the way in which this type of critique can be applied to mass advertising.[34] Similarly, Ariel Dorfman has applied this mode of analysis to various texts used in popular culture, including the portrayal of characters such as Donald Duck and Babar the Elephant. It is in his analysis of *Readers Digest* that Dorfman exhibits a dazzling display of the critical value of text analysis. In one example, for instance, he analyzes how *Readers Digest* uses a mode of representation that downplays the importance of viewing knowledge in its historical and dialectical connections. He writes:

> Just as with superheroes, knowledge does not transform the reader, on the contrary, the more he [sic] reads the *Digest,* the less he needs to change. Here is where all that fragmentation returns to play the role it was always meant to play. Prior knowledge is never assumed. . . .

From month to month, the reader must purify himself, suffer from amnesia, bottle the knowledge he's acquired and put it on some out-of-the-way shelf so it doesn't interfere with the innocent pleasure of consuming more, all over again. What he learned about the Romans doesn't apply to the Etruscans. Hawaii has nothing to do with Polynesia. Knowledge is consumed for its calming effect, for "information renewal," for the interchange of banalities. It is useful only insofar as it can be digested anecdotally, but its potential for original sin has been washed clean along with the temptation to generate truth or movement—in other words: change.[35]

I want to conclude by arguing that in order to develop a critical pedagogy around a form of cultural politics, it is essential to develop a discourse that does not assume that lived experiences can be inferred automatically from structural determinations. In other words, the complexity of human behavior cannot be reduced to merely identifying the determinants, whether they be economic modes of production or systems of textual signification, in which such behavior is shaped and against which it constitutes itself. The way in which individuals and groups both mediate and inhabit the cultural forms presented by such structural forces is in itself a form of production and needs to be analyzed through a related but different discourse and mode of analysis. In this case, I want to briefly present the nature and pedagogical implications of what I call the discourse of lived cultures.

Central to the discourse of lived cultures is the need to develop what can be loosely called a theory of self-production.[36] In the most general sense this would demand an understanding of how teachers and students give meaning to their lives through the complex historical, cultural, and political forms that they both embody and produce. A number of issues need to be developed within a critical pedagogy around this concern. First, it is necessary to acknowledge the subjective forms of political will and struggle. That is, the discourse of lived cultures needs to interrogate how people create stories, memories, and narratives that posit a sense of determination and agency. This is the cultural "stuff" of mediation, the conscious and unconscious material through which members of dominant and subordinate groups offer accounts of who they are and present different readings of the world. It is also part of those ideologies and practices that allow us to understand the particular social locations, histories, subjective interests, and private worlds that come into play in any classroom pedagogy.[37]

If we treat the histories, experiences, and languages of different cultural groups as particularized forms of production, it becomes less difficult to understand the diverse readings, responses, and behaviors that, let's say, students exhibit to the analysis of a particular classroom text. In fact, a cultural politics necessitates that a discourse be developed that is attentive to the histories, dreams, and experiences that such students bring to schools. It is only beginning with these subjective forms that critical educators can develop a pedagogy that confirms and engages the contradictory forms of cultural capital that consitute how students produce meanings that legitimate particular forms of life.

Searching out and illuminating the elements of self-production that characterize individuals who occupy diverse lived cultures is not merely a pedagogical technique for confirming the experiences of those students who are often silenced by the dominant culture of schooling; it is also part of a discourse that interrogates how power, dependence, and social inequality structure the ideologies and practices that enable and limit students around issues of class, race, and gender. Within this theoretical perspective, the discourse of lived cultures becomes valuable for educators because it can serve to illuminate how power and knowledge intersect not only to disconfirm the cultural capital of students from subordinate groups, but also how it can be translated into a language of possibility. That is, it can also be used to develop a critical pedagogy of the popular, one that engages the knowledge of lived experience through the dual method of confirmation and interrogation. The knowledge of the "other" is engaged not simply to celebrate its presence, but also because it must be interrogated critically with respect to the ideologies it contains, the means of representation it utilizes, and the underlying social practices it confirms. At stake here is to need to develop a link between knowledge and power, one that suggests realizable possibilities for students. That is, knowledge and power intersect in a pedagogy of cultural politics to give students the opportunity not only to understand more critically who they are as part of a wider social formation, but also to help them critically appropriate those forms of knowledge that traditionally have been denied to them.

In conclusion, each of the discourses I have briefly presented and analyzed involves a different view of cultural production, pedagogical analysis, and political action. And while each of these forms of production involves a certain degree of autonomy in both form and content, it is important that a critical pedagogy be developed around the inner connections they share within the context of a cultural politics. For it is within these interconnections that a theory of both structure and agency can construct a new language, point to new questions and possibilities, and allow educators as transformative intellectuals to struggle for the development of schools as democratic public spheres.

8

Culture, Power and Transformation in the Work of Paulo Freire: Toward a Politics of Education

By HENRY A GIROUX

Paulo Freire's work continues to represent a theoretically refreshing and politically viable alternative to the current impasse in educational theory and practice in North America. Freire has appropriated the unclaimed heritage of emancipatory ideas in those versions of secular and religious philosophy located within the corpus of bourgeois thought. He has also critically integrated into his work a heritage of radical thought without assimilating many of the problems that have plagued it historically. In effect, Freire combines what I have called the "language of critique" with the "language of possibility."

Utilizing the language of critique, Freire has fashioned a theory of education that takes seriously the relationship between radical critical theory and the imperatives of radical commitment and struggle. Drawing upon his experiences in Latin America, Africa, and North America, he has generated a discourse that deepens our understanding of the dynamics and complexity of domination. In this instance, Freire rightly argues that domination cannot be reduced exclusively to a form of class domination. With the notion of difference as a guiding theoretical thread, Freire rejects the idea that there is a universalized form of oppression. Instead, he acknowledges and locates within different social fields forms of suffering that speak to particular modes of domination and, consequently, diverse forms of collective struggle and resistance. By recognizing that certain forms of oppression are not reducible to class oppression, Freire steps outside standard Marxist Analyses; he argues that society contains a multiplicity of contradictory social relations, over which social groups can struggle and organize themselves. This is manifest in those social relations in which the ideological and material conditions of gender, racial, and age discrimination are at work.

Equally important is the insight that domination is more than the simple imposition of arbitrary power by one group over another. Instead, for Freire, the logic of domination represents a combination of historical and contemporary ideological and material practices that are never completely successful, always embody contradictions, and are constantly being fought over within asymmetrical relations of power. Underlying Freire's language of critique, in this case, is the insight that history is never foreclosed. Just as the actions of men and women are limited by the specific constraints in which they find themselves, they also make those constraints and the possibilities that may follow from challenging them.

Within this theoretical juncture Freire introduces a new dimension to radical educational theory and practice. I say new because he links the process of struggle to the particularities of people's lives while simultaneously arguing for a faith in the power of the oppressed to struggle in the interests of their own liberation. This is a notion of education fashioned in more than critique and Orwellian pessimism; it is a discourse that creates a new starting point by trying to make hope realizable and despair unconvincing.

Education in Freire's view becomes both an ideal and a referent for change in the service of a new kind of society. As an ideal, education "speaks" to a form of cultural politics that transcends the theoretical boundaries of any one specific political doctrine, while simultaneously linking social theory and practice to the deepest aspects of emancipation. Thus, as an expression of radical social theory, Freire's cultural politics is broader and more fundamental than any one specific political discourse such as classical Marxist theory, a point that often confuses his critics.

In fact, his represents a theoretical discourse whose underlying interests are fashioned around a struggle against all forms of subjective and objective domination as well as a struggle for forms of knowledge, skills, and social relations that provide the conditions for social and, hence, self-emancipation.

As a referent for change, education represents both a site and a particular type of engagement with the dominant society. For Freire, education includes and moves beyond the notion of schooling. Schools are only one important site where education takes place, where men and women both produce and are the product of specific social and pedagogical relations. Education represents, in Freire's view, both a struggle for meaning and a struggle over power relations. Its dynamic springs from the dialectical relation between individuals and groups who live out their lives within specific historical conditions and structural constraints, on the one hand, and those cultural forms and ideologies that give rise to the contradictions and struggles that define the lived realities of various societies on the other. Education is that terrain where power and politics are given a fundamental expression, where the production of meaning, desire, language, and values engage and respond to the deeper beliefs about what it means to be human, to dream, and to name and struggle for a particular future and form of social life. Education becomes a form of action that joins the languages of critique and possibility. It represents, finally, the need for a passionate commitment by educators to make the political more pedagogical, that is, to make critical reflection and action fundamental parts of a social project that not only engages forms of oppression but develops a deep and abiding faith in the struggle to humanize life itself. It is the particular nature of this social project that gives Freire's work its theoretical distinctiveness.

The theoretical distinctiveness of Freire's work can best be understood by examining briefly how his discourse stands between two radical traditions. On the one hand, the language of critique as it is expressed in Freire's work embodies many of the analyses that characterize what has been called the new sociology of education. On the other hand, Freire's philosophy of hope and struggle is rooted in a language of possibility that draws extensively from the tradition of liberation theology. It is from the merging of these two traditions that Freire has produced a discourse that not only gives meaning and theoretical coherence to his work, but also provides the basis for a more comprehensive and critical theory of pedagogical struggle.

The New Sociology of Education and the Language of Critique

The new sociology of education emerged in full strength in England and the United States over a decade ago as a critical response to what can be loosely termed the discourse of traditional educational theory and practice. The central question, against which it developed its criticism of traditional schooling as well as its own theoretical discourse, is typically Freirean: How does one make education meaningful so as to make it critical and, one hopes, emancipatory.

Radical critics, for the most part, agree that educational traditionalists generally ignore the question. They elude the issue through the paradoxical depoliticizing the language of schooling while reproducing and legitimating capitalist ideologies. The most obvious expression of this approach can be seen in the positivist discourse used by traditional educational theorists. A positivist discourse, in this case, takes as its most important concerns the mastery of pedagogical techniques and the transmission of knowledge instrumental to the existing society. In the traditional world view, schools are merely instructional sites.

Critical educational theorists argue that traditional educational theory suppresses important questions regarding knowledge, power, and domination. Furthermore, schools do not provide opportunities in the broad western humanist tradition for self- and social enpowerment in the society at large. In contrast, critical educators provide theoretical arguments and enormous amounts of empirical evidence to suggest that schools are in fact, agencies of social, economic and cultural reproduction. At best, public schooling offers limited individual mobility to members of the working class and other oppressed groups, but, in the final analysis, public schools are powerful instruments for the reproduction of capitalist relations of production and the legitimating ideologies of everyday life.

For the new sociology of education, schools are analyzed primarily within the language of critique and domination. Yet, since schools are viewed primarily as reproductive in nature, left critics fail to provide a programmatic discourse through which the opportunity for counterhegemonic practices could be established. The agony of the left in this case is that its language of critique offered no hope for teachers, parents, or students to wage a political struggle within the schools themselves. Consequently, the language of critique is subsumed within the discourse of despair.

Freire's earlier work shares a remarkable similarity with some of the major theoretical tenets found in the new sociology of education. By redefining and politicizing the notion of literacy, Freire develops a similar type of critical analysis in which he claims that traditional forms of education function primarily to objectify and alienate oppressed groups. Moreover, Freire explores in great depth the reproductive nature of dominant culture and systematically analyzed how it functions through specific social practices and texts to produce and maintain a "culture of silence" among the Brazillian peasants with whom he worked. Though Freire does not use the term "hidden curriculum" as part of his discourse, he demonstrates pedagogical approaches through which groups of learners can decode ideological and material practices whose form, content, and selective omissions contain the logic of domination and oppression. In addition, Freire links the selection, discussion, and evaluation of knowledge to the pedagogical processes that provide a context for such activity. In his view, it is impossible to separate one from the other, and any viable pedagogical practice has to link radical forms of knowledge with corresponding radical social practices.

The major difference between Freire's work and the new sociology of education is that the latter appears to start and end with the logic of political, economic, and cultural reproduction, whereas Freire's analysis begins with the process of production, that is, the various ways human beings construct their own voices and validate their contradictory experiences within specific historical settings and constraints. The reproduction of capitalist rationality and other forms of oppression is only one political and theoretical moment in the process of domination, rather than an all-encompassing aspect of human existence. It is something to be decoded, challenged, and transformed but only within the ongoing discourse, experiences, and histories of the oppressed themselves. It is in this shift from the discourse of reproduction and critique to the language of possibility and engagement that Freire draws from other traditions and fashions a more comprehensive and radical pedagogy.

Liberation Theology and the Language of Possibility

Central to Freire's politics and pedagogy is a philosophical vision of a liberated humanity. The nature of this vision is rooted in a respect for life. The hope and vision of the future that it inspires are not meant to provide consolation for the oppressed as much as to promote ongoing forms of critique and a struggle against objective forces of oppression. By combining the dynamics of critique and collective struggle with a philosophy of hope, Freire has created a language of possibility, what he calls a permanent prophetic vision. Underlying this prophetic vision is a faith, which Dorothée Soelle argues in *Choosing Life*, "makes life present to us and so makes it possible. . . . It is a great 'Yes' to life . . . [one that] presupposes our power to struggle."

Freire's opposition to all forms of oppression, his call to link ideology critique with collective action, and the prophetic vision central to his politics are heavily indebted to the spirit and ideological dynamics that have both informed and characterized the Liberation Theology Movement that has emerged primarily out of Latin America in the last decade. In truly dialectical fashion, Freire has both criticized and rescued the radical underside of revolutionary Christianity. As the reader will discover, Freire is a harsh critic of the reactionary church. At the same time, he situates his faith and sense of hope in the God of history and the oppressed whose teachings make it impossible, in Freire's words, to "reconcile Christian love with the exploitation of human beings."

Within the discourse of liberation theology, Freire fashions a powerful antidote to the cynicism and despair of many left radical critics. Though utopian, his analysis is concrete in its nature and appeal, taking as its starting point collective actors in their various historical settings and the particularity of their problems and forms of oppression. It is utopian only in its refusal to surrender to the risks and dangers that face all challenges to dominant power structures. It is prophetic in that it views the Kingdom of God as something to be created on earth but only through a faith in both other human beings and the necessity of permanent struggle. The notion of faith that emerges in Freire's work is informed by the memory of the oppressed, the suffering that must not be allowed to continue, and the need never to forget that the prophetic vision is an ongoing process, a vital aspect of the very nature of human life. By combining the discourses of critique and possibility Freire joins history and theology so as to provide the theoretical basis for a radical pedagogy that expresses hope, critical reflection, and collective struggle.

It is at this juncture that the work of Paulo Freire becomes crucial to the development of a radical pedagogy. For in Freire we find the dialectician of contradictions and emancipation. His discourse bridges the relationship between agency and structure, situates human action in constraints forged in historical and contemporary practices, while simultaneously pointing to the spaces, contradictions, and forms of resistance that raise the possibility for social struggle. I will conclude by turning briefly to those theoretical elements in Freire's work that seem vital to developing a new language and theoretical foundation for a radical theory of pedagogy, particularly in a North American context.

Two qualifications must be made before I begin. First, Freire's mode of analysis cannot be dismissed as irrelevant to a North American context. Although critics have argued that his experiences with Brazilian peasants do not translate adequately for educators in the advanced industrial countries of the West, Freire makes it clear through the force of his examples and the variety of pedagogical experiences he provides that the context for his work is international in scope. Not only does he capitalize on his experiences in Brazil, he also draws on his work in Chile, Africa, and the United States. Furthermore, he not only takes as the object of his criticism adult education, but also the pedagogical practices of the Catholic Church, social workers, and public education. As he has pointed out repeatedly, the object of his analysis and the language he uses is for the oppressed everywhere; his concept of the Third World is ideological and political rather than merely geographic.

This leads to the second qualification. In order to be true to the spirit of Freire's most profound pedagogical beliefs, it must be stated that he would never argue that his work is meant to be adopted unproblematically to any site or pedagogical context. What Freire does provide is a metalanguage that generates a set of categories and social practices. Freire's work is not meant to offer radical recipes for instant forms of critical pedagogy, it is a series of theoretical signposts that need to be decoded and critically appropriated within the specific contexts in which they might be useful.

The Discourse of Power

Power, for Freire, both a negative and a positive force, its character is dialectical, and its mode of operation is always more than simply repressive. Power works on and through people. Domination is never so complete that power is experienced exclusively as a negative force, yet power is at the basis of all forms of behavior in which people resist, struggle, and fight for a better world. In a general sense, Freire's theory of power and his demonstration of its dialectical character serve the important function of broadening the spheres and terrains on which power operates. Power, in this instance, is not exhausted in those public and private spheres by governments, ruling classes, and other dominant groups. It is more ubiquitous and is expressed in a range of oppositional public spaces and spheres that traditionally have been characterized by the *absence* of power and thus any form of resistance.

Freire's view of power suggests not only an alternative perspective to those radical theorists trapped in the straitjacket of despair and cynicism, it also stresses that there are always cracks, tensions, and contradictions in various social spheres such as schools where power can be exercised as a positive force in the name of resistance. Furthermore, Freire understands that power—domination—is not simply imposed by the the state through agencies such as the police, the army, and the courts. Domination is also expressed in the way in which power, technology, and ideology come together to produce knowledge, social relations, and other concrete cultural forms that indirectly silence people. It is also found in the way in which the oppressed internalize and thus participate in thier own oppression. This is an important point in Freire's work and directs us to the ways in which domination is subjectively experienced through its internalization and sedimentation in the very needs of the personality. What is at work here is an important attempt to examine the psychically repressive aspects of domination and the internal obstacles to self-knowledge and, thus, to forms of social and self emancipation.

Freire broadens the notion of learning to include how the body learns tacitly, how habit translates into sedimented history, and, most importantly, how knowledge itself may block the development of certain subjectivities and ways of experiencing the world. Ironically, emancipatory forms of knowledge may be refused by those who could most benefit from such knowledge. In this case, accommodation to the logic domination by the oppressed may take the form of actively resisting forms of knowledge that pose a challenge to their world view. Rather than a passive acceptance of domination, knowledge becomes instead an active dynamic of negation, an active refusal to listen, to hear, or to affirm one's own possibilities. The pedagogical questions that emerge from this view of domination are: How do radical educators assess and address the elements of repression and forgetting at the heart of this domination? What accounts for the conditions that sustain an active refusal to know or to learn in the face of knowledge that may challenge the nature of domination itself?

The message that emerges from Freire's pedagogy is relatively clear. If radical educators are to understand the meaning of liberation, they must first be aware of the form that domination takes, the nature of its location, and the problems it poses to those who experience it as both a subjective and objective force. But such a project would be impossible unless one took the historical and cultural particularities, the forms of social life, of subordinate and oppressed groups as a starting point for such an analysis. It is to this issue in Freire's work that I now turn.

Freire's Philosophy of Experience and Cultural Production

One of the most important theoretical elements for a radical pedagogy that Freire provides is his view of experience and cultural production. Freire's notion of culture is at odds with both conservative and progressive positions. In the first instance, he rejects the notion that culture can be divided easily into high, popular, and low forms, with high culture representing the most advanced heritage of a nation. Culture, in this view, hides the ideologies that legitimate and distribute specific forms of culture as if they were unrelated to ruling class interests and existing configurations of power. In the second instance, he rejects the notion that the moment of cultural creation rests solely with ruling groups and that dominant cultural forms harbor merely the seeds of domination. Related to this position, and also rejected by Freire, is the assumption that oppressed groups possess by their very location in the apparatus of domination a progressive and revolutionary culture waiting only to be released from the fetters of ruling class domination.

For Freire, culture is the representation of lived experiences, material artifacts, and practices forged within the unequal and dialectical relations that different groups establish in a given society at a particular historical point. Culture is a form of production whose processes are intimately connected with the structuring of different social formations, particularly those that are gender, age, racial, and class related. It is also a form of production that helps human agents, through their use of language and other material resources, to transform society. In this case, culture is closely related to the dynamics of power and produces asymmetries in the ability of individuals and groups to define and achieve their goals. Furthermore, culture is also an arena of struggle and contradiction, and there is no one culture in the homogeneous sense. On the contrary, there are dominant and subordinate cultures that express different interests and operate from different and unequal terrains of power.

Freire argues for a notion of cultural power that takes as its starting point the social and historical particularities that constitute the problems, sufferings, visions, and acts of resistance that comprise the cultural forms of subordinate groups. Cultural power then has a dual focus as part of his strategy to make the political more pedagogical. First, educators will have to work with the experiences that students bring to schools and other educational sites. This means making these experiences, public and private, the object of debate and confirmation; it means legitimating such experiences in order to give those who live and move within them a sense of affirmation and to provide the conditions for students and others to display an active voice and presence. The pedagogical experience here becomes an invitation to make visible the languages, dreams, values, and encounters that constitute the lives of those whose histories are often actively silenced. But Freire does more than argue for the legitimation of the culture of the oppressed. He also recognizes that such experiences are contradictory in nature and harbor not only radical potentialities but also the sedimentations of domination. Cultural power takes a twist in this instance and refers to the need to *work on* the experiences that make up the lives of the oppressed. Such experiences in their varied cultural forms have to be recovered critically so as to reveal both their strengths and weaknesses. Moreover, self-critique is complimented in the name of a radical pedagogy designed to unearth and critically appropriate those unclaimed emancipatory moments in bourgeois knowledge and experience that further provide the skills the oppressed will need to exercise leadership in the dominant society.

What is striking in this presentation is that Freire has fashioned a theory of cultural power and production that begins with popular education. Instead of offering abstract generalities about human nature, he rightly argues for pedagogical principles that arise from the concrete practices—the terrains on which people live out their everyday experiences. All of this suggests taking seriously the cultural capital of the oppressed, developing critical and analytical tools to interrogate it, and staying in touch with dominant definitions of knowledge so we can analyze them for their usefulness and for the ways in which they bear the logic of domination.

Freire, Transformative Intellectuals, and the Theory-Practice Relationship

Radical social theory has been plagued historically by the development of the relationship between intellectuals and the masses, on the one hand, and the relationship between theory and practice. Under the call for the unity of theory and practice, the possibility for emancipatory practice has often been negated through forms of vanguardism in which intellectuals effectively removed from the popular forces the ability to define for themselves the limits of their aims and practice. By assuming a virtual monopoly in the exercise of theoretical leadership, intellectuals unknowingly reproduced the division of mental and manual labor that was at the core of most forms of domination. Instead of developing theories of practice, which were rooted in the concrete experience of listening and learning with the oppressed, Marxist intellectuals developed theories for practice or technical instruments for change that ignored the necessity for a dialectical reflection on the everyday dynamics and problems of the oppressed within the context of radical social transformation.

Freire refutes this approach to the theory-practice relationship and redefines the very idea of the intellectual. Like the Italian social theorist, Antonio Gramsci, Freire redefines the category of intellectual and argues that all men and women are intellectuals. That is, regardless of social and economic function all human beings perform as intellectuals by constantly interpreting and giving meaning to the world and by participating in a particular conception of the world. Moreover, the oppressed need to develop their own organic and transformative intelletuals who can learn with such groups while simultaneously helping to foster modes of self-education and struggle against various forms of oppression. In this case, intellectuals are organic in that they are *not* outsiders bringing theory to the masses. On the contrary, they are theorists fused organically with the culture and practical activities of the oppressed. Rather than casually dispense knowledge to the grateful masses, intellectuals fuse with the oppressed in order to make and remake the conditions necessary for a radical social project.

This position is crucial in highlighting the political function and importance of intellectuals. Equally significant is the way it redefines the notion of political struggle by emphasizing its pedagogical nature and the centrality of the popular and democratic nature of such a struggle. This raises the important question of how Freire defines the relation between theory and practice.

For Freire, "there is no theoretic context if it is not in a dialectical unity with the concrete context." Rather than call for the collapse of theory into practice, Freire argues for a certain distance between theory and practice. He views theory as anticipatory in its nature and posits that is must take the concepts of understanding and possibility as its central moments. Theory is informed by an oppositional discourse that preserves its critical distance from the "facts" and experiences of the given society. The tension, indeed, the conflict with practice belongs to the essence of theory and is grounded in its very structure. Theory does not dictate practice; rather, it serves to hold practice at arm's length so as to mediate and critically comprehend the type of praxis needed within a specific setting at a particular time. There is no appeal to universal laws or historical necessity here; theory emerges within specific contexts and forms of experience in order to examine such contexts critically and then to intervene on the basis of an informed praxis.

But Freire's contribution to the nature of theory and practice and the role of the intellectual in the process of social transformation contains another important dimension. Theory must be seen as the production of forms of discourse that arise from various specific social sites. Such a discourse may arise from the universities, from peasant communities, from workers councils, or from within various social movements. The issue here is that radical educators recognize that these different sites give rise to various forms of theoretical production and practice. Each of these sites provides diverse and critical insights into the nature of domination and the possibilities for social and self-emancipation, and they do so from the historical and social particularities that give them meaning. What brings them together is a mutual respect forged in criticism and the need to struggle against all forms of domination.

Freire and the Concept of Historical Insertion

Freire believes that a critical sensibility is an extension of a historical sensibility. That is, to understand the present, in both institutional and social terms, educators must place all pedagogical contexts in an historical context so as to see clearly their genesis and development. History is used by Freire in a two-fold sense: it reveals in existing institutions and social relations the historical context that informs their meaning and the legacy that both hides and clarifies their political function. On the other hand, Freire points to the sedimented history that constitutes who we are as historical and social beings. In other words, the history that is anchored in the cultural forms that give meaning to the way we talk, think, dress, and act becomes subject to a form of historical analysis. History in this sense becomes dialectical in Freire's work because it is used to distinguish between the present as given and the present as containing emancipatory possibilities. Such a perspective makes the present as it constitutes our psyche and the wider society visible in terms of its revolutionary possibilities and in doing so points to the need for a critical awakening (what Freire might call the process of denunciation and annunciation) that is grounded in the capacity of social transformation.

In conclusion, Freire's work provides a view of pedagogy and praxis that is partisan to its core; in its origins and intentions it is for "choosing life." Moreover, Freire demonstrates once again that he is not only a man of the present, he is also a man of the future. His speech, actions, warmth, and vision represent a way of acknowledging and criticizing a world that lives perilously close to destruction. In one sense, Freire's work and presence is there to remind us not simply about what we are but also to suggest what we might become.

9

Teachers as Transformative Intellectuals

By HENRY A. GIROUX

Unlike many past educational reform movements, the present call for educational change presents *both* a threat and a challenge to public school teachers that appears unprecedented in our nation's history. The threat comes in the form of a series of educational reforms that display little confidence in the ability of public school teachers to provide intellectual and moral leadership for our nation's youth. For instance, many of the recommendations that have emerged in the current debate either ignore the role teachers play in preparing learners to be active and critical citizens or they suggest reforms that ignore the intelligence, judgment and experience that teachers might offer in such a debate. Where teachers do enter the debate, they are the object of educational reforms that reduce them to the status of high-level technicians carrying out dictates and objectives decided by experts far removed from the everyday realities of classroom life.[1] The message appears to be that teachers do not count when it comes to critically examining the nature and process of educational reform.

The political and ideological climate does not look favorable for teachers at the moment. But it does offer them the challenge to join in a public

121

debate with their critics as well as the opportunity to engage in a much-needed self-critique regarding the nature and purpose of teacher preparation, in-service teacher programs and the dominant forms of classroom teaching. Similarly, the debate provides teachers with the opportunity to organize collectively to improve the conditions under which they work and to demonstrate to the public the central role that teachers must play in any viable attempt to reform the public schools.

In order for teachers and others to engage in such a debate, it is necessary that a theoretical perspective be developed that redefines the nature of the educational crisis while simultaneously providing the basis for an alternative view of teacher training and work. In short, recognizing that the current crisis in education largely has to do with the developing trend towards the disempowerment of teachers at all levels of education is a necessary theoretical precondition for teachers to organize effectively and establish a collective voice in the current debate. Moreover, such a recognition will have to come to grips not only with a growing loss of power among teachers around the basic conditions of their work, but also with a changing public perception of their role as reflective practitioners.

I want to make a small theoretical contribution to this debate and the challenge it calls forth by examining two major problems that need to be addressed in the interest of improving the quality of "teacher work," which includes all the clerical tasks and extra assignments as well as classroom instruction. First, I think it is imperative to examine the ideological and material forces that have contributed to what I want to call the proletarianization of teacher work; that is, the tendency to reduce teachers to the status of specialized technicians within the school bureaucracy, whose function then becomes one of managing and implementing curricular programs rather than developing or critically appropriating curricula to fit specific pedagogical concerns. Second, there is a need to defend schools as institutions essential to maintaining and developing a critical democracy and also to defending teachers as transformative intellectuals who combine scholarly reflection and practice in the service of educating students to be thoughtful, active citizens. In the remainder of this essay, I will develop these points and conclude by examining their implications for providing an alternative view of teacher work.

Devaluing and Deskilling Teacher Work

One of the major threats facing prospective and existing teachers within the public schools is the increasing development of instrumental ideologies that emphasize a technocratic approach to both teacher preparation and classroom pedagogy. At the core of the current emphasis on instrumental and pragmatic factors in school life are a number of important pedagogical assumptions. These include: a call for the separation of conception from execution; the standardization of school knowledge in the interest of managing and controlling it; and the devaluation of critical, intellectual work on the part of teachers and students for the primacy of practical considerations.[2]

This type of instrumental rationality finds one of its strongest expressions historically in the training of prospective teachers. That teacher training programs in the United States have long been dominated by a behavioristic orientation and emphasis on mastering subject areas and methods of teaching is well documented.[3] The implications of this approach, made clear by Zeichner, are worth repeating:

> Underlying this orientation to teacher education is a metaphor of "production," a view of teaching as an "applied science" and a view of the teacher as primarily an "executor" of the laws and principles of effective teaching. Prospective teachers may or may not proceed through the curriculum at their own pace and may participate in varied or standardized learning activities, but that which they are to master is limited in scope (e.g., to a body of professional content knowledge and teaching skills) and is fully determined in advance by others often on the basis of research on teacher effectiveness. The prospective teacher is viewed primarily as a passive recipient of this professional knowledge and plays little part in determining the substance and direction of his or her preparation program.[4]

The problems with this approach are evident in John Dewey's argument that teacher training programs that emphasize only technical expertise do a disservice both to the nature of teaching and to their students.[5] Instead of learning to reflect upon the principles that structure classroom life and practice, prospective teachers are taught methodologies that appear to deny the very need for critical thinking. The point is that teacher education programs often lose sight of the need to educate students to examine the underlying nature of school problems. Further, these programs need to substitute for the language of management and efficiency a critical analysis of the less obvious conditions that structure the ideological and material practices of schooling.

Instead of learning to raise questions about the principles underlying different classroom methods, research techniques and theories of education, students are often preoccupied with learning the "how to," with "what works," or with mastering the best way to teach a *given* body of knowledge. For example, the mandatory field-practice seminars often consist of students sharing with each other the techniques they have used in managing and controlling classroom discipline, organizing a day's activities, and learning how to work within specific time tables. Examining one such program, Jesse Goodman raises some important questions about the incapacitating silences it embodies. He writes:

> There was no questioning of feelings, assumptions, or definitions in this discussion. For example, the "need" for external rewards and punishments to "make kids learn" was taken for granted; the educational and ethical implications were not addressed. There was no display of concern for stimulating or nurturing a child's intrinsic desire to learn. Definitions of *good kids* as "quiet kids," *workbook work* as "reading," *on-task time* as "learning," and *getting through the material on time* as "the goal of teaching"—all went unchallenged. Feelings of pressure and possible guilt about not keeping to time schedules also went unexplored. The real concern in this discussion was that everyone "shared."[6]

Technocratic and instrumental rationalities are also at work within the teaching field itself, and they play an increasing role in reducing teacher autonomy with respect to the development and planning of curricula and the judging and implementation of classroom instruction. This is most evident in the proliferation of what has been called "teacher-proof" curriculum packages.[7] The underlying rationale in many of these packages reserves for teachers the role of simply carrying out predetermined content and instructional procedures. The method and aim of such packages is to legitimate what I call management pedagogies. That is, knowledge is broken down into discrete parts, standardized for easier management and consumption, and measured through predefined forms of assessment. Curricula approaches of this sort are management pedagogies because the central questions regarding learning are reduced to the problem of management, i.e., "how to allocate resources (teachers, students and materials) to produce the maximum number of certified . . . students within a designated time."[8] The underlying theoretical assumption that guides this type of pedagogy is that the behavior of teachers needs to be controlled and made consistent and predictable across different schools and student populations.

What is clear in this approach is that it organizes school life around curricular, instructional, and evaluation experts who do the thinking while teachers are reduced to doing the implementing. The effect is not only to deskill teachers, to remove them from the processes of deliberation and reflection, but also to routinize the nature of learning and classroom pedagogy. Needless to say, the principles underlying management pedagogies are at odds with the premise that teachers should be actively involved in producing curricula materials suited to the cultural and social contexts in which they teach. More specifically, the narrowing of curricula choices to a back-to-basics format and the introduction of lock-step, time-on-task pedagogies operate from the theoretically erroneous assumption that *all* students can learn from the same materials, classroom instructional techniques and modes of evaluation. The notion that students come from different histories and embody different experiences, linguistic practices, cultures, and talents is strategically ignored within the logic and accountability of management pedagogy theory.

Teachers as Transformative Intellectuals

In what follows, I want to argue that one way to rethink and restructure the nature of teacher work is to view teachers as transformative intellectuals. The cagegory of intellectual is helpful in a number of ways. First, it provides a theoretical basis for examining teacher work as a form of intellectual labor, as opposed to defining it in purely instrumental or technical terms. Second, it clarifies the kinds of ideological and practical conditions necessary for teachers to function as intellectuals. Third, it helps to make clear the role teachers play in producing and legitimating various political, economic and social interests through the pedagogies they endorse and utilize.

By viewing teachers as intellectuals, we can illuminate the important idea that all human activity involves some form of thinking. No activity, regardless of how routinized it might become, can be abstracted from the functioning of the mind in some capacity. This is a crucial issue, because by arguing that the use of the mind is a general part of all human activity we dignify the human capacity for integrating thinking and practice, and in doing so highlight the core of what it means to view teachers as reflective practitioners. Within this discourse, teachers can be seen not merely as "performers professionally equipped to realize effectively any goals that may be set for them. Rather [they should] be viewed as free men and women with a special dedication to the values of the intellect and the enhancement of the critical powers of the young."[9]

Viewing teachers as intellectuals also provides a strong theoretical critique of technocratic and instrumental ideologies underlying an educational theory that separates the conceptualization, planning and design of curricula from the processes of implementation and execution. It is important to stress that teachers must take active responsibility for raising serious questions about what they teach, how they are to teach, and what the larger goals are for which they are striving. This means that they must take a responsible role in shaping the purposes and conditions of schooling. Such a task is impossible within a division of labor in which teachers have little influence over the ideological and economic conditions of their work. This point has a normative and political dimension that seems especially relevant for teachers. If we believe that the role of teaching cannot be reduced to merely training in the practical skills, but involves, instead, the education of a class of intellectuals vital to the development of a free society, then the category of intellectual becomes a way of linking the purpose of teacher education, public schooling and inservice training to the very principles necessary for developing a democratic order and society.

I have argued that by viewing teachers as intellectuals we can begin to rethink and reform the traditions and conditions that have prevented teachers from assuming their full potential as active, reflective scholars and practitioners. I believe that it is important not only to view teachers as intellectuals, but also to contextualize in political and normative terms the concrete social functions that teachers perform. In this way, we can be more specific about the different relations that teachers have both to their work and to the dominant society.

A starting point for interrogating the social function of teachers as intellectuals is to view schools as economic, cultural and social sites that are inextricably tied to the issues of power and control. This means that schools do more than pass on in an objective fashion a common set of values and knowledge. On the contrary, schools are places that represent forms of knowledge, language practices, social relations and values that are particular selections and exclusions from the wider culture. As such, schools serve to introduce and legitimate *particular* forms of social life. Rather than being objective institutions removed from the dynamics of politics and power, schools actually are contested spheres that embody and express a struggle over what forms of authority, types of knowledge, forms of moral regulation and versions of the past and future should be legitimated and transmitted to students. The struggle is most visible in the demands, for example, of right-wing religious groups currently trying to institute school prayer, remove certain books from school libraries, and include certain forms of religious teachings in the science curricula. Of course, different demands are made by feminists, ecologists, minorities, and other interest groups who believe that the schools should teach women's studies, courses on the environment, or black history. In short, schools are not neutral sites, and teachers cannot assume the posture of being neutral either.

In the broadest sense, teachers as intellectuals have to be seen in terms of the ideological and political interests that structure the nature of the discourse, classroom social relations, and values that they legitimate in their teaching. With this perspective in mind, I want to conclude that teachers should become transformative intellectuals if they are to educate students to be active, critical citizens.

Central to the category of transformative intellectual is the necessity of making the pedagogical more political and the political more pedagogical. Making the pedagogical more political means inserting schooling directly into the political sphere by arguing that schooling represents both a struggle to define meaning and a struggle over power relations. Within this perspective, critical reflection and action become part of a fundamental social project to help students develop a deep and abiding faith in the struggle to overcome economic, political and social injustices, and to further humanize themselves as part of this struggle. In this case, knowledge and power are inextricably linked to the presupposition that to choose life, to recognize the necessity of improving its democratic and qualitative character for all people, is to understand the preconditions necessary to struggle for it.

Making the political more pedagogical means utilizing forms of pedagogy that embody political interests that are emancipatory in nature; that is, using forms of pedagogy that treat students as critical agents; make knowledge problematic; utilize critical and affirming dialogue; and make the case for struggling for a qualitatively better world for all people. In part, this suggests that transformative intellectuals take seriously the need to give students an active voice in their learning experiences. It also means developing a critical vernacular that is attentive to problems experienced at the level of everyday life, particularly as they are related to pedagogical experiences connected to classroom practice. As such, the pedagogical starting point for such intellectuals is not the isolated student but individuals and groups in their various cultural, class, racial, historical and gender settings, along with the particularity of their diverse problems, hopes, and dreams.

Transformative intellectuals need to develop a discourse that unites the language of critique with the language of possibility, so that social educators recognize that they can make changes. In doing so, they must speak out against economic, political and social injustices both within and outside of schools. At the same time, they must work to create the conditions that give students the opportunity to become citizens who have the knowledge and courage to struggle in order to make despair unconvincing and hope practical. As difficult as this task may seem to social educators, it is a struggle worth waging. To do otherwise is to deny social educators the opportunity to assume the role of transformative intellectuals.

10

Curriculum Study and Cultural Politics

By HENRY A. GIROUX and ROGER SIMON

Any starting point for a new direction of curriculum study has to take into account the historical and sedimented division within most curriculum departments in North America. About sixty years ago educators began to clarify existing interests and assumptions in a manner that produced two quite different ways of thinking about curriculum study.[1] We are referring here to the classic division between "admistrative" and "scientific" interests, a schism perhaps most simply expressed in the difference between these questions: (1) What should teachers teach? and (2) What effective interventions can be derived from understanding human development and learning processes? We shall not critique or dwell on these orientations. They are familiar enough. Our interests are aligned with neither of them.

Rather, our concern is with the development of a new form of graduate study in curriculum that supports what we are calling the construction of a cultural politics. What program of study would articulate this concern, and with whom would such efforts be in alliance? Let us begin by being strategically practical. Any graduate program has to "speak to" a clientele. For those of us who are educators, we might as well face the social and economic structure of which we are part. We offer a commodity. We compete not only with other universities but also with our colleagues in other departments in our own institutions. Thus, this commodity logic forces us to ask, who are our clients? Who would find their interests addressed by curriculum study as cultural politics?

We think they are educators increasingly faced with the specification of practices rationalized through a logic of individual commodification that is dictated by an instrumental relation to the economy. They are educators who increasingly feel that they do not know what it means to be on the students' side but desperately want to be. They are educators whose contradictory location within a specific set of social relations results in the alternating raising an suppressing of questions such as: What counts as education?

What follows is premised on the notion that those of us in the universities have something useful to offer such a clientele (this very language signifies a problem built deep into the structure of our work, and we use the term self-consciously to raise the contradiction). Ironically, we who work within universities are forced to offer politics as a commodity! It is a familiar theme in Western society which always blunts the critical edge. It is a contradiction we must eventually address and will return to below. One may note that it is a contradiction that is easier to resolve in a research context where the growth of alliances is not as dependent on successful competition in the marketplace.

But now we want to be a bit more specific. For educators rethinking contemporary schooling the important issue that has to be faced is what programmatic approach to graduate study would be desirable? This is especially important in order for educators to consider what will have to be taken into account in formulating teaching and organizing practices that might counter the dominant discourse and ideology. In our view, such a programmatic approach to graduate study in curriculum would be one that grasps schooling: (1) as one form among many, (2) as a cultural and political site that embodies a project of transformation and regulation, and (3) as a productive form that constructs and defines human subjectivity through the repertoire of ideologies and practices it embodies. This formulation requires a form of curriculum study that stresses the historical and the cultural in relation to educative materials and practices. Moreover, it points to specific areas of study that would be crucial to this effort. Before examining the forms of discourse that would structure the study of curriculum, we want to comment on themes or areas of analysis that would be central to such a program.

Language

In many graduate schools of education, language (i.e., reading, writing, literature, second language learning, and so forth) is one of the specific foci or areas of concentration available to students entering a curriculum program. This exclusive delimitation of what defines a concern with language has always struck us as somewhat bizarre in that it legitimates and limits language issues as technical and developmental. While such concerns are clearly important, what is suppressed in this orientation is the essential question of the relation between language and power. We believe that graduate study supportive of the construction of a genuine oppositional cultural politics would have as one of its central themes the relation between language and power.

The rationale for such a position becomes clear if the acquisition of language (be it English, mathematics, physics, drama, or whatever) is viewed as a form of learning that not only instructs students into ways of "naming" the world but also introduces them to particular social relations. In other words, what is historically constructed as esteemed, approved, proper, and of instrumental value is learned in the "sense" of a particular discursive rendering of some aspect of our environment and ourselves. Expression is fully implicated in the accomplishment of experience, but "the rub" is that expression is never arbitrary utterance but is determined within the actual conditions that organize the social situation of the utterance.[2] Institutionally legitimated knowledge organizes and dis-organizes experience, and educators must know how to ask whose experience and whose interests are supported by different possible forms of education.

Popular and Subordinate Cultures

Another theme of study central to the construction of education as cultural politics is the relation of popular and subordinate cultures to the dominant modes of schooling. We have to come to grips with the implications of the fact that students' experience of school is intertwined with their lives at home and on the street. This is not a simplistic call for relevance; it is rather an assertion of our need to understand the traditions of mediation students bring to their encounter with institutionally legitimated knowledge. It is an attempt to construct a theoretical agenda through which educators may begin to take seriously the hopes, anxieties, experiences, and histories of subordinate groups and classes. We are using the term "culture" as the distinctive ways in which a social group lives out and makes sense of its "given" circumstances and conditions of life.[3] These may or may not be "unconscious"; certainly they are the product of collective historical processes and not of merely personal intention. In fact, individuals form their purposes and intentions within the frameworks provided by their cultural repertoire.

Theorizing the Social Formation

In order to decide on what to do, educators have to figure out why things are the way they are, how they got that way, and what conditions are supporting them. Furthermore, educators must be able to evaluate potentials for action that are embedded in actual relationships and practices. To do this demands thinking about education through its interrelation with the surrounding social formation. This form of analysis requires some familiarity with the questions posed by social theory and some understanding of the state as the agency through which schooling has been organized for the last 150 years. But most importantly it means learning how to analyze concrete situations in a way that shows how (and with what limitations) any social relationship or institutional form can be transformed through intentional action. How such analyses are formulated depends, of course, on specific views of how the social world is constructed. Indeed, this is an argument for the fundamental intersection of social and curriculum theorizing. It is also the call for a new form of curriculum discourse and language.

History

We are not interested here in chronology but rather in an understanding of how specific educational practices can be understood as historical constructions related to economic, social, and political events in a particular space and time. This is absolutely essential in order to be able to think about how specific instances of schooling and curriculum theory may represent one form among the many possible. Such a position not only highlights the specifically social and constructed nature of schooling, but also provides the basis for critical and oppositional thought and action. In short, it provides the basis for thinking in terms that might envision a different world and future. The substance here would have to be not only the history of schooling in one's own country, but comparison with others as well.

Pedagogy

This list of themes has perhaps been a bit one-sided. But we mean to give pedagogy its place. We support the term for the decidedly broad theoretical sweep and connection to practice it suggests. For us, pedagogy refers to a concern with materials and instruction in ways that speak about their integration, that give it a focus and purpose. This is where educators must collectively confront the question: What is to be done?

How might one think about reading a text to open its mythology?[4] How might one organize learning situations to minimize the symbolic violence of the dominant culture?[5] What new materials and activities might one emphasize that will give students a sense of alternative possibilities?[6] How might one work to make the experience and needs of students problematic so as to provide the basis for exploring the interface between their own lives and the constraints and possibilities of the wider society?

There are answers to such questions but they will always have to be contingently and collectively developed. To study pedagogy should never be confused with being told what to do, but it does require new forms of graduate study which fully implicate university faculty in real struggles to define educational projects that are truly transformative. It requires, as we shall see, ultimately abandoning the naming of our students as clientele.

We have tried to sketch briefly in the preceding section specific themes that we think should generate a *critical* discourse for the study of curriculum. We are attempting to provoke a new and critical discourse that defines the study of curriculum within the parameters of a theoretical culture that is linked to the dynamics of commitment and struggle. To that end, we want to proceed by highlighting some of the theoretical categories that we believe would be central to a critical view of the study of curriculum.

Theory as the Language of Critique and Possibility

As our themes above surely indicate, we think it is important to view curriculum thoery as a form of social theory. When curriculum theory is viewed in that light, it becomes evident that curriculum discourse is inextricably related to forms of knowledge and social practices that legitimate and reproduce particular forms of social life. Curriculum in this sense is seen as a theoretical discourse that makes the political a pedagogical act. That is, curriculum represents an expression of struggle over what forms of political authority, orders of representation, forms of moral regulation, and versions of the past and future should be legitimated, passed on, and debated in specific pedagogical sites. In this case, curriculum theory is not to be condemned for being political, but for being covertly or unconsciously political. Equally important is the related notion that curriculum discourse, in all of its variations, is a form of ideology that has an intimate relation to questions of power, particularly as these structure social relations around gender, racial, and class considerations.

Moreover, we think that the value of curriculum theory and practice should be linked to providing the conditions for students to understand it as a form of cultural politics, that is, as an expression of radical social theory. But a caveat must be inserted here. By linking curriculum theory and practice to radical social theory, we are not arguing that students should learn the discourse of, let's say, a specific doctrine such as Marxism. On the contrary, the notion of radical as we are using it in this context is much broader and more fundamental than any one version of Marxism or any other political doctrine. In fact, it suggests linking curriculum theory and practice with the deepest aspects of emancipation in which self and social empowerment are developed around the goals of fighting against all forms of subjective and objective domination. Similarly, it suggests struggling to produce forms of knowledge and skills that provide the conditions for a qualitatively better life for all. As such, curriculum discourse becomes, in this instance, valued for the ways in which its embraces both the language of critique and the language of possibility. Let us be more specific here.

Informed by the language of critique, curriculum studies would represent a site within the university where the partisan nature of human learning and stuggle would provide a starting point for linking knowledge to power. Commitment to the development of forms of community life would take seriously the notions of liberty, equality, and human solidarity.

Thus, curriculum studies would be organized around the goal of educating students to provide moral and intellectual leadership (not through vanguardism!). In this case, curriculum discourse would relate knowledge to power in a threefold sense. First, it would interrogate all knowledge claims for the interests that structure both the questions they raise and the questions they exclude. Second, knowledge claims about all aspects of schooling and society would be analyzed as part of wider cultural processes intimately connected with the production and legitimation of class, racial, gender, and aged social formations as they are reproduced within asymmetrical relations of power. Third, knowledge would be viewed as part of a collective learning process intimately connected to the dynamics of struggle and contestation both within and outside of the univeristy. Far from being treated as objective, as something simply to be mastered, knowledge claims in the curriculum field would be analyzed as part of a wider struggle over different orders of representation, conflicting forms of cultural experience, and diverse visions of the future.

Regarding the discourse of possibility, we are suggesting, as previously mentioned, that the study of curriculum be informed by a language that acknowledges curriculum as the introduction, preparation, and legitimation for forms of social life. That is, curriculum discourse would take seriously the social and historical particularities that constitute the cultural forms and boundaries that give meaning to the lives of students and other learners. In one sense, this points to the need to develop theories, forms of knowledge, and social practices that *work with* the experiences that people bring to the pedagogical setting. This means taking seriously and confirming the language forms, modes of reasoning, dispositions, and histories that give students an active voice in defining the world. In a second sense, the language of possiblity refers to the need to *work on* the experiences that constitute the lives of students. This means that such experiences in their varied cultural forms have to be recovered critically so as to reveal both their strengths and their weaknesses. Similarly this means teaching students how to critically appropriate the codes and vocabularies of different experiences so as to provide them with the skills they will need in order to define rather than simply serve in the modern world.

As the language of possibility, curriculum discourse would be linked to forms of self and social empowerment that embrace the struggle to develop active forms of community life around the principles of equality and democracy. It would infuse pedagogical work both in and out of schools with a discourse that can function so as to raise real hopes, forge democratic alliances, and point to new forms of social life that appear realizable.

Central to such a project would be a fundamental commitment to the notions of hope and emancipation. The importance, purpose, and study of curriculum as form of discourse and practice would be inextricably linked to a notion of educational practice that takes as its starting point a commitment to the welfare of the public good. Thus, curriculum study as an expression of specific forms of knowledge, values, and skills would take as its organizing principle the task of educating students to become active and responsible citizens; that is, citizens capable of the intellectual skills and civic courage needed to struggle for a self-determined, thoughtful and democratic life. The measure of success against which such a program would be judged would be based on the degree to which it provides successfully the ideological and material conditions for its implementation and the degree to which it demonstrates the central relationship between schooling and the idea of human emancipation.

Re-Constructing the Relation between Universities and Schools

As a critical theoretical discourse, curriculum studies will have to redefine the relationship between theory and practice, overcoming rather than reinforcing the division of labor between them. Particularly as it defines the connection between institutions of higher education and the public schools, curriculum study will have to be reconstructed in specific alliance with active forms of community life. This means recognizing that curriculum theory can be viewed as the production of forms of discourse that arise from specific social sites, and that while university people theorize out of one specific site, public school teachers, administrators, and others involved in pedagogical work theorize out of different but equally important contexts. These different sites give rise to various forms of theoretical production and practice. Each of these different institutional spheres provide diverse and critical insights into the problems of curriculum production and schooling, and they do so from the historical and social particularities that give them meaning. The key question is how these forms of theoretical production and practice can be linked within a common project informed by the languages of critique and possibility.

This link requires a rethinking of who we are as educators. It would redefine curriculum studies as supportive of teacher-educators as transformative intellectuals.[7] Educators would work in conjunction with specific social groups and movements around various emancipatory concerns. They would help such groups develop the tools for moral and intellectual leadership, and as such, their pedagogical role would be linked not merely to the production of ideas but also to forms of collective struggle around various economic, social, and political concerns. The importance of this has to be judged, in part, against the assumption that curriculum studies as currently constituted in most graduate programs have been stripped of a democratic vision—that they have, as a consequence, functioned to educate students less as intellectuals and reflective practitioners than as obedient civil servants and skillful technicians. Viewing teachers, administrators, and professors as transformative intellectuals provides the pragmatic opportunity to link emancipatory possibilities to critical forms of leadership by reformulating the role of curriculum work. By taking the category of intellectual seriously, graduate students, professors, and others would have to investigate and be made fully aware of their active role in mediating between the dominant society and everyday life. Equally important, they would have to be aware that their pedagogical role is decidedly political since they cannot escape the contradictory functions of legitimating or resisting dominant forms of ideology and culture. The category of organic intellectual also points to the ongoing daily struggle of educators over what constitutes the distinction between normality and deviance, over what counts as acceptable social and school practice, and over what counts as legitimate forms of language and knowledge.

But it must be stressed that the concept of transformative intellectual does more than suggest the political function curriculum work engages. It also provides a beginning for educators to examine their own histories, that is, those connections to the past and to particular social formations, cultures, and sedimented experiences that define who they are and how they structure school experiences. Similarly, the concept becomes a political referent for educators to take seriously the struggle to eliminate the divison between intellectual and manual labor, not only in our own work but also in the society at large. Lastly, the use of the concept as an organizing principle for curriculum discourse points to the importance of students and others to examine the multifaceted character of power as both an ideological and a material force. In other words, we need to understand how power works as both a positive and negative instance within the many contradictions that make up school life.[8] This suggests the need to develop concrete analyses within curriculum studies programs of how power functions to police and structure language, how it is used as a force to administer and shape the politics of the body, and how it is implicated in the organization of time and space. Central to these concerns is the constraining and enabling role that curriculum workers occupy as intellectuals.

Thus, we want to conclude this chapter by returning to one of the contradictions which is salient for academics seeking to articulate educational study and inquiry as a form of social inquiry and cultural politics. This is the contradiction, produced amid the commodity logic which structures our work, between our desire for the intellectual and entrepreneurial freedom of the unattached intellectual and the obligations and commitments of the organic intellectual. The following comments are meant to illuminate this contradiction and to point toward a way of mitigating it. There are not easy solutions.

The Social in Curriculum Studies

If we embrace, on the one hand, the notion highlighted earlier that curriculum be viewed as the expression of a form of struggle, we must ask the consequential questions: What is the nature of this struggle? What is it about? What form does it take? On whose side do we stand? and What needs to be done? Indeed, we would assert that curriculum study is defined through addressing these questions.

On the other hand, we must recognize that as academics we either work for the state or have a particularly close relationship with its ideologies and social practices. As employees of the state, for instance, we live off the surplus value created in the particular regions and areas of the country where we work. We live off this surplus value situated in a political economy defined by both the structural location of our worksite in universities and the concrete relations of our "profession." To the degree that academics want to acquire the scarce resources of this economy, which include tenured positions, desirable courses, interested students, space in journals, time to write, recognition from colleagues, and so forth, we must seek to define and control the "turf" on which we work.

But to the degree that academics do this individually, on their own terms, in competition with others who want similar resources, we become academic *petite bourgeoisie*. This is both a form of material practice and subjectivity that is indeed fostered by the very structure of work within universities.

We do recognize that the contradictory character of the setting of university work is at odds with the notion of curriculum study we have outlined above. But we seek to call into question and contest those ideological and material practices that, simultaneously, constitute the work lives and limit the practice of university intellectuals in curriculum departments. Furthermore, we submit that any program of curriculum study as cultural politics requires that we in some measure succeed.

We want to pose the question of how intellectuals can work through this contradiction: how they can foster collective academic life that allows for intellectual freedom, and yet remain connected to interests outside their own. We admit this phrase, "interests outside their own," sounds a bit paradoxical. We use it here in strict reference to the political economy we referred to above in that this economy defines and structures "our" interests. Why one should be interested in remaining connected to interests "outside their own" is an important matter. It relates to such questions as how we answer our family and friends when they ask how we justify what we do every day. To pursue this, however, would sidetrack us at this point. We have no comprehensive program, but we do want to raise and discuss a few ideas. This discussion will take place around three related issues: collegiality, program content, and the necessity of abandoning the notion of students as "clientele."

Collegiality

The competitive spirit is very much alive and well in academic life, and it structures much of our discourse and desire. There is far too little genuine social interaction (and thus far too little joy) in collective cultural production (multiple authorship of articles does not necessarily mean collective production)! As academics and intellectuals we must become increasingly deliberate about creating structures that support joint work both with regard to research/inquiry and with regard to co-teaching and co-writing. These structures may sound trivial, but in the concrete dynamics of everyday life they can take on frustratingly brute importance. They are represented by concerns such as making sure that course scheduling supports the possiblity of co-teaching, and, in cases where there may be discretionary funds to support research or travel, establishing priorities that give preference to joint work. Futhermore, it means providing technical support that can enhance joint work, for example, providing computer technology that would allow multiple authors to access the same file in order to create a truly common text that each could add to and alter.

In this same spirit, collective project work in terms of faculty and students needs to be encouraged. This is to be advocated both from the point of view of the limits of individual work (you can't do it all alone) and the importance of a form of graduate study that involves students and faculty in some genuine concrete inquiry that addresses an aspect of curriculum study. What we are implying is that *such efforts must be built into the structure of graduate study itself.* Moreover, course requirements should be set out to both allow and encourage students to fulfill program obligations through such collective project work. It is no small consequence that such a requirement would make the knowledge and skills necessary for collective work an explicit part of a program of graduate curriculum study.

Program Content

With regard to program content we agree with those who argue that curriculum study cannot be construed as an empty vessel. It has to be about something! But at the same time we believe that to organize curriculum study through identification with traditional subject-matter categories is antithetical to the type of curriculum program we are advocating. Our notions of basic course work are defined by the five content themes specified earlier (language, subordinate and popular cultures, theorizing the social formation, history, and pedagogy). What we suggest is the identification of more fluid "subject matter work groups." These are groups of faculty and graduate students whose interests at a given moment of time are collected around work on a particular subject. For example, at the Ontario Institute for Studies in Education in Toronto there are emerging work groups on work education, health education, and children's literature. Such groups meet both to read together and to support and criticize each other's work. The activity of these groups would have to be supported as a legitimate and central aspect of a program of study. Because a grade would not be assigned to participation in these groups they risk becoming extracurricular. This is a familiar problem. Their viability becomes a matter of available time, perceived legitimacy, and the importance of a group for providing identity to its members. There are specific ways to create these conditions, but this issue demands a level of specificity not appropriate for this essay.

Educators' Clientele

Finally, as we argued earlier, educators must abandon considering students as clientele. What this means is that the individual student no longer becomes dependent on faculty members for their expertise (the key word here is *dependent*, not expertise). Concretely, what might this mean?

One possibility is created by redefining the unit of admission into a graduate program so it becomes a *social* unit. That is, two or more people would become the admissible unit. Such a unit if it wishes to apply for admission must name a situation or project it wants to understand more about or work on (this does not imply that students once in a program have to be held to these ideas as they begin to go beyond the initial horizons for making sense of their personal and professional lives). This is a radical policy which redefines the purpose of Western liberal university education as no longer focused on individual development alone. Rather, it sets the condition for graduate study as collective inquiry. It would encourage groups of people from the same school or district, or who share a similar sense of frustration or dream, to engage with each other and to bring that engagement into play with faculty within a curriculum department. The personal dependency on faculty for expertise is altered as a common project becomes the focus of study.

Additionally, as we have previously stressed, educators must begin to see their work as part of an alliance with groups of people outside their particular focus. This is important for a program with a collective admission policy. A stress on joint faculty/student project work also needs, if it is to be a genuine form of cultural politics, a sense of how it articulates with efforts in other aspects of the public sphere. For instance, in Ontario collective faculty/student work is currently developing curriculum together with human rights groups committed to fighting racism in Canada. Such an alliance might also take the form of work with political groups whose agenda is not only electoral representation but the articulation of a social agenda within the public sphere. This would suggest alliances with ecology, feminist, or civil rights groups. As we argued earlier in this essay, curriculum study needs to make concrete a discourse that translates social theory into forms of praxis that contribute to the notions of civic courage and active citizenry. Such alliances not only provide the basis for collective work; they also link theory and practice to forms of social struggle.

What we are advocating is addressing curriculum study and teaching as something central to the practice of a cultural politics that has its basis in cooperative alliances among groups struggling to define a way of life. Indeed, we want to acknowledge this practice as *itself educative*. This is an educational forum that refuses customary separations of theory and practice, objective and subjective, knowing and doing. It is a way of working as an educator that rejects the fundamental dichotomy of bourgeois thought: the division between manual or practical labor and mental and theoretical labor. It is a form of professionalism that refuses what Wendy Simon, an elementary school teacher, has termed "peasant teacher status" by resisting the hierarchical trends in school board organization. In our view, the simultaneous transformation of circumstances and selves is the guiding theme of curriculum work and teaching as cultural politics. This assumes that we learn by discovery challenge, critique, and attempts to change, and that all these practices lead to reconceptualizing ourselves as having capacities, skills, forms of knowledge, and abilities which we have not previously realized. It is such activity that graduate study in curriculum can help stimulate and support.

11

The Need for Cultural Studies

By HENRY A. GIROUX, DAVID SHUMWAY,
PAUL SMITH, and JAMES SOSNOSKI

In North American Universities the study of culture[1] is so fragmented through specialization that concerted cultural critique is almost impossible. The historical development of insulated disciplines housed in segregated departments has produced a legitimating ideology that in effect suppresses critical thought. Rationalized as the protection of the integrity of specific disciplines, the departmentalization of inquiry has contributed to the reproduction of the dominant culture by isolating its critics from each other.[2] Under the banner of the academic freedom of experts to direct their own activity, specialists now bind themselves in discursive formations that generally circumscribe the nature of their inquiries.

The practitioners of disciplines investigating cultural phenomena— e.g., anthropology, sociology, history, literary studies—are limited in their ability to communicate with each other about their common concerns. Traditional literary study, for instance, has developed within formalistic parameters that set an almost impassable boundary between the study of a society and the study of a novel; similarly, sociologists make use of literature in ways that alienate traditional literary critics. And so on. The conventional wisdom for academics is to let members of other

143

departments do whatever they say is their work in whatever way they choose—as long as this right is granted to them. As a consequence of these developments, the study of culture is conducted in fragments, and, in so far as experts must define themselves over and against a public comprised of amateurs, specialization removes intellectuals from other public spheres.[3] Critique is thus disabled and the mechanisms of both social and cultural reproduction enabled.

The role of the specialist is not altogether compatible with the role of the intellectual. As Paul Piccone remarks,

> Unless one fudges the definition of intellectuals in terms of purely formal and statistical educational criteria, it is fairly clear that what modern society produces is an army of alienated, privatized, and uncultured experts who are knowledgeable only within very narrowly defined areas. This technical intelligentsia, rather than intellectuals in the traditional sense of thinkers concerned with the totality, is growing by leaps and bounds to run the increasingly complex bureaucratic and industrial apparatus. Its rationality, however, is only *instrumental* in character, and thus suitable mainly to perform partial tasks rather than tackling *substantial* questions of social organization and political direction.[4]

Our argument is that there is a need for cultural studies to engage critically exactly those social and political issues to which Piccone alludes, and to promote an understanding of both the enabling and constraining dimensions of culture. This suggests both the development of a critique and the production of cultural forms consonant with emancipatory interests. One important task for such a transformative critique is to identify the fissures in the ideologies of the dominant culture. In the absence of intellectuals who can critically analyze a society's contradictions, the dominant culture continues to reproduce its worst effects all the more efficaciously. And, without a sphere for cultural critique, the resisting intellectual has no voice in public affairs.

This chapter begins by showing how definitions of disciplines are historically arbitrary. It then goes on to argue that attempts to cut across the arbitrary boundaries set by disciplines and to develop interdisciplinary programs—American or Canadian studies, womens studies, black studies, etc.—have failed. Next the chapter argues that the traditional humanist rationale for the disciplinary study of culture is inappropriate in that it masks the role that members of a culture can play as agents in its formation. This leads us to argue for the necessity of a counter-disciplinary praxis. At this point, we introduce the notion of the transformative intellectual as an educational formation necessary to restore to academics their roles as intellectuals. The sections that follow sketch out some of the implications of our argument: a return of intellectuals from ivory-towered departments to the public sphere; and a movement away from individualist, esoteric research towards collective inquiries into social ills. The chapter concludes by outlining conditions for the development of cultural studies.

The Arbitrariness of Disciplines and the Failure of Interdisciplines

Most of us think of academic disciplines as the reflection of more or less natural categories of things which we call subjects. English is different from history because literature and history are two distinct sorts of thing. But if we consider the matter further we soon recognize that the identification of a discipline with natural objects doesn't explain very much. In the first place, a particular group of objects is the subject of any number of disciplines. The same text, *Uncle Tom's Cabin* for example, can be studied by both literary scholars and historians. Second, the particular objects which a discipline studies do not remain the same throughout its history. Literature has had its current reference—fiction, poetry, and drama—only since the early nineteenth century. Furthermore, the way in which categories are defined regularly changes. English has been recognized as a legitimate area of study only since the late nineteenth century, and new subdisciplines in physics or chemistry have been emerging at an ever increasing pace.

What is studied under the aegis of an academic discipline at any given time is not a natural subject matter, but a field which is itself constituted by the practice of the discipline. Such a field is not arbitrary in the sense that it develops randomly or on whim; rather, a field can be called arbitrary because it is contingent on historical circumstance. Hence it reflects cultural, social, and institutional demands. This is true of all academic fields, but especially so in fields outside the natural sciences. To understand why this is the case, it is necessary to look more closely at the formation of academic disciplines.

Michel Foucault has shown that discipline[5] as a particular strategy of social control and organization began at the end of the classical age and came into dominance in the modern period. Though Foucault is not directly concerned with academic disciplines, much of his analysis applies to these enterprises. What is characteristic of disciplinary technologies is their capacity simultaneously to normalize and hierarchize, to homogenize and differentiate. This paradox is explained by the control which discipline asserts over difference. Because norms are carefully established and maintained, deviation can be measured on a scale. The goal of the professional in a discipline is to move up this scale by differing only in the appropriate ways.

It does not require Foucauldian analysis to understand that a discipline limits discourse. To be part of a discipline means to ask certain questions, to use a particular set of terms, and to study a relatively narrow set of things. But Foucault's work does help us to see how these limitations, this discipline, are enforced by institutions through various rewards and punishments most of which pertain to hierarchical ranking. The ultimate punishment is exclusion. If one ceases to speak within the discourse of the discipline, one will no longer be considered part of it. This does not usually mean that heretics will be prohibited from teaching or even from publishing; rather, they are simply marginalized. The situation is similarly severe for the new Ph.D. for whom the price of admission into the academy is the same conformity with dominant academic discourses.

Even though the development of "normal science" in Kuhn's sense distinguishes the natural sciences from other disciplines, "The human sciences constantly try to copy the natural sciences' exclusion from their theories of any references to the [social and historical] background."[6] In the social sciences and humanities there has been an increasing normalization consistent with the professionalization of the various disciplines, but it is clear that no discipline has succeeded in completely excluding "background" from its theories. Formalizing techniques can make normal science possible in the social sciences and the humanities only by excluding the social skills, institutions, and power arrangements that make the isolation of attributes possible. This practice ignores the social practice and cultural interaction of social scientists and humanists.

Because social practice is not one of the objects constituted by the natural sciences, "it is always possible and generally desirable that an unchallenged normal science which defines and resolves problems concerning the structure of the physical universe establish itself, [but] in the social sciences such an unchallenged normal science would only indicate that an orthodoxy had established itself, not through scientific achievement, but by ignoring the background and eliminating all competitors."[7] Although humanistic disciplines allow a wider variety of activities than do the disciplines of the natural sciences, these activities themselves are hierarchically valued. In English, for instance, normal study under the New Critical "paradigm" was the acontextual interpretation of individual texts of the literary canon. Other kinds of scholarship were permitted and sometimes rewarded, but were never allowed to overshadow normal New Critical practice. Historical scholarship, in this instance, had its place, but it was regarded as subsidiary to New Criticism.[8]

Although work in the humanities does not pose as normal science, its disciplinary structure aims at producing specialists. The disciplinary structure of study in literature, history, sociology, and other divisions that often focus on culture, tends to prohibit these specialists from relating their knowledge to public spheres. Disciplinary study requires constant attention to those few questions that constitute its current specialized concern. These questions are very often far removed from the genuine controversies in a given culture.

Interdisciplinary movements such as American studies and women's studies have often developed out of the sense that the most important issues were being lost in the cracks between the rigid boundaries of the disciplines. As a consequence, American studies began with the agenda of retrieving such issues. It should be remembered that the nationalism which spawned American studies and Canadian studies was openly political, and that American studies books were critical of the ideological interests embedded in canonical documents of American culture. Nevertheless, American studies should be regarded as a cautionary example to those who would try to establish cultural studies as an interdisciplinary enterprise within the academy. The problem is that no solid alternatives to disciplinary structure have evolved within the academy and, as a result, movements such as American studies paradoxically must strive to become disciplines. Thus, while these movements often begin with a critical perspective, they retreat from radical critique as they become more successful. To the extent that such movements resist disciplines, their seriousness is questioned. Practitioners are regarded as dilettantes rather than real scholars, and their enterprises are written off as mere fads. In American studies, the idea of interdisciplinarity became a means for practitioners to challenge a particular hierarchy, but it did not offer an alternative to hierarchical order. And as American studies became more entrenched, interdisciplinarity receded in importance in the rhetoric of the movement.[9]

It would be a mistake to regard the failure of interdisciplinary movements to remain critical enterprises as the result of the suppression of political ideas. Because an intellectual's political views are posited as irrelevant to the work of disciplines themselves, speaking and thinking about political and social questions is construed as merely eccentric to the disciplinary study of culture. This failure to engage historical contexts and social particularities can be seen most clearly in the type of pedagogy that traditional disciplines institute.

Difficulties with the Traditional Rationale of the Study of Culture

Broadly speaking, the rationale of traditional humanistic education is that it offers students assured access to a storehouse of cultural materials which is constituted as a canon. Such a canon is relatively flexible in its definition insofar as it can incorporate and take cognizance of both marginal and recondite materials; as a thesaurus of sorts it cannot pass up anything of value. The values that are operational here do fluctuate according to specific ideological needs—witness the now quite secure incorporation of a women's studies canon or even a literary theory canon into some university curricula. But, at the same time, there is an always implicit "gold standard" by which these provisional incrementations and fluctuations are regulated. As the head of NEH, William Bennett conducted an *ad hoc* survey to discover what books every high school student "might reasonably be expected to have studied" before graduation. The list of such books, thirty in all, ranged from Plato's *Republic,* through some Virgil, Chaucer, Dickens, and Tolstoy, to *Catcher in the Rye.*[10] These books and authors represent the regulatory standard of a certain cultural currency by which the humanities and their productions are measured. A familiarity with the stable central core of the canon is said to enable students to absorb the values enshrined there, to the point that they could apply those values to its more marginal or provisional components. Most importantly, students would have access to a wealth which is "humanizing" in its effect; but that effect is a complicity with the economy which has produced that wealth for humanity.

Leaving aside the not unimportant questions of how this project for the humanities is effected ideologically and of how it relates in practice to students' lived lives (their individual socioeconomic histories), it is important to ask whether or not it would be desirable or even necessary for cultural studies to appropriate or exploit in any way the same kind of educational rationale. After all, and as the new right is quick to point out, that rationale has always taken seriously the ideological effect and function *for* students of what is taught. By learning the dominant culture, or imbibing its representative values, students are theoretically *enabled* in that they are given the wherewithal for particular manners of action and behavior within that culture. The argument can easily be made (as it is often made in women's studies, for example) that the teaching of an alternative substance, of a new canon, can effectively produce new ideological positions and thence political actions.

However, it must be remembered that the humanist rationale for the canon is based upon an hierarchical economy where cultural objects are ranked. Certain of those objects (Shakespeare's writing, for example) are assumed to be "the best" of western culture; they thus represent the *essence* of the culture. It is exactly this symbolic view of culture against which cultural studies should fight. The installation of a new canon, constructed on assumptions about what is most important and valuable for students to know or be familiar with, merely replicates the traditional hierarchical view of culture, albeit in a novel and perhaps minimally subversive form. Cultural studies, on the other hand, should be built upon a different economy, one which sees that cultural objects are, in fact, disposed *relationally*.

This is to say that cultural studies should look with suspicion upon any hierarchizing project through which culture is delimited to certain of its parts, whether such parts represent the culture's essential "best" or even if they represent what has been predetermined as politically or ethically important and valuable. Cultural studies should, in short, abandon the goal of giving students access to that which represents a culture. Instead, cultural studies has the possibility of investigating culture as a set of activities which is lived and developed within asymmetrical relations of power, or as irreducibly a process which cannot be immobilized in the image of a storehouse.

By investigating and teaching the claim that culture is in a real sense *unfinished*, cultural studies can secure its own political effectiveness. Students—particularly those marginalised by the values of the dominant culture—can be disabused of the notion that the culture they actually inhabit is somehow not theirs or available to them only through proper initiation into the values enshrined in representative texts. Cultural studies, taking new (i.e. necessarily noncanonical) objects and implicating them in a relational rather than hierarchical view, encourages a questioning of the premises of dominant educational and political practices. Most importantly, cultural studies can refuse to agree that "literature [and any other cultural object] . . . is distinct from politics"[11] and can thus reconsider the ideological and political appurtenance of a text or any set of texts.

Clearly, what is at stake here is the possibility that cultural studies could promote in students, not a striving after a predetermined or a once-and-for-all complacent accession to a given set of cultural values, but rather a continual analysis of their own conditions of existence. Such a praxis, founded in an overthrowing of the preassumptions of traditional disciplinary approaches to culture, is a prerequisite for self-conscious and effective resistance to dominant structures.

The Need for a Counter-Disciplinary Praxis

In the first section of the essay we pointed out that disciplines concerned with the analysis of culture, including those called humanistic, have attempted to model themselves on the pattern of normal science. Their aim is to describe culture, to accumulate knowledge about a culture. In the preceding section we argued that such an aim leaves the impression on students that a culture has a permanent character and that specific structures can be described in an essentialist manner. Such procedures are especially pernicious in those disciplines associated with the humanities since they suggest that the culture has already been formed rather than that it is in the process of transformation.

Cultural studies should resist such tendencies. This requires a movement away from our de-contextualized *conception of disciplinary practices* toward a *"conception of human Praxis,* emphasising that human beings are neither to be treated as passive objects,nor as wholly free subjects," since the study of human life is properly "the study of definite social practices, geared to human needs."[12]

Given the disciplinary mechanisms at work in the structure of Western universities, such a praxis is necessarily counter-disciplinary in the sense that it resists the notion that the study of culture is the accumulation of knowledge about it. In our view, the proper study of culture is "intrinsically involved with *that which has to be done*"[13] in societies rife with oppression. The precondition of such action is critical resistance to prevailing practices. However, resistance will not be effective if it is random and isolated; intellectuals must play the crucial role of mobilizing such resistance into a praxis that has political impact.

Transformative Intellectuals

Central to the emancipatory project that informs our notion of cultural studies is a reformulation of the role of the intellectual both within and outside the university. We concur with Gramsci that it is important to view intellectuals in political terms.[14] The intellectual is more than a person of letters, or a producer and transmitter of ideas. Intellectuals are also mediators, legitimators, and producers of ideas and social practices; they perform a function eminently political in nature. Gramsci distinguishes between conservative and radical organic intellectuals. Conservative organic intellectuals provide the dominant classes with forms of moral and intellectual leadership. As agents of the status quo, such intellectuals identify with the dominant relations of power and become, consciously or unconsciously, the propagators of its ideologies and values. They provide the ruling classes with rationales for economic, political, and ethical formations.

According to Gramsci, conservative organic intellectuals can be found in all strata of advanced industrial society—in industrial organizations, in universities, in the culture industry, in various forms of management, and so on. He claims that radical organic intellectuals also attempt to provide the moral and intellectual leadership for the working class. More specifically, radical organic intellectuals provide the pedagogical and political skills that are necessary to raise political awareness in the working class, and to help it develop leadership and engage in collective struggle.

Gramsci's analysis is helpful in formulating one of the central goals of cultural studies: the creation of what we want to call *transformative intellectuals.* This differs from Gramsci's notion of radical organic intellectuals; we believe that such intellectuals can emerge from and work with any number of groups which resist the suffocating knowledge and practices that constitute their social formation. Transformative intellectuals can provide the moral, political and pedagogical leadership for those groups which take as their starting point the transformative critique of the conditions of oppression. The epithet "organic" in our case cannot be reserved for those intellectuals who take the working class as the only revolutionary agent.

The notion of the transformative intellectual is important in the most immediate sense because it makes visible the paradoxical position in which radical intellectuals in higher education find themselves in the 1980s. On the one hand, such intellectuals earn a living within institutions that play a fundamental role in producing the dominant culture. On the other hand, radical intellectuals define their political terrain by offering to students forms of oppositional discourse and critical social practices at odds with the hegemonic role of the university and the society which it supports. In many cases, this paradox works in favor of the university:

> More often then not, [the] goal has been to elaborate disciplines rather than develop projects, to meld the bloodless tenets of semiology, systems theory, pragmatism and positivism with the archaicisms of historical materialism. The unflagging appetite of these leftist intellectuals to gain credibility within their respective disciplines, to be *au courant* and appreciated as its "left wing" and its most "forward looking tendency," is appalling evidence that what we lack is . . . a revolutionary intellectual movement.[15]

Bookchin's remarks remind us that critical scholarship is generally removed from any relation to concrete political movements; radical social theory becomes a mere commodity for academic journals and conferences; and radical intellectuals get safely ensconced within a tenure system that offers them as proof of the university's commitment to liberal pluralism.

Rather than surrender to this form of academic and political incorporation, cultural studies needs to define the role of the intellectual as a counter-hegemonic practice that can both avoid and challenge it. In general terms, we can point to the following pedagogical and strategic activities. First, cultural studies needs to develop a curriculum and a pedagogy that stress the mediating and political role of intellectuals. This means providing students with the critical tools they will need ot both understand and dismantle the chronic rationalization of harmful social practices, while simultaneously appropriating the knowledge and skills they need to rethink the project of human emancipation. Second, transformative intellectuals must actively engage in projects which encourage them to address their own critical role in the production and legitimation of social relations. Such projects are necessary not only to fight against conservative intellectuals and the multiple contexts in which legitimation processes occur, but also to broaden the theoretical and political movements outside the university. Transformative intellectuals must develop and work with movements outside of the limiting contours of the disciplines, symposia, and reward systems that have become the sole referents for intellectual activity. More importantly, such a project broadens the notion of education and takes seriously Gramsci's notion of all society as a vast school.[16] In addition, it encourages transformative intellectuals to play an active role in the many public spheres that are developing around various ideological conflicts.

Cultural studies thus posits the need for transformative intellectuals who can establish new forms of political relations within and outside the university. In this theoretical context, cultural studies echoes Gramsci's call for radical intellectuals to forge alliances around new historical blocs. Intellectuals can play an important role in empowering individuals and groups within oppositional public domains.

Public Spheres, Popular Culture, and Cultural Studies

The importance for cultural studies of participating in oppositional public spheres is an underlying premise of this essay. A counter-disciplinary praxis undertaken by transformative intellectuals would not be effective if it had as its only audience people in universities. Rather, it should take place more extensively in *public*. Although many universities are public institutions, we rarely consider them part of the public sphere.

If cultural studies is to be understood as an oppositional public sphere, it should not be conceived as a "department" or as part of the boundary separating professional activities from those of amateurs. Instead of thinking of cultural studies in terms which more properly characterize disciplines, we should reconceive traditional rationales in an effort to create counter practices. The classroom, to take one instance, is viewed traditionally as a place where information is transmitted to students. Experts in a discipline impart to apprentices the received knowledge about a particular subject matter; students are not agents in this process, but passive and overtly uncritical receptacles. However, as we have argued, if we grant students an active role in the process of cultural formation, they can become agents in the production of social practices. To accomplish this we should become involved in fostering forms of resistance; a critical pedagogy is required which will promote the identification and analysis of the underlying ideological interests at stake in the text and its readings. We are then engaged together as transformative intellectuals in a social practice that allows both parties to construe themselves as agents in the process of their own cultural formation. An obvious concretization of this praxis might be a woman resisting the view of women proffered in a canonical novel. This instance is a reflection of resistance to large-scale social practices that oppress women. Such resistance needs to be produced.

Rather than abandon scholarship, transformative intellectuals need to repoliticize it. Scholarly *publi*cations, the disciplinary criterion used to establish the merit of professional opinions against those of a public made up of amateurs, do not reach the public. Though it is not appropriate to argue the point here, we contend that the disciplines presently concerned with the study of culture are unduly bound to the premise that their task is to do disciplinary research, that is, to accumulate and store in a retrievable way descriptions of cultural phenomen. But, if we reconceive our activity as the production of (rather than the description of) social practices, then what we do in our classrooms is easily extended into public spheres. We cannot capitulate to the disciplinary notion that research has as its only audience other experts in the field. Transformative intellectuals must legitimate the notion of writing reviews and books for the general public, and they must create a language of critique balanced by a language of possibility that will enable social change.[17]

This means that we need to become involved in the political reading of popular culture. As Stanley Aronowitz remarks in *False Promises,* "It remains for us to investigate in what way mass culture becomes constitutive of social reality."[18] Training in disciplinary practices leads us away from the study of the relation between culture and society and toward the accumulation of descriptions of cultural material cut off from its connection to everyday life. As Aronowitz points out:

> To fully understand the ideological impact and manipulative functions of current media presentations, it is necessary to appreciate the multi-layered character of contemporary mass culture. In addition to the *overt* ideological content of films and television—transmitting new role models, values life styles to be more or less consciously emulated by a

mass audience—there is also a series of *covert* messages contained within them which appeal to the audience largely on the unconscious level. . . . Typically, [these] define the character of the spectator's experience of the spectacle in terms of the . . . gratification of his or her unconscious desires . . . . By creating a system of pseudo-gratifications, mass culture functions as a sort of social regulator, attempting to absorb tensions arising out of everyday life and to deflect frustrations which might otherwise actualize themselves in opposition to the system into channels which serve the system.[19]

It is because the effects of culture are so often unconsciously absorbed that the need for a cultural studies emphasising critique arises. As we pointed out earlier in this essay, the disciplines that claim selected aspects of culture as their subject restrict that subject arbitrarily—for instance, by constituting the field of literary study as a canon. Simultaneously, they have placed a wedge between professionals and the public in the service of the ruling classes as in the case of literary study, where so-called low culture is excluded from the research domain. Nor should we now continue to be fooled by the admission of films, popular novels, soap operas, and the like into the curricula of literature departments. As long as such cultural artifacts are examined as merely the materials that make up a fixed culture, their disciplinary description will do no more than create storehouses of knowledge having almost nothing to do with lived culture, much less its transformation. Only a counter-disciplinary praxis developed by intellectuals who resist disciplinary formation is likely to produce emancipatory social practices.

The problem with suggesting that cultural studies be counter disciplinary is that it cannot be housed in universities as they are presently structured. Hence the need for counter-institutions. There would be various sorts of collectives, variously membered—study groups, counter-disciplinary research groups, even societies and institutes.

It is unlikely that the disciplinary structures and mechanisms of universities will disappear in the near future. However, it would be a mistake to locate cultural studies within them. Our alternative would be to treat disciplines as peripheral to our main concerns while nonetheless obtaining some important concessions from their administrators. This is a tactical matter which has to be negotiated situation by situation. However, we can go even further and develop models of collaborative inquiry that extend beyong the university in order to combat hegemonic public spheres and to form alliances with other oppositional public spheres. In the context of cultural studies it will not be appropriate simply to generate idiosyncratic interpretations of cultural artifacts. The most important aim of a counter-disciplinary praxis is radical social change.

We should not be resigned to the roles that universities assign us. The transformative intellectual can develop a collective, counter-disciplinary praxis within the university that has a political impact outside it. The important tactical question at this moment in the history of North American universities is how to get cultural studies established as a form of cultural critique. Our suggestion has been the formation of institutes for cultural studies that can constitute an oppositional public sphere.

Conclusion

If cultural studies is to be informed by a political project that gives a central place to critique and social transformation, it will have to begin with a dual recognition. First, it is imperative to recognize that the university has a particular set of relations with the dominant society. These relations define the university as neither a locus of domination nor a locus of freedom. Instead, the university, with relative autonomy, functions largely to produce and legitimate the knowledge, skills and social relations that characterize the dominant power relations in society. Universities, like other public institutions, contain points of resistance and struggle, and it is within these spaces that the ideological and material conditions exist to produce oppositional discourses and practices. Such a recognition not only politicizes the university and its relation to the dominant society, it interrogates the political nature of cultural studies as both a sphere of critique and as a medium of social transformation. This leads to the second point.

If it is to be a radical social project, cultural studies must develop a *self-regulating discourse*; by this we mean a discourse that contains a language of critique and a concomitant language of possibility. In the first instance, it must lay bare the historically specific interests that structure the academic disciplines, the relations among them, and the manner in which the form and content of the disciplines reproduce and legitimate the dominant culture. This is a central task for cultural studies, for, if it is to promote an oppositional discourse and method of inquiry, it will have to embody interests that affirm rather than deny the political and normative importance of history, ethics and social interaction.

The discourse of cultural studies must resist the interests contained in the established academic disciplines and departments. It must interrogate the knowledge-claims and the modes of intelligibility central to the defense of the academic status quo in various departments and disciplines. Equally importantly, cultural studies must indict the interests embedded in the questions *not* asked within academic disciplines. It must develop methods of inquiry into how the present absences and structured silences that govern teaching, scholarship, and administration within academic departments deny the link between knowledge and power, reduce culture to an unquestioned object of mastery, and refuse to acknowledge the particular way of life that dominant academic discourse helps to produce and legitimate.

In order to retain its theoretical and political integrity, cultural studies must develop forms of critical knowledge as well as a critique of knowledge itself. Such a task demands resistance to the reification and fragmentation that characterizes the disciplines. Because of their constitution, disciplinary structures obstruct the overthrowing of technical and social divisions of labor of which they are part and which they help to produce. Cultural studies needs to develop a theory of the way in which different social formations are both produced and reproduced within the asymmetrical relations of power characterizing the dominant society. Similarly, it needs to develop a language of possibility, one in which knowledge would be viewed as part of a collective learning process connected to the dynamics of struggle both within and outside the university. Cultural studies, in this sense, must develop an oppositional discourse and a counter-disciplinary praxis to deal with struggles over different orders of representation, conflicting forms of cultural experience, and diverse visions of the future. Clearly, the interests that inform such a problematic cannot be developed within traditional departments. Currently, the structure of universities is inextricably tied to interests which suppress the critical concerns of intellectuals willing to fight for oppositional public spheres. Such interests can be dismantled in favor of more radical practices only through the collective efforts of transformative intellectuals.

12

Teacher Education and the Politics of Democratic Reform

By HENRY A. GIROUX and PETER McLAREN

First generation critical theorists such as Max Horkheimer, Theodor Adorno, and Walter Benjamin argue that in the Western democracies the capacity for critical reason is rapidly being eclipsed. Pointing to the encroachment of the State, the culture industry, and the concentration of wealth into fewer and fewer hands, these thinkers fear that the ideological and material conditions that made public interaction and critical thinking possible are being undermined through the growing standardization, fragmentation, and commercialization of everyday life. They further claim that as everyday life becomes more "rationalized" and cluttered with images of greed and a self-serving individualism, the discourse of democracy will recede from public life, eventually to be replaced by the language and logic of techno-culture.[1]

Jürgen Habermas and Herbert Marcuse take this critique further—illuminating how, in the twentieth century, reason has nearly been eliminated and reflective inquiry dangerously domesticated by the destruction of those classical public spheres that prevailed in eighteenth and nineteenth century Europe. Earlier, public spheres—political clubs, journals, coffee houses, neighborhood groups, and publishing houses—provided networks through which private individuals could assemble for debate, dialogue, and an exchange of opinion. Public spheres such as these were often transformed into a cohesive political force. For American pragmatists such as John Dewey, the public sphere provided the nexus for a number of important pedagogical sites where democracy as a social movement was embedded in an ongoing effort of numerous subordinate groups to meet and produce a social discourse and to ponder the implications of such a discourse for political action.[2] Extending Dewey's belief that intelligent social action holds the best promise for a more humane society, the social reconstructionists in the 1930s and 1940s argued for a politics of social individuality in which the imperatives of democracy could be sought not only in the schools but in all pedagogical sites that recognized the primacy of the political in everyday life. Beneath the logic of this position was an emphasis on the relationship between knowledge and power, doing and acting, and commitment and collective struggle. In effect, the public sphere not only served to produce the language of freedom, it also kept alive the hope that subordinate groups could one day produce their own intellectuals; in Gramsci's terms, this meant the creation of "organic intellectuals" who could bridge the gap between academic institutions and the specific issues and workings of everyday life. That is, such intellectuals could provide the moral and political skills necessary to fund institutions of popular education and alternative cultures and beliefs.[3]

Part of our intention in this chapter is to argue that teacher education institutions need to be reconceived as public spheres. Such institutions as they presently exist are damagingly bereft of both social conscience and social consciousness. As a result, programs need to be developed in which prospective teachers can be educated as transformative intellectuals who are able to affirm and practice the discourse of freedom and democracy.[4] Within this perspective, pedagogy and culture can be seen as intersecting fields of struggle. The contradictory character of pedagogical discourse as it currently defines the nature of teacher work, everyday classroom life, and the purpose of schooling can be subjected to more radical interrogation. More specifically, the problem we want to address centers around the issue of how radical educators can create a language that enables teachers to take seriously the role that schooling plays in joining knowledge and power. In short, we want to explore how a radicalized teaching force can provide for both empowering teachers and teaching for empowerment.

One of the great failures of North American education has been its inability to provide student teachers with the means and moral imperatives for fashioning a more critical discourse and set of understandings around the fundamental goals and purposes of schooling. Teacher education has rarely occupied a critical space, public or political, within contemporary culture, where the meaning of the social could be recovered and restated so that teachers' and students' cultural histories, personal narratives, and collective will could be permitted to coalesce around the development of a democratic counterpublic sphere.

Despite the early efforts of John Dewey and others to reform schooling to the logic of a radical democracy and the recent critical attempts by left educational theorists to link the ideology of schooling to the imperatives of the capitalist state, the political space which teacher education occupies today generally continues to deemphasize the struggle for teacher empowerment.[5] Furthermore, it generally serves to reproduce the technocratic and corporate ideologies that characterize dominant societies. In fact, it is reasonable to argue that teacher education programs are designed to create intellectuals who operate in the interests of the state, whose social function is primarily to sustain and legitimate the status quo.

Why do educators fail to seize whatever theoretical possibilities are available to them in order to rethink democratic alternatives and foster new emancipatory ideals? We believe that one major reason lies with the failure of left thinkers and other educators to move beyond what we refer to as the language of critique. That is, radical educators remain mired in a critical discourse that links schools primarily to the social relations of domination. From this, it follows that schools serve mainly as agencies of social reproduction which manufacture docile and obedient workers for the state; knowledge acquired in the classroom is generally considered to be part of the fabric of "false consciousness"; and teachers appear overwhelmingly trapped in a no-win situation. The agony of this position is that it has prevented left educators from developing a programmatic language in which they can theorize *for* schools. Instead, they have theorized primarily *about* schools and, in so doing have seldom concerned themselves with the construction of new, public spheres within school sites. Absent from their discourse is a language of possibility, one which, as Laclau and Mouffe point out, suggests the "constitution of a radical imaginary."[6] In our case, a radical imaginary represents a discourse that offers new possibilities for democratic social relations; it traces out linkages between the political and the pedagogical in order to foster the development of counterpublic spheres that seriously engage *with and in* articulations and practices of radical democracy. Our purpose here is not to rehearse the failures of left politics and educational reform, but to address the development of a new conceptualization of education and through it a more critical approach to teacher education.

Teacher Education and the Retreat from the Political

Teacher education constitutes a set of institutional practices that seldom results in the radicalization of teachers. Rarely do teacher education programs encourage student teachers to take seriously the role of the intellectual who works in the interest of an emancipatory vision. If and when teachers do decide to engage in forms of radical politics, it is invariably years after they leave their teacher education institutions. Our own experiences in teacher education—First as students and then as instructors—has confirmed for us what is generally agreed to be commonplace in most schools and colleges of education throughout North America: these institutions define themselves as service institutions. They are propelled by the logic of instructional technology and mandated by the state to provide requisite technical and managerial expertise. They undertake whatever pedagogical functions are deemed necessary by the various school communities in which students undertake their practicum or field placement experiences.[7]

This is not to imply that school critics have not put forth proposals designed to radicalize teacher education programs. Quite the contrary. The problem has been that when such proposals do appear, they are generally either confined to a celebration of more refined and reflective modes of inquiry and methods of instruction or they remain confined to the prison house of critique. One pressing concern emerging from this dilemma is the inability of liberals and radicals to constitute a new theory and social space for redefining the nature of teacher work and the social function of teaching. In other words, generally absent from the political project that informs these discourses is an attempt to link schooling to the wider struggle for radical democracy.

Educators on the more radical left generally do not fall into the trap of attempting to reform teacher education in order to make teachers more efficient puzzle solvers or more technically competent in their mastery of subject matter. These educators generally invoke the language of critique, self-reflexivity, and the linking of theory to practice. But despite their attempt to make knowledge problematic and to link theory to practice, this type of pedagogical endeavor lacks the capacity to conceptualize teacher education as part of a wider political project or social struggle in general. It fails to define teacher preparation programs as part of an extended counterpublic sphere that might work in some coordinated fashion to educate intellectuals who are willing to play a central role in the broad struggle for democracy and social justice. In effect, the language of critique that informs this type of discourse is overly pessimistic and tends to remain trapped within the logic of social reproduction. Their language fails to grasp and acknowledge the concept of counterhegemony as a moment of collective struggle because the programmatic suggestions that emerge from their discourse are primarily locked into the limitations of prevailing theories of resistance. The distinction between these two categories are worth elaborating.

Redefining Teacher Education

The term "counterhegemony," as distinct from the term "resistance," is one which we feel better specifies the political project we have defined as the creation of alternative public spheres.[8] As it is often used in the educational literature, resistance refers to a type of autonomous "gap" between the ineluctable widespread forces of domination and the condition of being dominated. Moreover, resistance has been defined as a personal "space," in which the logic and force of domination is contested by the power of subjective agency to subvert the process of socialization. Seen this way, resistance functions as a type of negation or affirmation placed before ruling discourses and practices. Of course, resistance often lacks an overt political project and frequently reflects social practices that are informal, disorganized, apolitical, and atheoretical in nature. In some instances it can reduce itself to an unreflective and defeatist refusal to acquiesce to different forms of domination; on some occasions it can be seen as a cynical, arrogant, or even naive rejection of oppressive forms of moral and political regulation.

Counterhegemony, on the other hand, implies a more political, theoretical, and critical understanding of both the nature of domination and the type of active opposition it should engender. More importantly, the concept not only affirms the logic of critique but also speaks to the creation of new social relations and public spaces that embody alternative forms of experience and struggle. As a reflective domain of political action, counterhegemony shifts the characteristic nature of struggle from the terrain of critique to the collectively constituted terrain of the counter-public sphere.

We have dwelled on this distinction because we believe that it points to ways in which teacher education programs have been and continue to be removed from a vision and set of practices that take seriously the struggle for democracy and social justice. Part of this problem stems from the lack of an adequate social theory that might provide the basis for rethinking the political nature of teacher work and the role of teacher education programs.

Many of the problems associated with teacher preparation today signal the curriculum's lack of emphasis on the issue of power and its hierarchical distribution and the study of critical social theory. Heavily influenced by mainstream behavioral and cognitive psychology, educational theory has been constructed around a discourse and set of practices that emphasize immediate, measurable, methodological aspects of learning. Absent are questions concerning the nature of power, ideology, and culture and how these constitute specific notions of the social and produce particular forms of student experience.[9] While a renewed interest in social theory has played a significant role in reconstituting radical educational theory, it has not made serious inroads into teacher education programs. This lack of attention to critical social theory has deprived student teachers of a theoretical framework necessary for understanding, evaluating, and affirming the meanings which their students socially construct about themselves and school and has therefore diminished the possibility of granting them the means to self-knowledge and social empowerment. For many student teachers who find themselves teaching working-class or minority students, the lack of a well-articulated framework for understanding the class, cultural, ideological, and gender dimensions of pedagogical practice becomes an occasion for the production of an alienated defensiveness and personal and pedagogical armor that often translates into a cultural distance between "us" and "them."

Social Theory and Teacher Education

Over the years, left educational theorists have increased our understanding of schooling as essentially a political enterprise, as a way of reproducing or privileging particular discourse, along with the knowledge and power they carry, to the exclusion of other theoretical or signifying systems. As a result, it has been possible for many educators to recognize schooling as a practice that is both determinate and determining. The conceptual core of the analyses undertaken by radical scholarship over the last decade has been strongly influenced by the rediscovery of Marx and has involved unpacking the relationship between schooling and the economic sphere of capitalist production. We are, in part, sympathetic with this position, and especially with Ernest Mandel's claim that the industrial nations are now entering a form of corporate capitalism in which capital has prodigiously expanded into hitherto uncommodified areas. We also concur with the notion that forms of power control have become more difficult to uncover and confront critically because they now saturate almost every aspect of the public and private dimensions of everyday life.[10] But we still believe that this position has failed to escape from the economic reductionism that it so prodigiously attempts to move beyond. Furthermore, such a reductionism in its more sophisticated forms is evident in the continuing work of some left educational theorists who overly stress the relationship between schools and the economic sphere at the expense of interrogating the determinate role of signs, symbols, rituals, and cultural formations in the naming and constructing of student subjectivity and voice.[11] Our position stems from the observation that state capitalism is regulated by more than a purely economic constraints and that the intervention of the state in the economic process has eventuated the evolution of new symbolic and cultural discourses which give rise to and sustain important areas of modern social life. This is particularly notable in the way in which the state mandates the form and content of teacher education programs through the legislation of certification requirements for prospective teachers. Thus, questions surrounding how students generate meanings and create their cultural histories cannot be answered with sole recourse to discussions of social class and economic determinism but must begin to address the ways in which culture and experience intersect to constitute powerfully determining aspects of human agency and struggle.

Burgeoning interest in the realm of culture as a mediator and generator of subjectivity and discourse is currently leaving its stamp on the theoretical project of critical pedagogy in North America. In recent years, radical educators have attempted with varying degrees of success to appropriate into their work key concepts formulated by European philosophers and social theorists. Derrida, Saussure, Foucault, Barthes, Lacan, Gadamer, and Habermas are slowly finding their way into educational journals and have had the cummulative effect of marshalling a massive assault on dominant modes of educational theorizing and practice. Extrapolating from the deconstructionist project of Derrida, the hermeneutical combat of Gadamer, Lacan's psychoanalytic reconstitution of the subject, Barthes' textual anarchy, and Foucault's notion of power and historical inquiry, critical educators are beginning to construct a new theoretical vocabulary. It is not uncommon today to encounter attempts at "deconstructing" the curriculum, reading the "text" of classroom instruction, and articulating the "discursive formations" embedded in educational research.[12]

Some educators have used these advances in social theory to help strip conventional thinking about schooling of its status as an objective, scientifically grounded discourse. Much of this work challenges the ideological view of the student as author and creator of his or her own destiny by describing how student subjectivity is inscribed and positioned in various pedagogical "texts." Such work constitutes a critical idiom through which oppositional behavior may be tested, political contestation made problematic, and "lived meaning" critically examined. Much of this new social theorizing can prove useful for understanding how students fashion their constructions of self and school through the politics of student voice and representation. To understand student voice is to grapple with the human need to give life to the realm of symbols, language, and gesture. Student voice is a desire, born of personal biography and sedimented history; it is the need to construct and affirm oneself within a language that is able to rebuild the privatized life and invest it with meaning and to validate and confirm one's lived presence in the world. It follows that to make a student voiceless is to make him or her powerless.

At the most general level, new advances in social theory have shifted the focus of ideology from the economistic logic of the Marxist tradition to the mutually determining categories of culture, ideology, and subjectivity. Student subjectivity and lived experience are now being interrogated as social practices and cultural formations that embody more than class domination and the logic of capital. On the other hand, these new theoretical approaches are now available for unravelling the complex relations among economic, cultural, and ideological productions.

But there are serious precautions that a radical pedagogy must take before it begins to weave these new strands of social theory into a programmatic discourse that can inform a more critical view of teacher education. Rather than endorse these movements in an unqualified manner, as some educators have done, the current task of radical pedagogy should be to selectively and critically appropriate key concepts in discourse theory, reception theory, poststructuralism, deconstructionist hermeneutics, and various other new schools of inquiry without becoming trapped in their often impenetrable language, arcane jargon, and theoretical cul-de-sacs. A radical pedagogy must adopt the critical potential of these movements but at the same time press them to account for their frequent apolitical, ahistorical, and overly structuralist undercurrents. Radical educators must continue to search within the semiotic revolution for a critical language that will enable relevant theoretical advances to be employed for the purpose of creating an emancipatory teacher education curriculum, without becoming sidetracked by debates on marginal issues. It also follows that critical pedagogy cannot really function unless it makes despair less acceptable by promoting the promise of a progressive acquisition of knowledge that would result in the emancipation of subordinated groups through a transformation of asymmetrical relations of power.

We applaud the emergence of poststructuralist and semiotic theories for bringing about a cross-fertilization and restructuring of ideas and theories which hitherto were only marginally or tenuously connected and acknowledged. Furthermore, these theoretical developments have been significant in creating an intellectual movement that has a fundamental interest in the production and representation of meaning within contemporary cultural formations. But we must nevertheless insist that whatever new developments these discourses generate, they must continue to speak to the central problems of power and politics, particularly as these are expressed in the domination and subordination of peoples within society. Given the development of these new theoretical trajectories within radical pedagogy, it is essential to understand that the power necessary to transform the social order cannot be brought about merely through the exercise of a particular discourse or a synthesis of discourses. Reform cannot exist as a practical possibility *outside* the lived dynamics of social movements. Discourse alone cannot bring about social change. It is with this understanding in mind that teacher education programs commit themselves uncompromisingly to issues of both empowerment and transformation, issues which combine knowledge and critique with a call to transform reality in the interest of democratic communities.

Cultural Politics and the Teacher Curriculum

A teacher-education curriculum as a form of cultural politics stresses the importance of making the social, cultural, political, and economic the primary categories for analyzing and evaluating contemporary schooling.[13] Within this context, school life is to be conceptualized as an arena brimming with contestation, struggle, and resistance. Furthermore, school life can be a plurality of conflicting discourses and struggles, a mobile terrain wherein classroom and streetcorner cultures collide and teachers, students, school administrators affirm, negotiate, and sometimes resist how school experience and practice are named and accomplished. The overriding goal of education is, then, to create the conditions for student self-empowerment and the self-constitution of students as political subjects.

The project of "doing" a curriculum of cultural politics as part of a teacher education program consists of joining radical social theory to a set of stipulated practices through which student teachers are able to dismantle and interrogate preferred educational discourses, many of which have fallen prey to a hegemonic, instrumental rationality that either limits or ignores the imperatives of a critical democracy. But, we are more concerned with harnessing this language of critique to a language of possibility in order to develop alternative teaching practices that are capable of shattering the logic of domination both within and outside of schools. In the larger sense, we are committed to articulating a language that can contribute to examining the realm of teacher education as a new public sphere, one that seeks to recapture the idea of critical democracy as a social movement for individual freedom and social justice. We want to recast teacher education as a political project, as a cultural politics, that defines student teachers as intellectuals whose will establish public spaces where students can debate, appropriate, and learn the knowledge and skills necessary to achieve that individual freedom and soical justice.

We think that reconceiving teacher education in this way is one method of countermanding the retrograde practice within educational bureaucracies of defining teachers as primarily technicians, pedagogical clerks who are incapable of making important policy or curriculum decisions. The derision and contempt directed by professional bureaucrats towards teachers who demand and exert the right to link the practical to the conceptual in an effort to gain some control over their work continues to haunt the discourse of the contemporary educational enterprise. The simultaneous characterization of intellectuals as ivory tower theorists, removed from the mundane concerns and exigencies of everyday life, by both school adminstrators and the public, is another serious obstacle that radical educators must come to understand as a first step toward surmounting it. A curriculum as a form of cultural politics encapsulates the belief that teachers can function in a pedagogical capacity as intellectuals, and it is to this issue that we will now turn.

The search for a radical pedagogy for teacher education involves as its primary task the creation of theoretical models that provide a critical discourse for analyzing schools as socially constructed sites of contestation actively involved in the production of lived experiences. Inherent in this approach is a problematic characterized by the need to define how ped- agogical practice represents a particular politics of experience, or, in more exact terms, a cultural field where knowledge, discourse, and power intersect so as to produce historically specific practices of moral and social regulation. This new emphasis within educational theory registers a wide range of cultural and political issues that are central to the future role of schooling and democracy.

Furthermore, this problematic points the need to interrogate how hu- man experiences are produced, contested, and legitimated within the dynamics of everyday classroom life. The theoretical importance of this type of interrogation is linked directly to the need for beginning teachers to fashion a discourse in which a comprehensive politics of culture, voice, and experience can be developed. At issue here is the recognition that schools are historical and cultural institutions that always embody ideo- logical and political interests. They signify reality in ways that are often actively contested by various individuals and groups. Schools in this sense are ideological and political terrains out of which the dominant culture "manufactures" its hegemonic "certainties"; but they are also places where dominant and subordinate groups define and constrain each other through an ongoing battle and exchange in response to the sociohistorical con- ditions "carried" in the institutional, textual, and lived practices that define school culture and teacher/student experience. Schools are anything but ideologically innocent, nor are they simply reproductive of dominant social relations and interests. At the same time, schools do exercise forms of political and moral regulation intimately connected with technologies of power that "produce asymmetries in the abilities of individuals and groups to define and realize their needs."[14] More specifically, schools establish the conditions under which some individuals and groups define the terms by which others live, resist, affirm, and participate in the construction of their own identities and subjectivities.

As sites of contestation and cultural production, schools embody representations and practices that promote as well as inhibit the exercise of human agency among students. This becomes clearer when we recognize that one of the most important elements at work in the construction of experience and subjectivity in schools is language. Language intersects with power in the way particular linguistic forms structure and legitimate the ideologies of specific groups. Intimately related to power, language functions to both position and constitute the way that teachers and students define, mediate, and understand their relation to each other and the larger society.

With the above theoretical assumptions in mind, we want to argue in more specific terms for the development within teacher education institutions of a curriculum that embodies a form of cultural politics. In effect, we want to press the case for constructing a pedagogy of cultural politics around a critically affirmative language that allows potential teachers to understand how subjectivities are produced within those social forms in which people move but of which they are often only partially aware. Such a pedagogy makes problematic how teachers and students sustain, resist, or accommodate those languages, ideologies, social processes, and myths that position them within existing relations of power and dependency. Moreover, it points to the need for both prospective and in-service teachers to recognize discourse as a form of cultural production, one which serves to organize and legitimate specific ways of naming, organizing, and experiencing social reality.

In this view the concept of experience is linked to the broader issue of how subjectivities are inscribed within discursive processes that develop with regard to the dynamics of production, transformation, and struggle. Understood in these terms, a pedagogy of cultural politics presents a twofold task for potential teachers. First, they need to analyze how cultural production is organized within asymmetrical relations of power in schools, (e.g., school texts, curricula, tracking, policy, pedagogical practices). Second, they need to construct political strategies for participating in social struggles designed to fight for schools as democratic public spheres.

In order to make these tasks realizable, it is necessary to assess the political limits and pedagogical potentialities of the different but related instances of cultural production that constitute the various processes of schooling. Note that we are calling these social processes instances of cultural production rather than using the more familiar concept of social reproduction. While the notion of social reproduction points adequately to the various economic and political ideologies and interests that get reconstituted within the relations of schooling, it lacks a comprehensive, theoretical understanding of how such interests are mediated, worked on, and subjectively produced, regardless of the various interests that finally emerge.

Reclaiming Citizenship Education for Teacher Education

We want to conclude by reemphasizing and extending some theoretical considerations for developing a critical theory of citizenship education for teacher education programs. Central to a politics and pedagogy of critical citizenship is the need to reconstruct a visionary language and public philosophy that puts equality, liberty, and human life at the center of the notions of democracy and citizenship. There are a number of aspects to this language that warrant some consideration. First, *it is important to acknowledge that the notion of democracy cannot be grounded in some ahistorical, transcendent notion of truth or authority.* Democracy is a site of struggle and is informed by competing ideological conceptions of power, politics, and community. This is an important recognition because it helps to redefine the role of the citizen as an active agent in questioning, defining, and shaping one's relationship to the political sphere and the wider society. As Laclau and Mouffe put it, the radical concept which democratic society introduces is that

> the site of power becomes an empty space; the reference to a transcendent guarantor disappears, and with it the representation of the substantial unity of soceity. . . . The possibility is thus opened up of an unending process of questioning: no law which can be fixed, whose dictates are not subject to contest, or whose foundations cannot be called into question. . . . Democracy inaugurates the experience of a society which cannot be apprehended or controlled, in which the people will be proclaimed sovereign, but in which its identity will never be definitely given but remain latent.[15]

Implicit in this position is a challenge to both liberal and right-wing notions of the concept of the political. That is, the notion of the political is not reduced to the liberal emphasis on following rules of legality and administrative procedure. Nor is it reduced to the right-wing view that politics is a private affair whose outcome has little to do with the public good and everything to do with the defense of the free-market economy, national defense, and an individualist definition of rights and freedom. But it is important to stress that in redefining the notion of the political, the left cannot merely reject out of hand the recent convergence of neo-liberal and right-wing view of democracy. Instead, it must "deepen and expand it in the direction of a radical and plural democracy."[16] For Laclau and Mouffe, this means acknowledging the importance of those funda-mental antagonisms among women, diverse racial and sexual minorities, and other subordinate groups who have opened up radical new political spaces around which to press for the extention of democractic discourse and rights. The emergence of these new democratic struggles demonstrates the need for a revitalized view of the meaning and importance of the notion of the concept of political. Benjamin Barber reinforces this view by correctly arguing that the American left needs to ground the notion of the political in historical traditions that both reveal the subversive and dignifying power of democratic discourse and support the overarching importance of the autonomy of political discourse in understanding and influencing important aspects of our daily lives. He writes:

> The alternative [for the Left] is a revitalization of the autonomy of politics, and of the sovereignty of the political over other domains of our collective existence. The tradition that yielded the American con-stitution saw civic equality as the crucial equality. According to this tradition, politics can remake the world, and political access, political equality, and political justice are the means to economic and social equality. The left's best weapons remain the American Constitution and the democratic political tradition it has fostered.[17]

Democracy in this view is seen as an active social movement based on ideological and institutional relations of power that call for a vigorous participatory politics steeped in the traditions of a Jeffersonian democracy. Before a radical notion of democracy can be part of the agenda in teacher education, the left needs to redevelop a concept of active citizenship, which could be forcefully advanced against liberal and conservative spokes-persons "who urge more moderation in democracy, measures to return the population to . . . a state of apathy and passivity so that 'democracy,' in the preferred sense, can survive."[18] In radical terms, active citizenship would not reduce democratic rights to mere participation in the process of electoral voting, but would extend the notion of rights to participation in the economy, the state, and other public spheres. Thomas Ferguson captures this sentiment in his observation that

> the prerequisites for effective democracy are not really automatic voter registration or even Sunday voting, though these would help. Rather, deeper institutional forces-flourishing unions, readily accessible third parties, inexpensive media, and a thriving network of cooperatives and community organizations—are the real basis of effective democracy.[19]

Second, *a radical language of citizenship and democracy entails a strengthening of the horizontal ties between citizen and citizen.* This calls for a politics of difference in which the demands, cultures, and social relations of diverse groups are recognized as part of the discourse of radical pluralism. As a form of radical pluralism, the category of difference is not reduced to the possessive individualism of the autonomous subject at the heart of liberal ideology. On the contrary, difference would be grounded in various social groups and public spheres whose unique voices and social practices contain their own principles of validity while simultaneously sharing in a public consciousness and discourse. Central to this form of radical pluralism is a public philosophy that recognizes the boundaries between different groups, the self and others, and yet creates a politics of trust and solidarity that supports a common life based on democratic principles that create the ideological and institutional preconditions for both diversity and the public good.[20]

This leads to our third consideration to revitalize the concept of citizenship and democracy for prospective teachers. *A revitalized discourse of democracy should not be based exclusively on a language of critique,* one that, for example, limits its focus on the schools to the elimination of relations of subordination and inequality. This is an important political concern but in both theoretical and political terms it is woefully incomplete. As part of a radical political project, the discourse of democracy also needs a language of possibility, one that combines a strategy of opposition with a strategy for constructing new social order. Such a project represents both a struggle over historical tradition and the construction of a new set of social relations between the subject and the wider community. Put more specifically, the left needs to situate the struggle for democracy in a utopian project that actively articulates a vision of the future grounded in a programmatic language of civic responsibility and public good. Ernst

Bloch paid significant attention to the importance of the utopian impulse in radical thought, and his notion of the production of images of that which is "not yet" is clearly captured in his analysis of daydreams.

> Dreams come in the day as well as at night. And both kind of dreaming are motivated by the wishes they seek to fulfill. But daydreams differ from night dreams; for the day dreaming "I" persists throughout, consciously, privately, envisaging the circumstances and images of a desired, better life. The content of the daydream is not, like that of the night dream, a journey back into repressed experiences and their associations. It is concerned with, as far as possible, an unrestricted journey forward, so that instead of reconstituting that which is no longer conscious, the images of that which is not yet can be phantasied into life and into the world.[21]

Bloch's emphasis on the utopian dimension of daydreams leads to a fourth consideration. In our view, *the insistance on incorporating the utopian notion of "unrealized possibilities" in radical theory provides a foundation for analyzing and constituting critical theories of schooling and citizenship.* Both schooling and the form of citizenship it legitimates can be deconstructed as a type of historical and ideological narrative which provides an introduction to, preparation for, and legitimation of particular forms of social life in which a vision of the future, a sense of what life could be like, is given a central place. Given the fundamental anti-utopianism that characterizes so much of radical discourse today, the incorporation of a utopian logic as part of a project of possibility represents an important advance in rethinking the role of teachers.

Finally, *educators need to define schools as public spheres where the dynamics of popular engagement and democratic politics can be cultivated as part of the struggle for a radical democratic state.* That is, radical educators need to legitimate schools as democratic public spheres, as places which provide an essential public service in the construction of active citizens, in order to defend them for their centrality in maintenance of a democratic society and critical citizenry. In this case, schooling would be analyzed for its potential to nourish civic literacy, citizen participation, and moral courage. A theory of critical citizenship for teacher education programs must begin to develop alternative roles for teachers as radical intellectuals both in and out of schools. This is an important issue because it highlights the necessity of linking the political struggle within schools to broader societal issues. At the same time, it underlies for prospective and classroom teachers how important it is to use their skills and insights in alliance with others who are attempting to redefine the terrain of politics and citizenship.

Developing a radical pedagogy for empowering future generations of students and teachers calls on school of education to rethink the nature of their programs and their practices. We acknowledge, however, that the project we are describing is an ongoing one. Student teachers require more time in classrooms—more than is usually provided in one or two years of teacher training—to explore the theoretical connections that we have been suggesting between schooling, subjectivity, citizenship, and power. And they also require a protracted exposure to a radical reorganization of teacher education institutions around the concepts of history, language, culture, and power.[22]

Of course, a radical agenda for school reform has to begin somewhere, and small coteries of teachers working in isolation in their respective schools is not enough to provide the conditions necessary for transforming schools into counterpublic spheres. Conditions for democratizing schools in the interest of empowering teachers and students must begin in schools and colleges of education through a reconstitution of teacher education programs in the manner that we have suggested. Equally important for radical reform is the need for teachers to acknowledge that counterpublic spheres cannot be created solely within teacher training institutions or school classrooms, but must eventually merge with other communities of resistance. The project we have described focuses on the role that teacher education programs and institutions might play in enlarging the discourse of democracy. But such a project goes far beyond these institutions and reveals the necessity for wider social movements and structural changes. In the end, wider reforms call not only for teachers to engage with new social movements, but for teacher education programs to redefine the nature of both why and how they function in society.

Conclusion

At the present time, public policy weighs heavily in favor of the values and interests of the rich and the privileged. Greed has replaced compassion, and the drive for profit relegates all social concerns to a form of individual and social amnesia. At risk in the new discourse of neoconservative and yuppie ideology are not only the poor, minorities, women, and the elderly, but also the nation's public schools, social services, and welfare agencies. The central message, as we have argued throughout this chapter, is that ultra conservatives have launched a full-scale attack on both the meaning and the possibilities for critical reasoning and democratic values. Those public spheres that might provide the critical space for the development of social movements or support oppositional social practices compatible with the most important impulses of democracy have become the object of ideological dismissal and scorn by right-wing groups both in and out of government and, in many cases, have been targeted in order to be removed from the landscape of American public policy. At one level, this has meant either eliminating or cutting funding for such institutions. At another level, it has meant launching a full-fledged ideological onslaught on the basic foundations of such institutions. This is clearly the case, for example, with respect to the various criticisms and policies offered to undermine the nation's public schools. Ultraconservatives would like to turn public schools into institutions approximating a mixture of the local Sunday School, company store, and "Old West" museum. Industrial ideology, religious sectarianism, and cultural uniformity provide the basis for reconstructing the public schools in the political image of the reactionary policy makers.

This should not suggest that the right wing has won the battle. What it does suggest is that educators should collectively organize in these trying times in order to fight for democracy as a way of life and to unite the imperatives of everyday life with forms of economic and political democracy that take the notions of liberty, freedom, and justice seriously. In more specific terms, this means that progressive educators of various ideological learnings need to make schools centers of democratic learning and purpose. Teacher education programs can play a powerful role in providing the leadership necessary to make public schools responsive to the need for American democracy to create a self-confident, organized, and empowered citizenry. Similarly, teacher education programs can play a major role in developing a public philosophy that links learning and empowerment to a vision of larger loyalites. Underlying such loyalties should be a public morality which stresses social responsibilities that are attentive to forms of community that combine respect for individual freedom and social diversity with a commitment to democratic public life.

The renewal of an American democratic public philosophy needs to be fueled by a vision that extends rather than restricts human possibilities. This assumes a sense that history that is open, uncertain, and worth fighting for; at issue here is a vision of the future in which history is not accepted simply as a set of prescriptions unproblematically inherited from the past. History can be named and remade by those who refuse to stand by passively in the face of human suffering and oppression. Educators can join together in order both to politicize the nature of what goes on in schools and to extend the political work of our classrooms to other public spheres.

13

Crisis and Possibilities in Public Education

By HENRY A. GIROUX

As the United States begins to move into the twenty-first century, it appears to face a dual crisis in public education. One aspect of the crisis is apparent in the rise of the New Right and its economic and ideological attacks on the schools.[1] The second aspect of the crisis centers on the failure of radical educators to match neo-conservative educational politics with a corresponding set of visions and strategies.[2] I believe that both crises offer critical educators the opportunity not only to rethink the nature and purpose of public education but also to raise ambitions, desires, and real hope for those who wish to take seriously the issue of educational struggle and social justice in the future. But for such hopes to become realizable, we need to assess not only the failures of left educational thinking in the past decade, but also the reasons for the success of neo-conservative educational policy and the "authoritarian popularism" upon which it has been able to construct a broad national consensus. In taking up such an analysis, I will first consider the nature and ideology of neo-conservative discourse regarding public education and how it has challenged some of the basic assumptions of radical educational theory. I will

177

finish the chapter by pointing briefly to some of the elements of a critical educational theory that, I believe, need to be developed in the future.

The most obvious aspect of the crisis in public education and the response it is engendering from neoconservatives is visible in the discourse currently being used to describe the role schools should play in American society. Schools are no longer being celebrated for their role as democratizing institutions. On the contrary, as the recent spate of commission reports illustrates, schools are now being viewed within the narrow parameters of human capital theory.[3] Simply stated, the traditional arm's-length relationship between schools and business is now being dismantled for the purpose of aligning schools more closely with short- and long-term business and corporate interests.

The turn towards public education as a citadel of corporate ideology comes at a specific historical conjuncture in the United States. For many, this conjuncture is both characterized and understood as an expression of the capitalist economic recession. This explanation is only partly true, and as such, fails to comprehend the popularity of neoconservative discourse on public education as part of both a struggle and response to a political and ideological crisis the nation currently faces. In other words, neoconservatives have not appeared out of thin air; they are part of a varied set of historical traditions that have congealed into a particular political and ideological force at this specific time in history. And in doing so they have realigned and reshaped the political nature of their discourse and the ideological configurations that inform it. Moreover, neoconservatives seem to make convincing sense to an American public that is worried and intimidated by the changes the country has gone through since the 1960s. At issue here is the paradox of how groups that so blatantly favor the rich, the upper classes, and the logic of unbridled individualism can so effectively mobilize the needs and desires of subordinate and oppressed groups such as working classes, minorities, and others.

Neoconservative discourse about public schooling not only taps into a wide range of discontents, it also takes a strong position on important educational issues such as standards, values, and school discipline. In mobilizing existing public discontent, it combines two aspects of conservative philosophy so as to add a powerful element of popular-cultural appeal to its theoretical discourse. In diverse ways, it embraces elements of community and localism in its support of the family, partriarchal authority, and religion. Similarly, these aspects of traditional conservative philosophy are combined successfully with the tenets of classical liberalism, with its stress on individualism, competition, and personal effort and reward.

Around the pro-family issue, for example, neoconservative discourse examines a whole range of issues related to the nature of the current economic and moral crisis as they define it. In this case, the family is seen as a "natural" entity that is God-given and exists beyond the bounds of history. Defined as the center of morality and order, the nuclear family is celebrated as a locus of civilization, community, and social control. As the primary unit of society, it is appealed to as a moral and political referent from which to mobilize and wage a constant struggle against its "enemies." Allen Hunter observes:

> A great many issues are . . . combined in the defense of the family. In this way family imagery acts as a "condensation symbol," and—like the "pro-family coalition"—is used to draw together a wide range of distinct issues and to give them a positive image. Enemies are lumped together, too. Feminists, youth culture and drugs, black music, homosexuals, abortion, pornography, liberal educators, liberal divorce laws, contraception, and a melange of other phenomena, are all assimilated to a common feature: they are destructive of the family, and along with it the society.[4]

Neoconservative discourse also fuels its celebration of the family with the ideology of individualism. While at first glance the ideology of militant individualism may appear to be at odds with support of the family and community, it is actually displaced to another sphere of society, in that it is used as an ideological prop to wage an attack against the state and other forms of bureaucratic intervention. In this case, the notions of mobility, liberty, and freedom are linked to the ability of individuals to cast their fate to the competitive dynamics of the marketplace. In contrast, it is argued that state and government intervention block this possibility and in doing so undermine the virtues of hard work and self sufficiency, while simultaneously eroding the economic well-being and spiritual and patriarchal privacy necessary to maintain family life.

What is interesting about neoconservative ideology is that it takes seriously the way in which the state and other institutions, including schools, either intrude into people's lives or, through the arrogance of administrative policy, function to exclude them from participating in vital issues which affect their experiences on a daily level. Needless to say, in many respects working-class people and others respond positively to anti-statist ideologies because they encounter state policy and social practices not as benefits but as demeaning and powerful bureaucratic impositions into their lives. On the other hand, many people have expressed an ambivalence about public education that neoconservatives have capitalized upon and redefined in their own interests.

For many people, schools occupy an important but paradoxical place between their daily experiences and their dreams of the future. In one sense, public education has represented one of the few possibilities for social and economic mobility. But because of the many problems plaguing school systems, whether they be school violence, absenteeism, falling standards, or the shrinking of economic resources, popular concern has shifted from the traditional emphasis on gaining access to public education to a concern for shaping and controlling school policy. Neoconservative ideology has been politically adroit in addressing these concerns, but it does so in a way that represents "them within a logic . . . which pulls them systematically into line with policies and class strategies of the right."[5]

In capitalizing upon popular sentiments and discontents, neoconservative discourse has conveniently argued for educational policies that promote traditional values and conservative forms of authority and discipline. Rather than denying the role of schools in promoting values, neoconservatives have argued that moral regulation should become a central dimension of the curriculum. Consequently, school curriculum has become a major focus of popular contestation and a site for a kind of competitive struggle. This becomes evident with neoconservatives arguing for the inclusion of religious practices, the banning of subversive books and areas of study, and a renewed involvement in forms in schooling that display an instrumental enterprise in developing curricula that enshrine goals and values that support the ideology of business pragmatism. In addition, as neoconservative policy promotes cutbacks in financial aid to public schools along with other forms of social service, it creates a new labor force of unpaid women, whom it argues belong in the home. At the same time, neoconservatives strongly support voluntary work to be done by mothers in the face of cuts among the ranks of teachers and ancillary staff.[6] In this case the attack on public education is buttressed by a discriminatory policy against women.

What this all adds up to is starkly revealed in the way neoconservative ideology separates public education from the discourse of self-empowerment and collective freedom. Rather than confronting the inequalities and real failures of public education, neo-conservative policy views public education within a model of reason that celebrates narrow economic concerns, private interests, and strongly conservative values.

It is instructive to note that the neoconservative discourse currently dominating the debate on education in the United States has partly strengthened its position by linking the crises in everday life with the failures of public education. What is particularly interesting here is that conservative coalitions have been able to intervene into popular concerns about schooling around a number of ideological issues in a way that has rendered radical educators almost invisible in the current debate. I believe that this says less about the credibility of neoconservative ideology than it does about the theoretical failure of radical educators to take seriously the social and historical particularities of people's lives. Radical education has for too long focused either on the question of who has access to public education or on providing often despairing accounts of how schools reproduce through the overt and hidden curricula the varied inequalities that characterize the dominant society. This should not suggest that left educators have not provided important insights into how schools work, but rather that these insights have often fallen far short of what is theoretically needed to develop a more comprehensive and critical theory of schooling. For the last decade, radical accounts of schooling have focused too heavily on critiques of schooling, while failing to provide the more difficult theoretical task of laying the groundwork for alternative modes of educational theory and practice.

The one-sided nature of radical educational theory is evident in the way in which it has treated the notions of power, social control, and popular struggle. For instance, power in these accounts has often been defined primarily as a negative force that works in the interest of domination. Treated as an instance of negation, power took on the characteristic of a contaminating force that left the imprint of either domination or powerlessness on whatever it touched. Consequently, the notion of social control became synonymous with the exercise of domination in schools, and the question of how schools could become the site for the production of new forms of opposing knowledge and social practices was largely ignored. It is clear, for example, that there has been a fundamental confusion around the issue of what constituted freedom within the discourse of radical pedagogy. This point is best seen in the underlying assumption in most radical educational theory that school discipline, authority and academic standards are representative of coercive impositions that limited the development of the natural, emotional, and intellectual abilities of students. Thus, freedom became synonymous with demystifying and eliminating the ideological and material restraints imposed by schools so students could discover their real abilities and possibilities for learning. In other words, freedom is defined as the absence of control and the student is presented as the embodiment of an individuality that has to mature as part of a natural developmental process. What is lost in this theoretical account is the understanding that education always functions in complex ways as either a positive or negative force to produce the very conditions under which individuality is constituted. My point is that freedom is not removed from power or from the issues of authority, standards, and discipline within schools. In fact, it is linked directly to the issue of how it both informs and emerges from those daily conditions in schools that help to produce students who are critically literate and socially responsible. Valerie Walkerdine cogently makes this point in her claim that "what educators need to understand is how that condition which we call individuality is formed within apparatuses of social regulation, including education."[7]

Radical educational theory provides many insightful criticisms about socially constructed nature of the school curriculum, but at the same time it fails to take seriously what implied in such a judgment. That is, school curriculum is not simply a social construction. It is also an historical expression of past struggles over what constituted political and cultural authority and the forms of ethical, intellectual, and moral regulation implied in specific forms of school authority. With few exceptions, radical educational theorists give little attention to the positive side of school life, i.e., to those dimensions of schooling that reached deep into the concerns of everyday experience. Neglected in this case are questions such as what constitutes critical knowledge, or how language and culture should be developed as part of a critical pedagogy. More specifically, what is ignored is the fundamental issue of how to define a positive notion of social control and responsibility from which to build and defend certain conceptions of school organization, classroom relations, and hierarchically organized bodies of school knowledge. I will finish this chapter by briefly focusing on some of these issues as they might be defined for a critical pedagogy applicable not only for the present but also for the future.

If schools are to be seen as active sites of intervention and struggle, in which exist the possibilities for teachers and students to redefine the nature of critical learning and practice, then the relationship between power and social control will have to be redefined. In this case, power will have to be viewed as both a negative *and* positive force, as something that works both *on and through* people. Its character will have to be viewed as dialectical, and its mode of operation as both enabling and constraining. This more dialectical view of power has significant implications for redefining the relationship between social control and schooling.

It is important to view social control as having both positive and negative possibilities. That is, when linked to interests that promote self and social empowerment, the construct of social control provides the theoretical starting point upon which to establish the conditions for critical learning and practice. Similarly, the notion of power that underscores this position begins with the assumption that if social control is to serve the interests of freedom it must function so as to empower teachers and students. As used in this context, social control speaks to the forms of practice necessary for the demanding task of designing curricula that give students an active and critical voice, providing them with the skills that are basic for analysis and leadership in the modern world.

But the notion of social control being used here speaks also to something more fundamental. It links the notion of freedom to forms of social structure and discipline that would be essential in creating and ordering new criteria for the development of the type of curriculum needed to promote forms of critical pedagogy. A critical notion of social control cannot elude the tough issue of responsibility, of providing the context and conditions for the development of emancipatory forms of schooling.

Connected to this notion of social control is the need for radical educators to take seriously the relationship between schooling and what I call "cultural power." Traditionally, school culture has operated primarily within a logic that defends it as part of the fabric of high culture. The teacher's job was to transmit this form of culture to students in the hope that it would offset those cultural forms reproduced on the terrains of popular culture and subordinate class experience. Left educators countered this view of culture by arguing that high culture was itself developed out of the fabric of domination and mystification and as such had to be rejected. As part of an oppositional educational task, the culture of oppressed groups had to be rescued and re-presented so as to offset the worst dimensions of dominant culture. The key notion here was that radical educators had to work with the experience of oppressed groups. As insightful as this concept is in both criticizing dominant culture and giving a voice to subordinate cultures (the working class, blacks, women), it failed to develop a critical method and pedagogy for dealing with both dominant and subordinate cultures. In other words, it failed to take seriously the need to not only work with subordinate cultures, but also to work on them. Thus, "to work on them. meant not just to confirm subordinate cultural experiences, but also to interrogate them critically so as to recover their strengths as well as weaknesses. Similarly, if the notion of cultural power is to provide the theoretical basis for forms of critical pedagogy, it has to become a referent for examining what students and others need to learn outside of their own experiences. This points to the need to redefine the role of knowledge within the contexts of cultural and curriculum studies.

A critical pedagogy, then, would focus on the study of curriculum not merely as a matter of self-cultivation or the mimicry of specific forms of language and knowledge. It would stress forms of learning and knowledge aimed at providing a critical understanding of how social reality works; it would focus on how certain dimensions of such a reality are sustained; it would focus on the nature of its formative processes; and it would also focus on how those aspects of it that are related to the logic of domination can be changed. Stuart Hall provides a more specific idea of the kind of skills this type of critical pedagogy would involve. He writes:

> It is the skills which are basic, now, to a class which means to lead, not simply to serve, the modern world. They are the basic, general skills of analysis and conceptualization, of concepts and ideas and principles rather than of specific and outdated "contents," of abstraction and generalization and categorization, at whatever level it is possible to teach them.[8]

Similarly, this approach to critical pedagogy would be based on a dialectical notion of what counts as really useful knowledge and school practice in the building of an emancipatory curriculum. It would be developed around knowledge forms that challenge and critically appropriate dominant ideologies, rather than simply rejecting them outright; it would also take the historical and social particularities of students' experiences as a starting point for developing a critical classroom pedagogy; that is, it would begin with popular experiences so as to make them meaningful in order to engage them critically. As critical educators begin thinking about pedagogical strategies for the twenty-first century, they will have to develop some clarity about what kind of curriculum is needed to build a critical socialist democracy. This means redefining the notion of power, school culture, and really useful knowledge. Such a task does not mean debunking existing forms of schooling and educational theory, it means reworking them, contesting the terrains on which they develop, and building upon them the democratic possibilities inherent both in schools and in the visions that guide our actions.

What I have suggested in this chapter points to the need to infuse educational theory and practice with a vision of the future, one that is matched, I hope, by the willingness of educators to struggle and take risks. The nature of such a task may seem utopian, but the stakes are too high to ignore such a challenge.

14

Reproducing Reproduction: The Politics of Tracking

By HENRY A. GIROUX and PETER McLAREN

As early as 1922, George S. Counts called into question the democratic principles which allegedly structured the nature and practices of American schooling. In analyzing academic achievement in public schools, Counts was able to uncover and document a clear relationship between educational opportunity and class structure:

> It seems . . . probable that the selection is sociological first and psychological second; that children enter and remain in high school because they come from the homes of the influential and more fortunate classes, not because of their greater ability. . . . Why should we provide at public expense those advanced educational opportunities for Y because his father is a banker and practically deny them to X because his father cleans the streets of the city? We must distinguish between that education which is for all, and that which is for the few. At present our secondary education is of the first type in theory, and of the second in practice.[1]

Although sixty-five years have passed since Count's study, schools continue to reproduce class, gender, and racial inequality. The problem is most clearly evident in institutionalized tracking.

While the debate over school tracking appears to surface every decade, it often is shunted aside or marginalized by budgetary or administrative concerns that seem more pressing. Jeannie Oakes's book, *Keeping Track,* promises to reinstate the tracking issue as a prime subject for debate. A senior research associate at UCLA's Education Graduate School, Oakes has marshalled an impressive array of data to interrogate an old but important theme: the structuring of school curricula and pedagogy in such a manner as to privilege some groups over others on the basis of race, gender, and class distinctions.[2]

Oakes's book comes at an important time in our history, given the scope of debate and reform activity surrounding American education today. In this debate conservatives have dominated the early rounds, and the discourse of educational reform has been narrowed to the reductionist logic of economic advancement and individual achievement. Given those circumstances, the appearance of *Keeping Track* in the educational marketplace is especially welcome, if only to remind educators and the public of the culpability of school organization and administration in the production of inequality and injustice.

Oakes begins her study with an earnest attempt to "unlock the tradition" of educational tracking by tracing the development of ability grouping and tracking in American schools over the last 100 years. The influx of unskilled immigrants from southern and eastern Europe in the early 1900s, paralleled by the enforcement of child-labor laws and compulsory education, precipitated the birth of the comprehensive high school. This new type of schooling necessitated abandonment of "the nineteenth century notion of the need for common learnings to build a cohesive nation" in favor of curriculum differentiation in the form of tracking and homogeneous grouping.[3] Social Darwinism provided the legitimating ideology for characterizing ethnic minorities and the poor as standing lower on the evolutionary ladder and as less fit in moral development than the Anglo-Protestant majority. Coupled with a growing concern for preserving the dominant white Anglo-Saxon culture against the "depravity" of the immigrant population, Social Darwinism thus supported the trend toward Americanization which eventually dominated the school curriculum.

American industry was to provide the logic for this new kind of education by presenting schools with a factory model of learning. As a consequence, and with encouragement from a burgeoning industrial economy, production and efficiency became the guiding ideological principles for the establishment of vocational education as the appropriate alternative curriculum for students not bound for college. The development of IQ tests further provided the objective rationale needed to classify students into various programs on the basis of their ethnic, racial, and economic backgrounds. Undertaken "in the spirit of scientific efficiency," educational testing was viewed as meritocratic since it helped to sort students into specialized programs where they would receive what was thought of as the best possible education, given the opportunities available in the industrial workplace.

After providing an historical account of tracking, Oakes unravels certain inegalitarian myths and practices surrounding school tracking. In analyzing the radical disjunction between the democratic values that schools espouse and the authoritarian, reproductive ideologies inherent in the morphology and practices of tracking, Oakes works from a large, complex sample of data taken from a late 1970s study of 25 desegregated junior and senior high schools (297 classrooms) which John Goodlad developed into his well-known study, *A Place Called School*.[4] Arguing that "school people must not fall into the trap of thinking that early preparation for an unjust world requires early exposure to injustice,"[5] Oakes seeks to show us that schools provide benefits unequally. Invariably, she maintains, students who are poor and from a minority background are most disempowered and disenfranchised by school tracking procedures.

This effect derives in part from the way in which school knowledge is distributed within high-track and low-track groups. Oakes maintains that students in low-track groups are more likely than others to be from poor and minority backgrounds and to be taught behaviors that will make them suitable for low-status jobs. In other words, low-track students are taught low-status knowledge which has "little exchange value in a social or economic sense."[6]

Oakes also analyzes opportunities for learning. Her data reveal that students in high-track groups enjoy distinct educational advantages over those in low- and middle-track groups: for the high-track groups, more time is set aside by teachers for learning; more actual class time is spent on learning activities; more attention to homework is expected; fewer students are permitted to be off-task; and more instructional practice is given. In short, for high-track students, learning takes place in an environment that confirms the students' high-track identity and, as such, structures time, activity, and place so as to privilege *their* sense of self and achievement.

For low-track students, time in school may be more a burden than an asset. Such students often view knowledge as unrelated to their lives and instruction as an assault on their time. School becomes a place for enduring time rather than using it in the interests of self and social empowerment. It is to Oakes's credit that she analyzes the reactions of low-track students to the ways in which schools administer and disrupt their lives. If such students learn anything, it is in spite of the degradation they endure.

Tracking does more than alienate students from schooling; it also undermines their social aspirations and sense of self-worth. Oakes suggests that students at the bottom of the social hierarchy adjust their aspirations downward without being aware that schools are treating them unjustly. Oakes's position takes a cruel turn here, unfairly translating a social failure into a personal one and obscuring our sense of how such failures can be rectified in the future. In essence, schools play a major role in the legitimation of inequality, in socializing students to accept the unequal features of the larger society.

Oakes also examines vocational education and claims that vocational programs function primarily to segregate poor and minority students into occupational training programs, thereby preserving the academic curriculum for middle- and upper-class students. Consequently, vocational education is crucial to the schools' reproduction of race, gender, and class inequalities characteristic of the larger economic order. Not surprisingly, Oakes discovers that nonwhites more than whites are directed in vocational training toward futures in lower-class social and economic positions.

Near the end of *Keeping Track,* Oakes shifts from the language of criticism to the language of possibility. She analyzes the legality of tracking and identifies characteristics that might be the focus of legal action. Her premise is that

> tracking is a governmental action that classifies and separates students and thereby determines the amount, the quality and even the value of the government service (education) that students receive. The classifications made are both durable and stigmatizing. Further, they do not appear to be essential to the process of providing educational services. In fact, for some students they may interfere with the educational process.[7]

Clearly, Oakes's discussion of litigation as a means to challenge the discriminatory effects of tracking is designed to suggest a preliminary strategy that might lead to state-legislated equality.

We do not wish to quarrel with Oakes's general propositions and conclusions: namely, that school knowledge is unequally distributed and qualitatively different from track to track; that tracking limits the economic and social mobility of students; and that schooling colonizes the attitudes of students and teaches them to accept their low-track status as unquestionable and inviolable. However, we do wish to draw attention to some theoretical problems Oakes encounters as she relies uncritically on reproduction theory in her attack on tracking.

Oakes draws upon the works of reproduction theorists such as Bowles and Gintis and radical theorists such as Paul Willis, Basil Bernstein, and Pierre Bourdieu and Jean-Claude Passeron, to support her conclusions.[8] Not content to rely on the ideological thrust of her own data, she reiterates the major claims of the reproductionists: that schooling legitimates inequality; that low-track status corrodes self-esteem; that schools, as sorting machines, prepare students for adult roles, thus helping to maintain the social structure and organizational patterns of the wider society; that schools constitute and distribute students according to race, class, and gender; and that disaffected students usually end up in the same low status jobs as their parents. But while Oakes does not hesitate to use reproduction theory, she fails to address its more radical implications. She does not call attention, for example, to the crippling effects of the logic of capital in general, or the way in which this logic gets produced in the process of tracking itself. In other words, Oakes's analysis gives no sense of how the ideological and material forces of capital actually structure—through the intervention of the state, business, and the ideology of individual success and competitiveness—various interests operating in schools, to the benefit of capitalist social relations. She does not acknowledge that without major shifts in the distribution of economic and political power in the wider society, school reform toward equity is virtually impossible. Martin Carnoy, by contrast, puts the issue well:

> The hierarchial system of capitalist production structured on class, race, and gender divisions in our society will not be altered by the higher and equal quality of basic education unless concurrent efforts are made to democratize the economy and state bureaucracy. And if the workplace is not democratized, some groups of children will receive equal education with a much lower social return. Unless menial, repetitive jobs are rotated, for example, among all citizens, we will have very intellectual, very dissatisfied dishwashers working at low wages. Appeals that ask them to regard their education as an end in itself can only be made by those who sit in ivory towers and are paid well to do so.[9]

Oakes' disinclination to consider "broad social reconstruction" leads her to offer suggestions for more immediate reform. In a disquieting appeal to pragmatic politics, she adopts a stance that translates loosely as follows: if we can't realistically create an authentic democracy, at least we can attempt to create equality in the schools. Consequently, she asserts that schools must "cease to sort and select students for future roles in society." Furthermore, they should "relinquish their role as agents in reproducing inequalities in the larger society."[10]

As Oakes's plan for reform unfolds, we are presented with a pedagogical model based, rather predictably, on mandatory heterogeneous grouping and a common curriculum, one which is, surprisingly, guided by an uncritical celebration of "high-status" knowledge. Oakes claims that

> the reorganization of schools so that the predominant pattern becomes the use of heterogeneous groups could equalize students' educational experiences in several ways. First, if students were given a common curriculum ideally comprised largely of the high-status knowledge now primarily reserved for students in high-tracks, the closing off of students' access to future opportunities would be considerably postponed and perhaps lessened. All students would be at least exposed to those concepts and skills that permit access to higher education. And if some students do not grasp the concepts as quickly or comprehensively as others, they will have been given a beginning, a chance.[11]

Because differences in knowledge acquisition still would occur within heterogeneously grouped classes, Oakes develops what she considers to be alternative pedagogical strategies ideally suited for teaching heterogeneous groups. One alternative is to use criterion-referenced tests rather than testing that compares one student with another. In addition, learning tasks would be restructured to foster cooperative learning, enabling students to avoid the individualistic and competitive models of instruction that most teachers currently employ. Cooperative learning structures, Oakes claims, offer three distinctive advantages: "(1) a built-in incentive for students to interact with one another as learning resources; (2) a means of accomodating learner differences in the learning process; and (3) a way of greatly minimizing or eliminating the effects of initial differences in students' skill levels or learning rates in the assigning of rewards for learning."[12]

Lost in Oakes's vision of school reform is a critical analysis of the nature of high status knowledge. Oakes does not see that uncritical acceptance of the primacy of high-status knowledge might lead to a devaluation of popular cultural formations and subcultural knowledge and to a disconfirmation of the cultural capital of working-class students. In other words, Oakes shows no theoretical understanding of the relationship between culture, power, and learning. There is little sense in her discourse of how schools embody a dominant culture that often functions at the level of everyday school life to disconfirm, marginalize, or actively silence the "voices" of students from subordinate groups. We are given no analysis of the relationship between language and power, of the way in which language functions to introduce students into particular ways of life, and, in doing so, how it constructs and engages particular forms of subjectivity. Reproduction theory in general and Oakes's analysis in particular fail to develop a theory of subjectivity and a politics of student experience linked to the dynamics of practical learning.

In effect, what we are offered is a new liberal strategy without the benefit of radical insights provided by the very reproduction theorists that Oakes both endorses and criticizes. Oakes ultimately sacrifices the primacy of the political by constructing a notion of teacher reform that removes the central categories of culture, ideology, and power from the pedagogy she points to as a way to make schools democratic sites of equal opportunity. What we end up with is more Rogerian and interactionist than any form of radical pedagogy that has evolved in the United States so far. We are told, for example, that the form and content of school subject matter should be reorganized in a more equitable fashion and that, since students act or interact with one another in a way largely determined by how teachers structure learning goals, teachers need to be more attentive to the organization of classroom tasks and to the allocation of rewards for learning. But we are given little contextual description of how a student's own voice and cultural capital are both mediated and constituted by school experience or how student voice and cultural capital get constructed within larger sociocultural formations.

At its best, the vision of equality outlined by Oakes is one in which students from all racial and class backgrounds would stand an equal chance to survive economically in an unjust world. Oakes herself admits that she is unclear about whether or not her vision of equality in the schools would in the long term have the effect of discouraging societal inequalties. At the very least, Oakes thinks that students would have a better start than they have now on the road to job success. But any proposal for school reform that doubts its own power to affect reality outside the school itself—beyond helping students to find a place in the capitalist market place—shortchanges us by obscuring the possibility that teachers might organize collectively outside of school, in alliance with other social movements, in order to effect political and structural changes that can address both the schools and society at large. Oakes poses no questions about whether the persistence of the dominant view of education—which she links loosely to "employment opportunities"—is ethically warranted. Of course, Oakes's dilemma is not new. It reflects the major impasse in liberal educational reform: How can schools give students a taste of democracy, so that they will be motivated to create a more just and more equitable social order once they leave, while rejecting as too unrealistic, or too radical, suggestions or strategies for sweeping changes in the wider society?

Oakes's formulations on the nature and purpose of democratic schooling are not made problematic enough. In Oakes's view, an education system bereft of inequality would be one organized to ensure "increased academic achievement, more positive attitudes toward instructional activities, and enhanced intergroup and interpersonal relationships."[13] There is some logic to this. But without sustained and systematic analysis of the wider social and economic system that is responsible for inequality in the schools, the model of the democratic school that Oakes endorses represents no more than an ideological factory streamlined for "democratic" efficiency. What we end up with is less a matter of democratic empowerment than a form of schooling in which students from all class and racial groups are socialized equally into the imperatives of the dominant culture. In Oakes's vision of reform all students would have a greater chance to acquire high status knowledge and better employment opportunities, but the schools as such would remain as handmaidens of the dominant culture.

This suggests for us a problem as well as a confusion in which Oakes appears to be trapped. Oakes seems to confuse the *procedural nature of democracy* with the issue of *empowering for democracy*. It is one thing to argue that schools should become more democratic settings, but such a call is theoretically hollow if it isn't accompanied by an attempt to spell out the forms of knowledge, values, and 'social practices students will need in order to understand how a particular society works, where they are located in it, and what its more inequitable characteristics are. In effect, Oakes presents an argument for democracy as a setting that lacks any agents. It would be a democracy of empty forms.

The concept of good schooling should transcend pedagogical considerations that focus on such concerns as "time on task," "student involvement with learning tasks," and the "degree of intensity of student engagement." Equal opportunity should come to mean more than simply giving both genders, all classes, and all races the same chance to be equally socialized for upper-class occupations. Both concepts require us to reconsider the relationship between knowledge and power. We need to learn how authority works in schools to fashion subjectivity according to the logic of the dominant society.

In light of current political realities, Oakes's narrow focus on the immediacy of school organization and bureaucracy may provide an opportunity for the New Right and others to mobilize around issues that affect schools in an indirect but powerful way. The abolition of tracking is one precondition of democratic schooling. But Oakes's failure to take seriously the need for schools to function politically as public spheres or to make links with popular constituencies, such as workers' movements, feminist groups, and anti-armament groups, aligns her recommendations perilously close to those of another recent proposal for a completely one-track system of schooling that also has a humanistic and high-status focus, the *Paideia Proposal*.

In the final instance, the concept of equality which Oakes espouses remains uncritical and undifferentiated. Inequality is not simply "caused" by structural and administrative arrangements or by the unreflective adherence of well-intentioned teachers to myths that erroneously promote the tracking of students. Rather, inequality is best understood contextually, by reference to sets of social practices and negotiations among social actors within certain structural, historical, and ideological constraints. As Connell et al. point out, inequality can't be understood

> by a kind of arithmetic of advantage and disadvantage. If anything, the analogy should be with chemical compounding rather than with addition and subtraction. We need tools with which to think about qualitative changes, leaps and discontinuities, as our means of penetrating into the *essence* of the system.[14]

The notion of causes of inequalities should, we think, be played down in favor of efforts to understand the social relationships and patterns that work through the educational system, including the contradictions and tensions within these patterns, and an understanding of how people relate to and mediate these patterns and relationships. Rather than attempting to manipulate the causal factors of inequality, as Oakes does, Connell et al. prefer to speak "in terms of the *potentials* that a given situation has for the people in it, and the *constraints* on what they can do with it."[15]

In other words, the notion of cause is fruitless unless it is examined in the context of social action. Seen from this perspective, tracking is more a product of how power and knowledge work through institutional arrangements and sociocultural formations than it is a result of some undirectional institutional cause. Oakes's book for all its data and good intentions, brings us only marginally closer to answering the question that Counts posed back in 1922. It therefore seems only fitting that we allow the spirit of Counts to echo our final concern, that educators need to make a choice between schooling and democracy or schooling and domination. Oakes fails to bring us to an adequate understanding of schools as possible sites for and about democracy. She addresses the issue of whether or not schools can function in the interest of democracy, but she does so with a theoretical and political temerity that suggests the need for a new model of radical educational theory and practice. In looking for answers, Oakes stands the recent tradition of radical educational theory on its head and mistakes the beginning of radical educational theory in its reproduction phase as its culminating moment. This is theoretically misleading and politically wrong. We suggest that educators take advantage of the new discourse and concerns that radical educational theory has advanced. It is an approach that links theory to practice, combines the language of critique with the language of possibility, and analyzes schools in ways that disclose how they might produce new subjects, new subjectivities, and the courage needed for wider institutional reform.[16]

15

Antonio Gramsci: Schooling for Radical Politics

By HENRY A. GIROUX

Almost forty five years after his death, Antonio Gramsci finally looms as one of the great theoreticians of Marxist social theory. But the almost global preoccupation with Gramsci's writings has been accompanied by a paradox that remains to be resolved. Though Gramsci's work is currently accessible to scholars far beyond the reach of his native Italy, there is little agreement about the meaning or importance of his work. Interpreted and reinterpreted, Gramsci's work has been elaborated and popularized to the degree that it has sometimes been deprived of its most important features. Amidst the confusion and sloganizing, Gramsci's name has become a halo used to rationalize the most banal theoretical claims.

The sources of this problem are both the nature of Gramsci's writing and the genre in which he expressed his ideas. His earlier work consisted mostly of journalistic endeavors that, while insightful, were somewhat limited by the genre in which they were composed. The more celebrated prison writings were written under the scornful eye of a Fascist prison censor and are at best fragmentary and unfinished. This is not to suggest the absence of a rich vein of insight and analysis in these writings; the latter are there, but demand a patient and systematic reading in which often contradictory and underdeveloped ideas have to be placed within the wider parameters of Gramsci's world view in order to be fully understood.

The contextualization of Gramsci's ideas is particularly relevant regarding his writings on education. Theoretical and abstract, they are marred both by coded language and by incomplete and shifting perspectives. For example, a large part of Gramsci's prison notes on curricular change and pedagogy were written as a response to Gentile's proposed school reforms of 1923. The importance of these writings can only be fully appreciated within Gramsci's overall position on hegemony, intellectuals, and "war of position." Not to do so runs the risk of supporting a simplistic reading of Gramsci's position on education, one that wrongly describes him as a supporter of a conservative mode of schooling. The latter is particularly misleading since such an analysis parades under the commonly used cliches of traditional and progressive education. This type of categorization is ahistorical and undialectical and simply cannot accommodate the notion that what was labelled as progressive educational policy in Italy in the 1920s might be considered quite "conservative" by some "radical" educators in the 1980s. When abstracted from the sociohistorical contexts in which they were used these terms become inapplicable in assessing the value of Gramsci's contribution to critical educational theory and practice. Thus, the real issue is not, in the conventional ahistorical sense, one of labeling elements of traditional or progessive pedagogy in Gramsci's work. Instead, the important theoretical starting point for evaluating Gramsci's educational writings is whether or not his problematic on schooling, the questions he raises, and the suggestions he proposes, provide the conceptual building blocks for a critical pedagogy consistent with both his own aims for radical social change and the political needs of the working class in the advanced industrial countries of the West during the 1980s and 1990s.

Harold Entwistle's work represents one of the first fully fledged efforts to explore the relevance of Gramsci's writings for developing a foundation for critical educational theory and practice. Entwistle approaches this task by first examining in detail Gramsci's writings and notes on schooling. He then compares his own analysis of these writings against the way Gramsci's work has been interpreted and used by the so-called new sociologists of education as well as other radical educational theorists. After resurrecting the "real" Gramsci, Entwistle proceeds to dismiss those "radical" critics who have allegedly misinterpreted Gramsci's work. He further proves that the lesson to be learned from Gramsci's work is that schools do not provide the setting for "a radical, counter-hegemonic education."[1] Entwistle's analysis of Gramsci provides one with the opportunity to articulate some of the major assumptions that characterize his work, to criticize a particularly conservative appropriation of these assumptions, and to indicate the relevance Gramsci's work might have for educators.

In this view, critical pedagogy rests exclusively with institutions designed for adult education, i.e. workplaces, trade unions, etc. Thus, in the name of Gramsci, we are treated to a rather strange dualism: on the one hand, schooling for children is seen as an exercise in imposing discipline, drudgery, and "objective" facts; that is, it becomes a place where teachers can mechanically instill in working-class students the tools and "virtues" of "traditional" culture and history. On the other hand, education for adults is characterized by self-reflection, critical thinking, and teacher-student relationships in which both parties are actively engaged as learners in the pursuit of truth and social change.

In the most important sense, the dualism which characterises Entwistle's view of Gramsci and schooling represents the key to understanding the methodology he uses to develop his thesis. It is a methodology that is as reductionistic as it is undialectical. Its raison d'être begins not with a problem or issue to be explored but with a messianic fervor, the purpose of which appears to be to impose a positivistic reading on Gramsci, one that unfortunately makes him appear to be nothing more than a crude apologist for the most reactionary mode of pedagogy. Entwistle also appears to have used this book to exorcise the 'evil' influence of the new sociologists of education and neo-Marxist critical educators. In both cases, the interpretation is at odds with the reality.

Entwistle's reading of Gramsci reveals him as a "stern" taskmaster whose views on discipline, knowledge, and hegemony render him more in tune with Karl Popper and Jacques Barzun (both of whom are referred to positively) than the likes of Karl Marx, Paulo Freire, or, for that matter, even John Dewey. For instance, if we are to take Entwistle's version of Gramsci seriously as a model for socialist education, then we will have to accept the claim that Gramsci believed that human knowledge was objective in the view adopted by Karl Popper. That is, knowledge is "independent of anybody's claim to know, and that there exist objective, intractable laws to which man must adapt if he is to master them in his turn."[2]

In making this epistemological claim, Entwistle obscures Gramsci's distinction between the natural sciences, which involve "objective things" in the natural world that corresponds to attributes marked by linguistic conventions and knowledge of the social world which involves perceptions of social reality construed out of the way in which human beings constitute and confer meaning upon the world. Popper's "knowledge without a subject" and his notion of logic which operates independently of human volition bear little resemblance to Gramsci's thought, which rejected the false distinction between knowledge and human interests.[3] Moreover Gramsci's position cannot be construed as an argument for the type of relativism enshrined by the early proponents of the new sociology of education and rightly criticised by Entwistle.[4] Nor can it be used to support Popper's view of knowledge with its underlying support of technocratic organisational forms designed "so that objective, ahistorical and abstract knowledge may be employed in controlling historical events."[5] Gramsci was very clear about surrendering human action and social practice to projections based on statistical laws and models of objectivity and prediction. He argued that such a view not only reinforced passivity among the masses, it also supported the false notion that the future could be *predicted* through a mechanical reading of the past.[6] The point here is to argue against an objectivism that bleaches Gramsci's epistemology and Marxism of its subjectivity, history, and humanism. Gramsci's concern with "facts" and intellectual rigor in his educational writings makes sense only as a rightly argued critique of those forms of pedagogy that separate facts from values, learning from understanding, and emotion from the intellect.

It was no mystery to Gramsci that the pedagogy of the Gentile reforms, which stressed "feeling," "emotion," and the most "immediate needs of the child" to the exclusion of content and modes of critical reasoning, represented a form of domination operating in the guise of a libertarian educational theory. It is only within the context of Gramsci's own dialectical pedagogy that his critique of vocational schooling, his concern with linking scholarship with arduous self-discipline, and his rejection of the "immediate" testify to an epistemology that rejected a positivist rendering of social reality and human nature with its false dualisms and its image of a self-subsistent world of fact structured in lawlike manner. Entwistle's reading of Gramsci does not penetrate the source of this dualism, he simply reverses it. That is, he substitutes a one-sided celebration of the immediacy of needs with an equally one-sided celebration of the immediacy of "facts."

Radical pedagogy for Gramsci was historical, dialectical, and critical. Rather than adulate the "immediacy" of human needs or the "immediacy" of facts, it rejected mere factuality and demanded that schooling be "formative, while being 'instructive'."[7] For Gramsci, the pedagogical task was, in part, "mitigating and rendering more fertile the dogmatic approach which must inevitably characterise these first few years."[8] Such a task was not easy and demanded, on the one hand, the necessity "to place limits on libertarian ideologies," while, on the other hand, it was necessary to recognize that "the elements of struggle against the mechanical and Jesuitical school have become unhealthily exaggerated."[9] Underlying Gramsci's pedagogy is an educational principle in which a comfortable humanism is replaced by a hard headed radicalism, not a radicalism that falsely separates necessity and spontaneity, discipline and the learning of important basic skills from imagination, but, instead, one that integrates them.[10] There is no question that drill, drudgery, and discipline find support in Gramsci's pedagogy. But, as Philip Simpson points out, "the necessary drudgery is not the principle he finds in work, so much as its transforming power."[11] The interconnections between discipline and critical thinking in Gramsci's view of schooling only lend support to a conservative notion of pedagogy if the concept of physical discipline and self-control is abstracted from his emphasis on the importance of developing a counterhegemony, one "which demands the formation of a militant, self-conscious proletariat that will fight unyieldingly for its right to govern itself. . . ."[12] In other words, Gramsci's claim that "it will always be an effort to learn physical self-discipline and self-control, the pupil, has, in effect, to undergo psycho-physical training" gets seriously distorted unless understood within the context of his other remarks on learning and intellectual development.[13] For instance, he wrote in 1916:

We must break the habit of thinking that culture is encyclopedic knowledge whereby man is viewed as a mere container in which to pour and conserve empirical data or brute disconnected facts which he will have to subsequently pigeonhole in his brain as in the columns of a dictionary so as to be able to eventually respond to the varied stimuli of the external world. This form of culture is truly harmful, especially to the proletariat. It only serves to create misfits, people who believe themselves superior to the rest of humanity because they have accumulated in their memory a certain quantity of facts and dates which they cough up at every opportunity to almost raise a barrier between themselves and others.[14]

Entwistle rightly criticizes Gramsci's relativism, his failure to situate knowledge historically, and his linear reading of hegemony as an imposition of meaning as serious flaws in both their interpretation and use of Gramsci's educational principles. But in the attempt to buttress his position that Gramsci argued against developing a radical pedagogy in which schools would be sites for counterhegemonic struggles, Entwistle develops a critique of radical schooling that is misleading.

Entwistle argues that Gramsci's notion of the hegemonic function of the school "lies in its organisation rather than in its curriculum, or in the 'hidden curriculum' implicit in teaching method."[15] That is, the hegemonic function of the school has nothing to do with how or what it teaches, but rather with how it prevents working-class students from gaining access to a traditional humanistic education.[16] In this rather "remarkable" view, questions concerning how schools function within the larger system of power relations in order to maintain the dominance of ruling groups are glibly dismissed as either inconsequential or misleading. By ignoring the issue of how the imposition of meanings and values distributed in schools are dialectically related to the mechanisms of economic and political control in the dominant society, Entwistle depoliticizes the relationship between power and culture. In doing so, he trivializes the role that schools play in defining what is legitimate knowledge and social practice. Consequently, his own analysis ends up as a form of management ideology, one that substitutes questions concerning the relationship between knowledge and power for questions which are limited to how a *given* body of knowledge is to be taught and learned in the classroom encounter.

A significant point is partially developed by Entwistle in his claim that Gramsci's notion of hegemony has been badly interpreted and applied by a number of radical educators. By viewing hegemony as simply the imposition of meanings, they have trivialized the concept by defining it merely as a form of inculcation. This is an important corrective in understanding how the mechanisms of domination mediate between the larger society and the school, particularly as they manifest themselves in the material practices of classroom social relationships, in the ideoligial practices of teachers, in the attitudes and behavior of students, and the classroom materials themselves.

Gramsci's notion of ideological struggle was much too critical to suggest that teachers should simply transmit mainstream culture. He argued that traditional humanistic culture should be mastered, but in the dialectical sense that it had to be understood in order to be criticized and rearticulated according to the needs of a radical working class. Opposition, not transmission, is the critical theme Gramsci posits as the key pedagogical task of radical schooling. This suggests making neither a clean sweep of the existing culture nor "replacing it with a completely new and already formulated one. Rather, it consists of a process of transformation (aimed at producing a new form) and rearticulation of existing ideological elements."[17] Again, the dominant culture had to be critically understood before it could be transformed. This is a significant issue in Gramsci's notion of education for it has important implications for teacher-student relationships in a critical theory of pedagogy, implications that are in opposition to the views that Entwistle attributes to Gramsci.

Gramsci clearly understood, as Femia points out, that "revolutionary consciousness was not to be pumped into the working class from without, it must be mobilised from within."[18] This does not imply, as Entwistle claims, that there is no working-class culture. Nor does it suggest, on the other hand, that radicals should argue for the equivalency of working-class culture with the dominant culture. Both positions are reductionistic and ignore the complex mediations and modes of resistance that exist between the dominant culture and various modes of working-class culture. Entwistle's rebuke of working-class culture not only ignores its moments of resistance and its possibilities as a partial source of counterhegemony, it also suggests that domination in schools is relatively total. Such a view misconstrues the notion of hegemony as well as the ability of people to resist domination. The latter position also ignores Gramsci's view on the relationship between "common sense" and "good sense," as well as his view that the interconnection between the two provides a fundamental instance as a source of counterhegemonic pedagogy around which to structure teacher-student relationships. For Gramsci, common sense did not suggest simply a mystified consciousness; instead, it referred to the terrain where men acquired consciousness of themselves. Put more simply, working-class culture is not to be equated with passivity and one-dimensionality; instead it is to be seen as a mode of practice unable "to break with the given world and transform it."[19] Far from being passive, such a world view is simply "disjointed and ambivalent."[20]

The task of critical educators is not to deny working-class culture, but to use it as a starting point in order to understand how particular students give meaning to the world. Students must be able to speak with their own voices, before they learn how to move outside of their own frames of reference, before they can break from the common sense that prevents them from understanding the socially constructed sources underlying their own self-formative processes and what it means to both challenge the latter and to break with them. Gramsci's notion that common sense contains the seeds of a more rational view of the world reinforces his view that the task of the intellectual is to develop counterhegemonic struggles by using popular consciousness as a starting point in any pedagogic relationship. When Gramsci argues that "every teacher is always a pupil and every pupil a teacher"[21] he is not abandoning the call for disciplined pedagogy. What he is doing is introducing an educational principle into the teacher-student relationship that leaves no room for elitism or sterile pedantry. The notion that the teacher is always a learner places intellectuals in the position of not only helping students to appropriate their own histories, but also to look critically at the nature of their own relationship with students of the working class, as well as with other oppressed groups. Gramsci's notion that "the popular element 'feels' but does not always know or understand; the intellectual element 'knows' but does not always understand and in particular does not always feel"[22] puts into high relief two important dimensions of hegemony that must be contested in schools. On the one hand, ideologies must be combatted and dereified, whether these be in the overt or the hidden curricula. On the other hand, the hegemonic practices that are sedimented in the social relations of the classroom encounter, part and parcel of the very texture of our need structure and personalities, must be transformed through concrete social formations that allow critical communication and action.[23] Only within this type of pedagogy will critical educators be able to understand how the seeds of social and cultural reproduction are contained within the very nature of student resistance, and how they might, for instance, use that insight to transform what is often misdirected cultural resistance into forms of political awareness and social action.

16

Solidarity, Ethics, and Possibility in Critical Education

By HENRY A. GIROUX

The necessity of hope as a precondition for radical thought and struggle is not generally characteristic of prevailing forms of radical educational theory in North America. In part, what currently passes for much of radical educational theory represents a language of critique, devoid of any language of possibility, which, in turn, represents a view of politics without the benefit of a substantive moral discourse or a programmatic vision of the future. There is a growing tendency, especially among a second generation of radical educational theorists, to eschew a logic of hope and possibility as the basis for theoretical and political engagement. Whereas the larger sphere of radical social theory draws upon various sophisticated currents in order to define its project, radical educational theory still appears tied to a legacy of scienticism and ideological reductionism that tends to manifest itself either as a variant of vulgar Marxism or as simply bad scholarship. One of the most striking aspects of much of radical educational theorizing is its increasing celebration of theory as method and verification. Radical educational theorists now speak of the importance of theory being empirically secure, or of its value as a coherent structure of assertions. Some radical educators argue in Popperian fashion for radical educational theory to stand up to the test of being either empirically confirmed or falsified.[1] This is not to suggest that the issues of coherency, internal logical consistency, or empirical verification are not important. But theory should first be valued for its political project, its socially relevant criticism, its estranging quality. In other words, it should be valued for its potential to liberate forms of critique and to establish the basis for new forms of social relations. Critical educational theory cannot be reduced to the deadening and politically harmless issue of consistency and reliability, a peculiar obsession of dominant social theory; on the contrary, its value should be assessed by its ability to confront the discourse and social practices of oppression with what Benjamin once called "potentially liberating images of freedom."

In part, the profoundly anti-utopian nature of much of contemporary radical educational theory is due to the isolation of theorists from larger social movements and sources of social criticism as well as to the pessimism of those academics who distrust any form of struggle or theorizing that might emerge in public spheres outside the university. In some cases, this takes the form of an outright refusal to grant any hope or possibility that teachers and others might be able to wage counterhegemonic struggles in the schools. We have the exaggerated claims, for example, by some theorists that any form of struggle for democratic reform and student empowerment within schools only leads to a kind of "false consciousness." Focusing primarily on a discourse that stresses the overwhelming logic of domination or the failure of teachers to act in the face of domination, these theorists appear merely to recycle the ethos of reproduction theory without acknowledging how its ideological assumptions shape their own pronouncements.[2] This is the language of noncommitment buttressed as ideological critique—a language that lacks even the slightest glimmer of political engagement. Similarly, another group of radical theorists performs the paradoxical feat of calling for educational change by celebrating reform from the "bottom up," at the same time displaying little faith or understanding in either the efforts of teachers or the power of social theory to contribute to such change.[3]

The despair and reductionism of such approaches is also manifest in their refusal to consider the possibility of developing political strategies in which schools can be linked to other social movements and public spheres. Brandishing their orthodox Marxist credentials in good classical fashion, some radical educators go so far as to argue that critical educational theory has given too much attention to issues of race, gender, and age considerations; if one wants to be really radical it is important to get down to business by emphasizing the primacy of class as *the* universal and major determination in the struggle for freedom.[4] This is more than dull theorizing, it also sometimes accompanied by forms of academic discourse that exchange the imperatives of critical analyses with sweeping, stylistic insults. Radical traditions are perfunctorily dismissed as mere "inspirational interludes"; complex radical analyses are blithely termed "preachy exaggerations and . . . didactic simplifications."[5] In addition to casual dismissal of certain educational traditions and schools of thought there has emerged a meanness of spirit that abstracts and reifies the pain and suffering that take place in schools. That is, amidst "scientific" analyses regarding the labor conditions of teachers, the perils of schooling and capitalism, and the political economy of textbooks, there is little attention given to a politics of the body, to concrete human suffering, or to forms of collective empowerment among teachers and/or students as they emerge out of various struggles against domination inside of schools. In fact, the disappearance of a discourse of the body, one that illuminates and points to concrete instances of suffering and opposition, is a crucial theoretical absence because it points to the disappearance of the discourse of politics and engagement. Instead of developing a political project and ethics that embody critique *and* hope, that connect schools and other institutions to forms of ongoing struggle, these newly emerging strains of critical educational theory appear to be suffocating in ideological narcissism, tied more closely to the self-serving tenets of vanguardism and despair than to anything else.

Social theory itself needs to be resuscitated and deepened so as to provide a more critical and comprehensive basis for educators to rethink the underlying nature of their political and ethical project. It ought to provide the theoretical signposts necessary for teachers to understand their role as social activists whose work is both supported and informed by wider social movements and struggles. A number of recent critical works have helped to illuminate these issues for a renewed form of radical social and educational theory. Two recent books, by Terry Eagleton and by Sharon Welch, in particular, establish important theoretical insights for centering and focusing the meaning and possibilities for a reconstructed critical social theory which gives central attention to the notions of democratic public sphere and the discourse of critical ethics.[6] It is significant that, while each author deals with different aspects of political struggle and social criticism, they are united in the potentially transformative and radically utopian discourse they exhibit.

Eagleton's book is especially welcome because he attempts to provide a view of social criticism as a set of historical practices inextricably connected to issues of power and control. In addition, he is able to situate criticism as a social practice within a historically changing analysis of the various public spheres which provided it with institutional support. Eagleton argues that social criticism was born of struggle in the seventeenth and eighteenth centuries in England between the rising middle classes and the political imperatives of royal absolutism. Pitting itself against "the arbitrary diktats of the autocracy," the middle classes fashioned a bourgeois public sphere comprising "a realm of social institutions—clubs, journals, coffee houses, periodicals—in which private individuals assemble for the free, equal interchange of reasonable discourse, thus welding themselves into a relatively cohesive body whose deliberations may assume the form of a power political force."[7]

The classic public sphere has an important dialectical quality for Eagleton. First, it defines social criticism as part of a larger discourse concerned with cultural politics and public morality and in doing so invokes the Enlightenment principles of rational argument and free exchange of ideas to challenge notions of authority rooted in superstition, tradition, and absolutist decrees. The classic public sphere established a legacy in which writing, the study of literature, and social criticism had a "broadly civilizing function."[8] Second, the classic public sphere ultimately buttressed and mystified bourgeois social relations and the power of the state. Infusing the public sphere with a false egalitarianism, its bourgeois supporters denied the underlying structure of privilege and ultimately dissociated politics from knowledge by arguing that the public sphere was a place where all men and women could voice their ideas regardless of social class. As Eagleton makes clear, reason and rationality rather than power and domination became the ideology used to both hide and confirm the system of inequality that gave the classic public sphere its legitimacy and rationale for existence.

With the rise of industrialism in England, the classic public sphere was invaded by the forces of the market, the waning legitimacy of its own neutrality, and the emergence of public spheres among subordinate classes and groups. Consequently, the bourgeois critic could no longer speak unchallenged as the universal voice of reason. So, the very nature of criticism changed, especially literary criticism, which now escaped to the university where it became institutionalized in English departments, losing its connection with everyday life and its potentially critical role as a basis for a form of cultural politics.

Eagleton is at his best in explaining how this occurred. Criticism, he shows, not only radically divorced itself from social life but also lost any claim to a legitimating view of authority rooted in its capacity as a social practice inextricably linked to the welfare of the wider community of everyday experience. It may have gained security in academe but it did so ultimately by committing political suicide. This is not to say the university and its attendant intellectuals do not perform any social and political function. Eagleton's point is that they no longer produce forms of social criticism that are emancipatory in nature, criticism with active political links to the wider society. Instead, criticism is now either so tame that it serves as an apology for the state or it has degenerated into arcane forms of Marxist theorizing that substitute literary struggles for actual political battles that involve real rather than imaginary relations of power. For Eagleton, the university as a public sphere failed in a dual ideological sense. While traditional academic criticism tries "to train students in the effective deployment of certain techniques, in the efficient mastery of a certain discourse, as a means of certificating them as intellectually qualified recruits to the ruling class,"[9] left criticism as it emerged in the universities, especially in the 1970s, takes on a highly abstract and theoretically questionable position regarding the purpose of social criticism. For Eagleton, the various structuralisms of a deconstruction and postmodernist variety degenerated into a "liberalism without a subject."[10] Questions of power and struggle are often reduced to analyses of texts and structures, while issues of authority and subjective struggle are canceled out in a play of infinite differences and indeterminations.

According to Eagleton, the broad political and civilizing function of criticism is neither characteristic of academics nor of the university in general. Although such an claim merely seems to recycle a critique often heard in the student revolts of the 1960s, Eagleton adroitly uses it to analyze how intellectuals within the university might assert the primacy of the political nature of their work by linking it to broader politico-cultural projects. At issue here is the concern that, in the absence of a vital public sphere, criticism has no opportunity to be debated and institutionalized in a collective context that allows it to become a mobilizing political force. Eagleton attempts to substantiate his point theoretically by analyzing the political effects of the work of Raymond Williams, one of England's foremost socialist writers. Though Williams had by 1979 sold over 750,000 copies of his books in Britain alone, there was little opportunity for him to organize his readership politically in the absence of a socialist counterpublic sphere. Eagleton comments:

> In the effective absence of a working-class theatre movement, Williams's political drama found a home instead, for both good and ill, in the capitalist media; in the absence of working-class institutions of literary and intellectual production, one of the most vital tasks of the socialist intellectual—that of the resolute popularization of complex ideas, conducted within a shared medium which forbids patronage and condescension—was denied him. For genuine political popularization involves more than producing works which make socialist theory intelligible to a mass audience, important though that project is; such a readership must be institutionalized rather than amorphous, able to receive and interpret such work in a collective context and to ponder its consequences for political action.[11]

Central to Eagleton's own political project is a language of both critique and possibility. He provides a historical and critical analysis of the social function of criticism and the intellectuals who practice it within different institutionalized settings. Yet he is quite clear in arguing that, if university intellectuals are to play an active counterhegemonic role on the terrain of cultural politics, they will have to give up their stance as lonely intellectuals reduced to the production of criticism. In fact, such intellectuals need to reassert a new politics of sociality in which their work is developed and nourished through a lived set of concrete relations with those groups with which they side politically. Put bluntly, such intellectuals will have to become part of a larger social movement linked to existing public spheres.

Underlying Eagleton's call for educators to link their work to public spheres is an important recognition: given the present nature of the culture industry and the ever-encompassing power of the State the classic public sphere of the seventeenth and eighteenth centuries cannot provide the political and ideological model upon which to develop public spheres in the industrialized countries of the west. The classic public sphere was developed around a notion of rationality and discussion that generally substituted polite discourse and debate for dialogue aimed at developing forms of solidarity and political organizations. Eagleton argues that public spheres by political necessity need to move beyond such a notion of rationality, and he finds alternative models in two sources. The first source is historical and points to the various public spheres organized by the working classes in the Weimar Republic. As Eagleton points out

> the working-class movement was not only a redoubtable political force; it was also equipped with its own theatres and choral societies, clubs and newspapers, recreation centres and social forums. It was these conditions which helped to make possible a Brecht and a Benjamin, and to shift the role of critic from isolated intellectual to political functionary. In the Britain of the 1930s, agitprop groups, the Unity Theatre, the Workers' Film and Photo League, The Workers' Club, the London Workers' Film Society and a range of other institutions reflected elements of this rich counter culture.[12]

The women's movement represents for Eagleton a second mode of politics and form of sociality at work in which the logic of public spheres can be identified. What is striking about Eagleton's analysis is his identification of critical elements of the women's movement with what he calls a politics of the body, a form of sociality that links rationality with power and desire and not merely with discursive structures. Of considerable importance here is a politics in which everyday experience, interests, desires, and needs configure as part of a cultural politics attempting to broaden and deepen the notion of both oppression and emancipation. In the end, Eagleton links intellectual work and political practice with the development of public spaces where new forms of subjectivity can be constructed amidst a new form of politics. Eagleton's historical inventory of the nature of social criticism and its attendant and legitimating forms of intellectual practice provide a glimpse of the social and political forces at work that separate knowledge from power and critical theory from concrete political practice. Similarly, such an analysis points to the power of the university in producing intellectuals, for whom in the absence of a public sphere, despair, and cynicism often become mistaken as central elements of critical theory and practice. Of course, Eagleton's *call* for intellectuals to broaden and develop their work within public spheres engaged in an ongoing struggle for radical democracy, provides new hope in defining the terms of a cultural politics suitable for the latter part of the twentieth century.

What Eagleton does not do is provide the ontological grounding for the type of intellectual work that posits a strong committment to overcoming instances of suffering and developing concrete forms of sociality that buttress rather than detract from a critical cultural politics. It is this issue which Sharon Welch admirably addresses, and to which I will now turn in the remainder of this chapter.

> The sheer weight of the apocalypse obliterates utopia. The catastrophe no longer conjures up images of redemption. Instead it produces cynicism, which is no less ideological. Cynicism is the total embrace of the power of reality as fate, or as a joke, the "unhappy consciousness" of powerlessness. It is the hardened, wizened posture: detached negativity which scarcely allows itself any hope, at most a little irony and self pity.[13]

> Fear in particular, says Sartre, is a state which cancels out the person; accordingly the animatingly opposite is true, subjectively and especially objectively, of hope. And even if in the building of mere castles in the air the total expenditure one way or the other scarcely matters . . . hope with plan and with connection to the. . . . possible is still the most powerful and best thing there is. And even if hope merely rises above the horizon, whereas only knowledge of the Real shifts it in solid fashion by means of practice, it is still hope alone which allows us to gain the inspiring and consoling understanding of the world to which it leads, both as the most solid, the most tendency-based and concrete understanding.[14]

Conservative educators now employ the language of radical critique in order to cancel out the suffering of history. They argue that the development of critical consciousness among the populace translates *tout court* into an unjustified assault on tradition while simultaneously promoting a nihilistic, self-serving individualism. According to this view, critical reason appears incapable of taking as its object the specific formative history of a particular culture in order to interrogate the interplay of its dominant and emancipatory traditions. Instead, reason is collapsed into political inertia. At the same time, critical reason remains separated from social empowerment so as to deny the possibilities for collective struggles organized around the contradictions of everyday life and the legacy of radical historical memories that have been excluded from the dominant cultural discourse. Hope, in this case, is rendered untenable and impracticable.[15]

Now, some radical educators argue that the notion of hope as the basis of a language of possibility is really nothing more than a "trick of counterhegemony," employed for ideological effect rather than for sound theoretical reasons.[16] In other words, hope as a vision of possibility contains no immanent political project and as such has to be sacrificed on the altar of empirical reality. Ironically, this position makes the very notion of counterhegemony untenable, since all struggle implicitly signifies an element of utopian possibility. It is not surprising that such a position ends up defining critical social practice as nothing more than "a persistent skepticism toward reform from within the status quo."[17] In this case, the concept of hope is used to disclaim political action. Such a theoretical and political dead-end is the antithesis of what it means to speak the language of possibility while engaging in critical practice, that is, it runs counter to challenging oppression while simultaneously struggling for a new kind of subjectivity and alternative forms of community.

The crucial issue that confronts educators is that a growing fundamental anti-utopianism among some elements on the left has now joined ideological hands with a new right. Such an unholy alliance produces a discourse that assaults democratic logic by narrowing the possibility for intellectuals to become part of those social movements currently engaged in defending and advancing the universal values of freedom and life. That is, the new right/left discourse in education represents a theoretical tendency that denies the very grounds on which intellectual practice can be legitimated.[18]

Amidst the deeping crisis in democracy facing the industralized nations of the West, it is imperative that the political and social function of the relationship between intellectuals and emancipatory social movements be given serious consideration by critical educators. As I pointed out earlier, theorists such as Terry Eagleton have argued persuasively that the university no longer encourages the discourse of moral leadership and social criticism. Consequently, the call for the development of counterpublic spheres outside of the university points to the need to reconstruct a cultural politics in which critical educators and other intellectuals can become part of any one of a number of social movements in which they use their theoretical and pedagogical skills in the building of historical blocs capable of emancipatory social change. On one level, this suggests that such intellectuals can work to analyze specific historical struggles waged by various radical social movements around the political importance of education in the battle for economic and social justice. This type of analysis not only illuminates the activities of social movements outside of the university, which have struggled for knowledge and forms of critical practice, it also provides the basis for considering what types of public spheres might be useful politically in the current historical juncture.

This is an important argument because it provides the theoretical grounds for developing counterpublic spheres as a defense and transformation of public education itself, rather than as a long-term substitute for the system of public education and higher education. By expanding the notion of education and extending the possibilities for pedagogical activity within a variety of social sites, critical educators can make the policies, discourses, and practices of schooling open to criticism and thus available to a greater number of people who otherwise are generally excluded from such a discourse. It is imperative for educators to consider how social institutions may be understood and developed as part of a wider political and educational struggle; moreover, by combining the language of critique with a language of possibility such educators can develop a political project that broadens the social and political contexts in which pedagogical activity can function as part of a counterhegemonic strategy. Essential to this project is the question of how specific forms of democratic practice can be supported by a particular version of justice and morality. Educators must be clear about the moral referents for justifying how particular forms of experience can be legitimated and accomplished as part of both the development of democratic public spheres and radical social change in general. Clearly, the discourse of social change needs to develop a critical conception of democracy as a practice that operates out of particular social forms and is rooted in a specific set of moral and political interests. It is this issue to which I will now turn.

Writing in the 1920s, Ernst Bloch attempted to counter the eighteenth century Enlightenment perspective in which the concept of utopia was dismissed because it could not be legitimated through reason and grounded in an immediate empirical reality. Bloch argued that Utopia was a form of "cultural surplus" in the world, but not of it: "it contains the spark that reaches out beyond the surrounding emptiness."[19] Sharon Welch's attempt to develop a feminist theology of liberation is highly indebted to Ernst Bloch, though she does not rely directly on his work.[20] Like Bloch, she develops her analysis of traditional Christianity within a language of critique that rejects universal abstractions about the goodness of humanity and focuses instead on concrete instances of suffering, the acts of resistance they often engender, and the role traditional Christianity has played in either ignoring such suffering or directly contributing to it. At the same time, she posits a notion of hope that is mediated by forms of struggle in which "alternative visions of society, humanity, institutional structures, orders of knowing . . . are brought into play."[21]

For Welch, hope is both a referent for social change and pedagogical struggle and the basis for reconstructing a radical theology, one that combines the vision of liberation theology, with its focus on the oppressed, with the radical feminist goal of reconstructing social identities and subjectivities within new forms of community. Welch writes:

> This theology emerges from the struggle to create, not merely to proclaim, a human community that embodies freedom. The verification of this struggle is not conceptual, but practical: the successful process of enlightenment and emancipation, a process that is open and self-critical. This theology emerges from an effort to live on the edge, accepting both the power and the peril of discourse, engaging in a battle for truth with a conscious preference for the oppressed . . . . It is a discourse imbued with the particular tragedy of human existence— the dangerous memory of despair, barrenness, suffering—and with the particular moments of liberation—the equally dangerous memory of historical actualizations of freedom and community . . . . [This] type of theology . . . affirms with Bloch "that learned hope is the signpost for this age—not just hope, but hope and the knowledge to take the way to it."[22]

Central to Welch's political project is the discovery of a language that gives central expression to the primacy of experience, power, and ethics. Her goal is to move beyond the "hollow space" of Enlightenment rationality which limits experience to perception in order to develop a discourse that provides historical and social understanding of how experience is shaped, legitimated, and accomplished within particular social forms as these are organized within particular relations of power. In Welch's view, experience is both historical construction and lived practice. It connects the need to understand how social forms position and produce experience with the further imperative of interrogating how experience in its contradictory and often less than coherent moments is felt and inhabited. For Welch, suffering cannot be reduced to statistical reports churned out by the State and centers of Church power; it is a lived experience that links desire, pain, suffering, and hope.

Welch's experience as a feminist provides part of the basis for her criticism of the rituals and theologies of established Christianity as a religion of the middle classes. Welch recalls that her own experience of both patriarchy and nonsexist forms of sociality led her to question the practices of the traditional Christian Church. These experiences, including her actual insurrection against sexist practice, provided Welch with the basis for analyzing the Christian Church's view of sin as an expression of male ideology. It also enabled her to develop a theoretical critique of traditional Christianity's refusal to develop a discourse that takes seriously the historically contingent nature of truth, doctrine, and redemption. Operating behind a discourse of absolutes and universal essences, traditional Christianity, in Welch's view, failed to develop a view of faith and ecclesia based on a commitment to those marginal and excluded groups who were exploited and oppressed. But rather than rejecting Christianity completely (as was done by Marx, Proudhon, Bakunin, and many contemporary radicals), Welch chooses to reconstruct and extend those dimensions of Christian hope that point to the possibility for human struggle and happiness. In this case, she argues that within Christianity there are discourses that do not accept the role of the traditional Church and the fundamental institutions of dominant society. It is these excluded and marginalized discourses that need to be recovered today. Welch uses this issue to demonstrate how deeply the struggle for religious control inscribes itself in a particular language and culture. Moreover, her own choice of a distinctive discourse, one based on a radical reading of faith and social practice, not only illuminates the assumptions of a radical feminist theology, but also questions the historical and ideological contingency of knowledge and its relationship to power. By critically appropriating Foucault's notion of the relationship between power and language, Welch demonstrates through her own reading of Christianity how language offers a series of subject positions, a range of discourses out of which historical understanding develops and particular forms of knowledge and social practice become legitimated. For Welch, it is imperative that a major element of radical theology recognize language as a social construction, linked to apparatuses of power and particular definitions of the truth. One of the major strengths of the book resides in her argument that language has to be seen in its historical and socially formative dimensions as part of a politics of identity, ethics, and struggle.

> In liberation theology one chooses to think and act from the perspective of the oppressed. I believe that the option is chosen, not imposed. To be a feminist theologian of liberation is to recognize the constitutive role of one's matrix-participation in resistance struggles-and to choose to continue to think and act from this perspective, recognizing the contingency of that choice. . . . The context of these theologies is one stratum within the whole Christian tradition, a particular option that is critical of society and of the institutional church. This stratum is a

practical, communal, revolutionary form of ecclesia. Theologies of liberation are rooted in the memory of the revolutionary struggles and hopes expresed in the "underground Bible" and the history of heresies. They are rooted in communities of faith that are continuous with those aspects of the Christian tradition that have been committed to liberation within history and to solidarity with the oppressed. [23]

One of the strengths of liberation theology is its redefinition of the theory and practice relation. Theory is defined through its ability to recall and legitimate standards of ethical practice which best serve human needs and hopes. Welch grounds her notion of radical practice in a theory of faith constructed around a particular view of human suffering, solidarity, and human community.

This relationship is worth elaborating. In the first instance, Welch argues that radical practice begins with an identification of the needs and desires of dominated groups and their ongoing attempts to end their suffering and oppression. This is not merely a reflection on human suffering as much as it is a moral referent for political action rooted in an affirmation of the importance of human life and the necessity to address injustices caused by class discrimination, sexism, racism, and other forms of exploitation. In addressing her own experiences working with abused women, Welch forcefully demonstrates this issue by acknowledging the context of human suffering as a field of struggle and hope.

> I am pulled back from self-indulgent ennui and despair only as I remain in community with those who are oppressed and are struggling against that oppression. To live in community with women helping other women and children recover from the trauma of rape, incest, and wife-abuse, with men working against rape by identifying and challenging the equation of sexuality and violence in male socialization, with women and men trying to create communities of nonviolence in a violent world reminds me that suffering is real, that it must be addressed even if one is not certain of its causes or aware of the best means of healing its damage. To remember the reality of oppression in the lives of people and to value those lives is to be saved from the luxury of hopelessness. [24]

Central to the affirmation of human life is a double-sided notion of critique. First, there is the need to develop forms of critical analyses that illuminate how the concrete mechanisms of power work within different ideological and institutional relations of domination. Second, there is the emphasis on analyzing critique itself as a particular type of practice in which men and women challenge oppressive and dominating institutions. Critique in this view is linked to acknowledging as part of any radical project the historical and cultural specifics that constitute the nature of particular types of resistance.

Welch's notion of solidarity is a central category for organizing a radical notion of faith around a specific conceptualization of struggle and as a lived engagement with collective action. Welch conceives solidarity as a form of sociality that is experienced in actual participation "in the resistance struggles of the oppressed."[25] As a participatory act, solidarity provides the theoretical basis for critically developing new forms of sociality based on a respect for human freedom and life itself. As such, solidarity as a lived experience and form of critical discourse serves as a referent for criticizing oppressive social institutions and as an ideal for developing the material and ideological conditions neccessary for creating communities in which humanity is affirmed rather than denied.

Closely linked to Welch's views regarding human suffering and solidarity is her notion of redeemed communities, which can be more clearly understood against her critique of traditional Christianity's discourse of abstract universals. By speaking of universals such as human rights and universal peace, the traditional Church refused to address the particulars of pain, suffering, and struggle within the concrete communities in which people experienced daily life. Echoing Foucault, Welch argues that Christianity has refused to acknowledge the process by which power is embodied and installed within concrete conditions of oppression and in doing so often fails to alleviate the suffering of its victims. Behind the traditional Church's discourse of universals, there is a structured silence.

The type of humanity and subjectivity that Welch believes is consistent with her own feminist theological principles represents a form of community that has to be fought for rather than demanded through an appeal to Scripture. Welch clearly understands that the power of love, work, and justice emerges not through discourse alone but through a struggle within and for specific social and economic conditions. Welch rightly insists that the notion of community does not represent an a priori form of social organization that needs to be established for the oppressed. On the contrary, the notion of redeemed community represents a struggle for a particular kind of subjectivity and social existence the outlines of which are defined by the historical processes through which people actually struggle, develop concrete forms of sociality, and promote the discourse of self and social liberation. Inherent in Welch's notions of suffering,

solidarity, and redeemed community are principles of political and pedagogical practice which highlight a specific view of the relationship between
power, knowledge, and cultural struggle. Welch makes this clear in the
following statement:

> To challenge the truth of oppression is not to point to its intellectual
> or conceptual frailties, but to expose its frailties of practice, to disclose
> and nurture alternate forms of human community that challenge it on
> the level of daily operations of power/knowledge. To challenge oppres-
> sion effectively is to point to its failure to determine the nature of
> human existence and to seek to extend the sphere of influence of alternate
> structures . . . . The temptation to define others' hopes for liberation
> must be avoided. The cultural genocide of an imperialistic Christianity
> is not accidental, but is grounded in such an arrogant approach to
> liberation. It is oppressive to "free" people if their own history and
> culture do not serve as the primary sources of the definition of their
> freedom. [26]

Welch is not content merely to challenge traditional Christianity's
notion of truth in her politics of redeemed communities; rather, she
attempts a fundamental reconsideration of the concept, one that is central
to her entire theoretical edifice. Welch's articulation of a politics of truth
resonates the empowering spirit found in the writings of Ernst Bloch and
Michel Foucault. Bloch argues against a transcendental grounding of truth
since it is the logic of such a priori rationalizations that is often used to
legitimate the status quo. For Bloch, truth should be directed against
the world and located in the ongoing dialectics of human interaction and
community. As Bloch notes,

> There exists a second concept of truth . . . which is instead suffused
> with value (*Wertgeladen*)—as, for example, in the concept "a true
> friend," or in Juvenal's expression *Tempestas poetica*—that is, the kind
> of storm one finds in a book, a poetic storm, the kind that reality has
> never witnessed, a storm carried to the extreme, a radical storm and
> therefore a true storm. [27]

Welch's own formulation of the concept of truth as rooted in the most
fundamental aspects of experience and solidarity clearly rejects, along
with Bloch, the Enlightenment notion of truth as a universal way of
knowing and ordering experience. But whereas Bloch provides Welch
with a notion of truth as radical critique, Foucault links truth with the
most fundamental workings of power and knowledge and in doing so

provides a radically new way to conceptualize the role of the intellectual and intellectual practice.

In Foucault's terms truth does not exist outside of power, nor is it a product and reward of those intellectuals who have freed themselves from ignorance. Truth is part of a political economy of power. In Foucault's own words,

> Truth is a thing of this world: it is produced only by virtue of multiple forms of constraint. And it induces regular effects of power. Each society has its regime of truth, its "general politics" of truth: that is, the types of discourse which it accepts and makes function as true; the mechanisms and instances which enable one to distinguish true and false statements, the means by which each is sanctiond; the techniques and procedures accorded value in the acquistion of truth; the status of those who are charged with saying what counts as true . . . . It seems to me that what must now be taken into account in the intellectual is not the "bearer of universal values." Rather, it's the person occupying a specific position—but whose specificity is linked, in a society like ours, to the general functioning of an apparatus of truth.[28]

Foucault's analysis of the political economy of truth and his study of the discursive and institutional ways that "regimes of truth" are organized and legitimated, provides Welch with a theoretical basis upon which to develop the concept of intellectual practice as a form of cultural politics. Welch argues that intellectuals have to be seen in terms of their social and political function within particular "regimes of truth." That is, intellectuals can no longer deceive themselves into believing they are serving on behalf of truth, when, in fact, they are deeply involved in battles "about the status of truth and the economic and political role it plays."[29]

In developing this view Welch further argues that, if intellectual practice is to create an alternative and emancipatory politics of truth, it needs to be grounded in forms of moral and ethical discourse and action that address the suffering and struggles of the oppressed. This is one of the most striking formulations Welch develops. It is impressively produced through a critical appropriation of the most fundamental radical tenets of liberation theology and feminist theory. Of equal importance is Welch's attempt to point to specific forms of intellectual practice consistent with her view of legitimating ethics.

Welch's pedagogical formulations emerge from her conviction that intellectuals need to reconsider the relationship between knowledge and power. This is particularly clear in her critique of the shortcomings of the traditional Marxist view of ideology.[30] In the classical Marxist view, power relates to knowledge primarily through the ways in which it serves to distort or mystify the truth. Consequently, ideology critique mainly serves to examine the underlying economic and social conditions of knowledge or the ways in which knowledge can be analyzed for its distortions and mystifications. According to Welch, what is lost in this formulation is any understanding of the productive role that power plays in generating forms of knowledge that produce and legitimate particular forms of life, resonate with people's desires and needs and construct particular forms of experience. Extending Foucault's important insight, Welch argues that the knowledge/power relation produces dangerous "positive" effects in the way it creates particular needs, desires, and truths.

It is here that her analysis can provide educators with the basis for reconstructing a critical social theory that links pedagogy to forms of critique and possibility. By illuminating the productive effects of power, it becomes possible for teachers as intellectuals to develop forms of practice that take seriously how subjectivities are constructed within particular "regimes of truth"; it also highlights the importance of developing a theory of experience as a central aspect of radical pedagogy. This also points to the role that educators can play as bearers of dangerous memory. As transformative intellectuals, educators can serve to uncover and excavate those forms of historical and subjugated knowledges that point to experiences of suffering, conflict, and collective struggle. In this sense, teachers as intellectuals can begin to link the notion of historical understanding to elements of critique and hope. Such memories keep alive the horror of needless exploitation as well as the constant need to intervene and to struggle collectively to eliminate the conditions that produce it.

Finally, Welch argues convincingly that radicals need to engage in counter-hegemonic struggles as "specific intellectuals." Such a formulation requires that intellectuals think not in terms of civility, professionalism, and tenure promotions, but redefine their role within the specificity of political, economic and cultural sites where "regimes of truth" are produced, legitimated, and distributed. It is within such contexts that intellectuals can confront the microphysics of power and work to build alternative public spheres that have an ongoing organic connection to the dynamics of everyday life.

Eagleton and Welch respectively develop and demonstrate the importance of making a discourse of ethics and hope, on the one hand, and the ongoing struggle for developing democratic public spheres in and outside of schools, on the other, central aspects of a critical educational theory. Whereas Eagleton critically interrogates and reconstructs the relationship between social criticism and the public sphere, Welch provides the moral referents linking theory and practice to ongoing political and pedagogical struggles with oppressed and subordinate groups. Both authors furnish the outlines of a political project that is not only at odds with the anti-utopianism displayed by many conservative and radical educators, but also raise real hopes for developing educational theory and practice within a discourse that joins schooling to a politics in which criticism and hope are grounded in a practical project of possibility.

Notes

Foreword

1. For an extended commentary on *Education Under Siege,* see my essay review in *Educational Studies* 17 (1986): 277–89. For a joint discussion of *Education Under Siege* and *Theory and Resistance in Education,* see Peter McLaren, "Education as Counter-Discourse," *Review of Education* 13 (Winter 1987): 58–68. Small portions of these reviews have been reproduced in the present essay.

2. See Henry A. Giroux and Roger Simon, "Critical Pedagogy and the Politics of Popular Culture," in *Critical Pedagogy and Popular Culture,* eds. Henry A. Giroux and Roger Simon (South Hadley, Mass.: Bergin & Garvey Publishers, forthcoming).

3. See Bill Reynolds, "Henry Giroux Has The Working-Class Blues," *Sunday Journal Magazine* (Rhode Island), May 15, 1985, pp. 4–7.

4. See Giroux's forthcoming book, *Schooling and the Struggle for Public Life: Critical Pedagogy in the Modern Age* (Minneapolis: University of Minnesota Press).

5. Henry A. Giroux, *Ideology, Culture, and the Process of Schooling* (Philadelphia: Temple University Press, 1981).

6. Henry A. Giroux, *Theory and Resistance in Education* (South Hadley, Mass.: Bergin & Garvey Publishers, 1983). See also Samuel Bowles and Herbert Gintis, *Schooling in Capitalist America* (New York: Basic Books, 1976).

7. For a related discussion of ideology, see Peter McLaren, "Ideology, Science, and the Politics of Marxian Orthodoxy: A Response to Michael Dale," *Educational Theory* 37 (1987): 301–26; and Peter McLaren, "The Politics of Ideology in Educational Theory," *Social Text* (forthcoming).

8. Giroux uses the terms oppositional public sphere and counterpublic sphere to mean generally the same thing. Stanley Aronowitz and Henry A. Giroux, *Education Under Siege* (South Hadley, Mass.: Bergin & Garvey Publishers, 1985).

9. Stanley Aronowitz, *The Crisis in Historical Materialism* (New York: Praeger, 1981).

10. Giroux, *Schooling and the Struggle for Public Life.*

11. Giroux and Simon, "Critical Pedagogy and Politics of Popular Culture."

12. Ibid.

13. See Peter McLaren, "The Anthropological Roots of Pedaogy: The Teacher as Liminal Servant," *Anthropology and Humanism Quarterly* (forthcoming).

14. Jessica Benjamin, "Shame and Sexual Politics," *New German Critique* 27 (Fall 1982): 152.

15. *Ibid.,* 153.

16. Richard Smith and Anna Zantiotis, "Practical Teacher Education and the Avante Garde," *Schooling, Politics, and the Struggle for Culture,* Henry A. Giroux and Peter McLaren, eds. (Albany: State University of New York Press, forthcoming).

Introduction

1. The most celebrated texts that emerged in the 1970s were: Michael F.D. Young, ed., *Knowledge and Control* (London: Collier-Macmillan, 1971); Basil Bernstein, *Class, Codes, and Control,* vol. 3 (London: Routledge & Kegan Paul, 1977); Samuel Bowles and Herbert Gintis, *Schooling in Capitalist America* (New York: Basic Books, 1976); Michael Apple, *Ideology and Curriculum* (London: Routledge & Kegan Paul, 1977).

2. For an analysis of this position, see Henry Giroux, *Ideology, Culture, and the Process of Schooling* (Philadelphia: Temple University Press, 1981).

3. The most celebrated example of this position can be found in Bowles and Gintis, *Schooling in Capitalist America.* The literature on schooling and the reproductive thesis is critically reviewed in Henry A. Giroux, *Theory and Resistance.*

4. For recent analyses of this position, see Henry A. Giroux and David Purpel, *The Hidden Curriculum and Moral Education* (Berkeley: McCutchan Publishing, 1983); Jeannie Oakes, *Keeping Track: How Schools Structure Inequality* (New Haven: Yale University Press, 1985).

5. Apple, *Education and Power.*

6. The most influential book on this position has been Pierre Bourdieu and Jean-Claude Passeron, *Reproduction in Education, Society, and Culture* (Beverly Hills, Calif.: Sage, 1977).

7. More recent examples of this position include Arthur Wise, *Legislated Learning* (Berkeley: University of California Press, 1979); Martin Carnoy and Henry Levin, *Schooling and Work in the Democratic State* (Stanford, Calif.: Stanford University Press, 1985).

8. The relationship between schooling and democracy is brilliantly explored within a liberal perspective in John Dewey, *Democracy and Education* (New York: Free Press, 1916). Both a critique and a radical extension of this position can be found in Stanley Aronowitz and Henry A. Giroux, *Education Under Siege* (S. Hadley, Mass.: Bergin & Garvey, 1985).

9. The notion of the transformative intellectual was first used in Aronowitz and Giroux, *Education Under Siege.*

10. For a discussion of the notion of liberating memory as part of the tradition of liberation theology, see Rebecca S. Chopp, *The Praxis of Suffering* (New York: Orbis Press, 1986).

11. Michael Foucault, *Power and Knowledge: Selected Interviews and Other Writings*, ed. C. Gordon (New York: Pantheon, 1980), p. 82.

12. See Henry A. Giroux and Roger Simon, "Curriculum Study and Cultural Politics," in this volume.

13. Foucault, *Power and Knowledge*.

14. Sharon Welch, *Communities of Resistance and Solidarity: A Feminist Theology of Liberation* (New York: Orbis Press, 1985), p. 63.

Chapter 2

1. Quentin Skinner. "The Flight from Positivism." *New York Review of Books* 25 (June 15, 1976): 26.

2. Emancipatory intentions in this case can be generally construed as a paradigm that combines theory and practice in the interest of freeing individuals and social groups from the subjective and objective conditions that bind them to the forces of exploitation and oppression. This suggests a critical theory that promotes self-reflection aimed at dismantling forms of false consciousness and ideologically frozen social relations, all of which usually parade under the guise of universalistic laws. Thus, emancipation would render complementary critical thinking and political action. This suggests a learning process in which thought and action would be mediated by specific cognitive, affective, and moral dimensions.

3. Decent collections of writings on the movement can be found in: William F. Pinar, editor. *Curriculum Theorizing: The Reconceptualists* (Berkeley, Calif.: McCutchan Publishing, 1975); James Macdonald and Esther Zaret, ed., *Schools in Search of Meaning* (Washington, D.C.: ASCD, 1975). The best book on the subject published in this country is Apple, *Ideology and Curriculum*. The continental influence can be found in Jerome Karabel and A.H. Halsey, ed., *Power and Ideology in Education.* (New York: Oxford University Press, 1977).

4. William F. Pinar, "Notes on the Curriculum Field 1978," *Educational Researcher* 7 (September 1978): 5–11.

5. Herbert M. Kliebard, "Bureaucracy and Curriculum Theory," *Curriculum Theorizing*, pp. 51–69.

6. Young, *Knowledge and Control*.

7. Michael W. Apple and Nancy King, "What Do Schools Teach?" *Humanistic Education,* Richard Weller, ed., (Berkeley, Calif.: McCutchan Publishing, 1977), p. 36. See also Henry A. Giroux and Anthony N. Penna, "Social Education in the Classroom: The Dynamics of the Hidden Curriculum," in this volume.

8. This should not suggest that the new sociology of curriculum supports the separation of theory from empirical work or rejects empirical investigations altogether. Such a characterization is crude and vulgar. Theory as it is being described in this chapter has its center of gravity in its social potential for insight into the nature of truth and the meaning of life. It is linked to specific interests and situates its assumptions and modes of inquiry in *both* understanding and determining ends. What the new sociology of curriculum rejects is empiricism, that is, the use of theory to boost scientific methodology as the ultimate definition of meaning and truth. Empiricism is theory reduced to the instrumentality of finding means for ends that go unquestioned. It stands convicted of ideology in that it is incapable of identifying its own normative foundation or the interests that it serves. See Jürgen Habermas, *Toward a Rational Society* (Boston: Beacon Press, 1970).

9. Fenwick W. English, "Management Practice as a Key to Curriculum Leadership," *Educational Leadership* 36 (6): 408–13; March 1979. An in-depth response to the positivist ideology inherent in English's model can be found in Henry A. Giroux. *"Schooling and the Culture of Positivism"* 1981 in *Ideology, Culture and the Process of Schooling* (Philadelphia: Temple University Press, 1981), pp. 37–62.

10. Paulo Freire, *Pedagogy of the Oppressed* (New York: Seabury Press, 1973).

11. Howard Zinn, *The Politics of History* (Boston: Beacon Press, 1970), pp. 10–11.

12. Freire, *Pedagogy of the Oppressed.*

13. Thomas Kuhn, *The Structure of Scientific Revolutions,* 2nd ed. (Chicago: University of Chicago Press, 1970).

14. Thomas Popkewitz, "Educational Research: Values and Visions of Social Order," *Theory and Research in Social Education* 6 (Dec. 1978): 19–39.

15. Karabel and Halsey, *Power and Ideology,* pp. 1–85.

16. Apple, *Ideology and Curriculum*; Henry A. Giroux, "Beyond the Limits of Radical Educational Reform: Toward a Critical Theory of Education," *Journal of Curriculum Theorizing* 2(1): Winter 1980, pp. 20–46. in press; Henry A. Giroux, "Paulo Freire's Approach to Radical Educational Reform," *Curriculum Inquiry* 9 (3): (Fall 1979), pp. 257–72.

17. Rachel Sharp and Anthony Greene, *Education and Social Control: A Study in Progressive Primary Education* (Boston and London: Routledge and Kegan Paul, 1975).

18. Herbert Marcuse, *The Aesthetic Dimension* (Boston: Beacon Press, 1978), p. 9.

Chapter 3

1. Charles E. Silberman, *Crisis in the Classroom: The Remaking of American Education* (New York: Random House, 1970); Joel Spring, *The Sorting Machine: National Educational Policy Since 1945* (New York: David McKay, 1976), pp. 93–139.

2. Gene Lyons, "The Higher Illiteracy," *Harper's* 253 (Sept. 1976): 33–40; Ben Brodinsky, "Back to the Basics: The Movement and Its Meaning," *Phi Delta Kappan* 58 (March 1977): 522–27.

3. Pinar, "Notes on the Curriculum Field."

4. Bourdieu and Passeron, *Reproduction in Education*; Bernstein, *Class, Codes, and Control,* vol. 3; Young, *Knowledge and Control.*

5. Michael W. Apple, "Curriculum as Ideological Selection," *Comparative Education Review* 20 (June 1975): 210–11.

6. Robert Dreeben, *On What is Learned in Schools* (Reading, Mass.: Addison-Wesley, 1968); Philip N. Jackson, *Life in Classrooms* (New York: Holt, Rinehart & Winston, 1968); Norman Overly, ed., *The Unstudied Curriculum* (Washington, D.C.: Association of Curriculum and Supervision, 1970); Michael W. Apple, "The Hidden Curriculum and the Nature of Conflict," *Interchange* 2 (1971): 27–40; Apple and King, "What Do Schools Teach?"

7. Henry A. Giroux, "Writing and Critical Thinking in the Social Studies," *Curriculum Inquiry* (March 1979): 291–310.

8. Peter Stern and Jean Yarbrough, "Hannah Arendt," *American Scholar* 47 (Summer 1978): 371–81.

9. Talcott Parsons, "The School Class as a Social System: Some of Its Functions in American Society," *Harvard Educational Review* 29 (Fall 1959): 297–318; Dreeben, "The Contribution of Schooling."

10. Michael W. Apple, "Some Aspects of the Relationships between Economic and Cultural Reproduction," paper presented at Kent State Invitational Conference on Curriculum Theory, Nov. 11, 1977.

11. Karabel and Halsey, *Power and Ideology*, p. 3.

12. John O' Neill, "Embodiment and Child Development: A Phenomenological Approach," in *Childhood and Socialization*, Hans Peter Dreitzel, ed. (New York: International Publishers, 1973), p. 65.

13. Young, *Knowledge and Control*; Nell Keddie, ed., *The Myth of Cultural Deprivation* (Baltimore: Penguin, 1973); Chris Jenks, ed., *Rationality, Education, and the Social Organization of Knowledge* (London: Routledge & Kegan Paul, 1977); John Eggleston, *The Sociology of the School Curriculum* (London: Routledge & Kegan Paul, 1977).

14. Sharp and Greene, *Educational and Social Control*.

15. Sharp and Greene, *Educational and Social Control*, p. 21.

16. Antonio Gramsci, *Selections from the Prison Notebooks*, Quinton Hoare and Geoffrey Smith, eds. and trans. (New York: International Publishers, 1971); Harold Entwistle, "Antonio Gramsci and the School as Hegemonic," *Educational Theory* 28 (Winter 1978): 23–33.

17. Richard LaBreoque, "The Correspondence Theory," *Educational Theory* 28 (Summer 1978): 194–201.

18. Dreeben, *The Contribution of Schooling*, p. 24.

19. Stephen Arons, "The Separation of School and State: Pierce Reconsidered," *Harvard Educational Review* 46 (Feb. 1976): 98.

20. Ralph Tyler, *Basic Principles of Curriculum and Instruction* (Chicago: University of Chicago Press, 1949), p. 35.

21. Paulo Freire, *Pedagogy of the Oppressed* (New York: Seabury Press, 1973), p. 15.

22. Dreeben, "The Contribution of Schooling," p. 13.

23. Ibid., p. 66.

24. Bernstein, *Class, Codes, and Control*, vol. 3.

25. Stanley Aronowitz, *False Promises: The Shaping of the American Working-Class Consciousness* (New York: McGraw-Hill, 1973), p. 75.

26. Apple, "The Hidden Curriculum"; Giroux and Penna, "Social Relations in the Classroom."

27. Jerome Bruner, *The Relevance of Education* (New York: Norton, 1973), p. 115.

28. Bowles and Gintis, *Schooling in Capitalist America*, p. 265.

29. Apple, "The Hidden Curriculum"; Jean Anyon, "Elementary Social Studies Textbooks and Legitimating Knowledge," *Theory and Research in Social Education* 6 (Sept. 1978): 40–54; Thomas S. Popkewitz, "The Latent Values of the Discipline-Centered Curriculum in Social Education," *Theory and Research in Social Education* 5 (April 1977): 41–60.

30. Apple, "The Hidden Curriculum"; Popkewitz, "Latent Values."

31. Popkewitz, "Latent Values," p. 58.

32. Jackson, *Life in Classrooms*.

33. Ibid., p. 16.

34. Ibid., p. 18.

35. Bowles and Gintis, *Schooling in Capitalist America*, p. 40.

36. Ibid., p. 41.

37. Keddie, *Myth of Cultural Deprivation*; Sharp and Greene, *Educational and Social Control*.

38. Dan C. Lortie, *Schoolteacher: A Sociological Study* (Chicago: University of Chicago Press, 1975), p. 54.

39. Ivan Illich, "After Deschooling, What?" in Alan Gartner et al., *After Deschooling, What?* (New York: Holt, Rinehart & Winston, 1973); Bernstein, *Class, Codes, and Control*, vol. 3.

40. Jackson, *Life in Classrooms*, p. 33.

41. Paulo Freire, *Pedagogy in Process* (New York: Seabury Press, 1978).

42. Karl Marx, "Theses on Feurrbach," in Loyd D. Easton and Kurt H. Guddart, *Writings of the Young Marx on Philosophy and History* (New York: Doubleday, 1967), p. 402.

43. Elizabeth Cagan, "Individualism, Collectivism, and Radical Educational Reform," *Harvard Educational Review* 48 (May 1978): 261.

44. Harry Braverman, *Labor and Monopoly Capital* (New York: Monthly Review Press, 1974); Stuart Ewen, *Captains of Consciousness* (New York: McGraw-Hill, 1976).

45. Philip Slater, *The Pursuit of Loneliness* (Boston: Beacon Press, 1970); Cagan, "Individualism, Collectivism, and Radical Educational Reform."

46. Norman Daniels, "The Smart White Man's Burden," *Harper's* 247 (Oct. 1973): 24–26ff.; Brigitte Berger, "A New Interpretation of the I. Q. Controversy," *The Public Interest* 50 (Winter 1978): 29–48; J. B. Biggs, "Genetics and Education: An Alternative to Jensenism," *Educational Researcher* 7 (April 1978): 11–17.

47. Bernstein, *Class, Codes, and Conrol*, vol. 3, pp. 88–89.

48. Lortie, *Schoolteacher*.

49. Bowles and Gintis, *Schooling in Capitalist America*.

50. Freire, *Pedagogy of the Oppressed*.

51. Lortie, *Schoolteacher*.

52. Stanley Aronowitz, "Mass Culture and the Eclipse of Reason: The Implications for Pedagogy," *Harvard Educational Review* 46 (April 1977): 768–74.

53. Ivan Illich, *Deschooling Society* (New York: Harper & Row, 1971).

Chapter 4

1. The term schools as it is used in this chapter should not suggest fixed and rigid theoretical positions among the two movements analyzed or the many marginal movements that take positions on the design of course objectives. The various movements represent schools in the sense that their members share core assumptions. Needless to say, while differences do exist among members of the respective schools, such differences are outweighed by their agreements. One interesting look at the humanistic and behaviorist objectives schools can be found in Leonard Gardner, "Humanistic Education and Behavioral Objectives: Opposing Theories of Educational Science," *School Review* (May 1971): 376–94. See also David R. Krathwohl and David Payne, "Defining Educational Objectives," in *Educational Measurement*, Robert L. Thorndike, ed. (Washington, D.C.: ACE, 1971), pp. 17–45.

2. One glaring example of this can be found in W. James Popham, "Probing the Validity of Arguments against Behavioral Goals," *Behavioral Objectives and Instruction*, ed. Robert J. Kibler et al. (Boston: Allyn and Bacon, 1970), pp. 115–16. In defending the behavioral objectives position, Popham made the following statement, "Yet as a partisan in the controversy, I would prefer unanimous support of the position to which I subscribe. You see, the other people are wrong. Adhering to a philosophic tenet that error is evil, I hate to see my friends wallowing in sin."

3. Michael W. Apple, "The Adequacy of Systems Management Procedures in Education and Alternatives," in *Perspectives on Management Systems Approaches in Education*, Albert H. Yee ed. (Englewood Cliffs, N.J.: Educational Technology Publications, 1973), pp. 97–110; also see Maxine Greene, "Curriculum and Consciousness," in Pinar, *Curriculum Theorizing*, p. 304.

4. Jean Bethke Elshtain, "Social Relations in the Classroom: A Moral and Political Perspective," *Telos* (Spring 1976): 97–100.

5. The relationship between the formal and hidden curricula is explored in Giroux and Penna, "Social Relations in the Classroom."

6. The most comprehensive understanding of this position can best be achieved by examining its historical roots. To my knowledge, the best book on the subject is by Raymond Callahan, *Education and the Cult of Efficiency* (Chicago: University of Chicago Press, 1962).

7. M. Greene, "Curriculum and Consciousness," p. 299.

8. Michael F. D. Young, "Knowledge and Control," *Knowledge and Control*, p. 10.

9. Apple, "Curriculum as Ideological Selection," pp. 210–11.

10. For a sophisticated treatment of the relationship between theory and "facts," see Max Horkheimer, *Critical Theory* (New York: Seabury Press, 1972), pp. 188–244.

11. Trent Shroyer, "Toward a Critical Theory for Advanced Industrial Society," in *Recent Sociology* No. 2, ed. Hans Peter Dreitzel (London: Collier-Macmillan, 1970), p. 211.

12. Russell Jacoby, *Social Amnesia* (Boston: Beacon Press, 1975), p. xviii.

13. Bernstein, *Class, Codes, and Control*, vol. 3; also see Bourdieu and Passeron, *Reproduction*.

14. Paulo Freire, *Education for Critical Consciousness* (New York: Seabury Press, 1973), pp. 1–58.

15. Max Horkheimer, *Eclipse of Reason* (New York: Seabury Press, 1974), p. 73.

16. Erich Fromm, *Beyond the Chains of Illusion* (New York: Holt, Rinehart & Winston, 1968), p. 173.

17. Discussions of the hidden curriculum can be found in the following sources: Jackson, *Life in Classrooms*; Dreeben, *On What is Learned in Schools*; Overly, *The Unstudied Curriculum*.

18. Bowles and Gintis, *Schooling in Capitalist America*, pp. 131–48.

19. Lynne B. Iglitzin, "Political Education and Sexual Liberation," *Politics and Society* 2 (Winter 1972): 242.

20. Herbert Marcuse, *Counter-Revolution and Revolt* (Boston: Beacon Press, 1972), p. 28.

21. Mihailo Markovic, *From Affluence to Praxis* (Ann Arbor: University of Michigan Press, 1974), p. 23.

22. Lawrence Kohlberg, "Moral Development and the New Social Studies," *Social Education* 37 (May 2, 1973): 371.

Chapter 5

1. The now-famous *Newsweek* article, "Why Johnny Can't Write," Merrill Shiels (Dec. 1975), simply brought the problem to the public's attention. See also Nan Elsasser and Vera P. John-Steiner, "An Interactionist Approach to Advancing Literacy, *Harvard Educational Review* 47 (Aug. 1977): 355–69; Lyons, "The Higher Illiteracy."

2. A.D. Van Nostrand, "The Inference Construct: A Model of the Writing Process," *ADE Bulletin*, no. 54 (May 1978): 1–27.

3. See Janet Emig, "Writing as a Mode of Learning," *College Composition and Communication* 28 (May 1977): 122–28; James Britton et al., *The Development of Writing Abilities* (London: Macmillan, 1975); Gary Tate, ed., *Teaching Composition: Ten Bibliographic Essays* (Fort Worth, Texas: Texas Christian University Press, 1976).

4. Lev S. Vygotsky, *Language and Thought* (Cambridge, Mass.: MIT Press, 1962), p. 100.

5. Braddock et al., *Research in Written Composition* (Champaign, Ill.: National Council of Teachers of English, 1963); W.B Elley et al., "The Role of Grammar in a Secondary School English Curriculum," *Research in the Teaching of English* 10 (Spring 1976): 18.

6. Richard Ohmann, *English in America* (New York: Oxford University Press, 1976), p. 136.

7. John Simon, "The Language," *Esquire* (June 1977): 18.

8. Ibid.; see also R. Verland Cassill, *Writing Fiction* (Englewood Cliffs, N.J.: Prentice-Hall, 1975).

9. A.D. Van Nostrand, "English I and the Measurement of Writing," speech given at the National Conference on Personalized Instruction in Higher Education, March 21, 1975.

10. Sidney Simon et al., *Values Clarification through Writing: Composition for Personal Growth* (New York: Hart Publishing, 1973); George E. Newell, "The Emerging Self: A Curriculum of Self Actualization," *English Journal* 66 (Nov. 1977): 32–34.

11. Jacoby, *Social Amnesia,* p. 67.

12. One of the most devastating critiques on these educators who overly stress the interpersonal dimension in pedagogy has been made by Elshtain, "Social Relations in the Classroom."

13. Britton et al., *Development of Writing Abilities,* pp. 1–18.

14. Sheils, "Why Johnny Can't Write," p. 61; see also Janet Emig, *The Composing Process of Twelfth Graders* (Urbana, Ill.: National Council of Teachers of English, 1971.)

15. Van Nostrand, "The Inference Construct," p. 2.

16. For an excellent comment on the relationship between knowledge and values, see Young, *Knowledge and Control.* Michael Apple has written extensively on the latter subject, and his article, "The Hidden Curriculum and the Nature of Conflict," deals directly with the social studies field. See also Jonathon Kozol, *The Night Is Dark and I Am Far from Home* (Boston: Houghton Mifflin, 1975), pp. 63–73.

17. For an excellent description of this type of pedagogy, see Freire, *Pedagogy of the Oppressed,* and Giroux and Penna, "Social Relations in the Classroom."

18. Marcuse, *Counter-Revolution,* p. 27.

19. There are many sources that treat this position seriously. One of the best is Bowles and Gintis, *Schooling in Capitalist America.* See also Martin Carnoy and Henry M. Levin, *The Limits of Educational Reform* (New York: David McKay, 1976), pp. 52–82, 219–44.

20. Martin Jay, *The Dialectical Imagination* (Boston: Little, Brown, 1973), p. 65.

21. This approach has been widely popularized through the works of Hilda Taba, *Teacher's Handbook for Elementary Social Studies* (Reading, Mass.: Addison-Wesley, 1967); J. Richard Suchman, *Inquiry Box: Teacher's Handbook* (Chicago: Science Research Associates, 1967); Joseph J. Schwab, *Biology Teacher's Handbook* (New York: Wiley, 1965).

22. Alvin J. Gouldner, *The Dialectic of Ideology and Technology* (New York: Seabury Press, 1976), p. 49.

23. Fredric Jameson, *Marxism and Form* (Princeton, N.J.: Princeton University Press, 1971), p. xx.

24. Jean-Paul Sartre, *Literature and Existentialism,* 3rd. ed. (New York: Citadel Press, 1965).

25. See Apple and King, "What Do Schools Teach?" pp. 29–63, and Bowles and Gintis, *Schooling in Capitalist America.* A decent collection of articles can be found in Overly, *The Unstudied Curriculum.*

26. Freire, *Education for Critical Consciousness.*

27. See David Swartz, "Pierre Bourdieu: The Cultural Transmission of Social Inequality," *Harvard Educational Review* 47 (Nov. 1977): 545–55; Bourdieu and Passeron, *Reproduction*; Bernstein, *Class, Codes, and Control,* pp. 85–156. For a good, general study

on the politics of language, see Claus Mueller, *The Politics of Communication* (New York: Oxford University Press, 1973).

28. M. Greene, "Curriculum and Consciousness," p. 304.

29. See Henry A. Giroux et al., *The Process of Writing History: Episodes in American History* (Providence, R.I.: Center for Research in Writing, 1978). All the writing concepts used in this chapter are adapted from A.D. Van Nostrand et al., *Functional Writing* (Boston: Houghton Mifflin, 1978).

30. Giroux et al., *Process of Writing History,* p. 13.

31. Ibid., p. 14.

32. Freire, *Education for Critical Consciousness,* pp. 32–89.

33. Giroux et al., *Process of Writing History,* p. 24.

34. Ibid., p. 33.

35. Paulo Freire, "Conscientization," in *The Goal Is Liberation* (Geneva: United Council of Churches, 1974), p. 2.

36. Freire, *Education for Critical Consciousness,* pp. 5–6.

Chapter 6

1. Herbert Marcuse, *One Dimensional Man* (Boston: Beacon Press, 1964); Horkheimer, *Eclipse of Reason*; David F. Noble, *America by Design* (New York: Knopf, 1977); Aronowitz, *False Promises.*

2. J.W. Freiberg, "Critical Social Theory in the American Conjuncture," in J.W. Freiberg, ed., *Critical Sociology* (New York: Irvington Press, 1979), pp. 1–21.

3. Todd Gitlin, "Media Sociology," *Theory and Society* 6 (1978): 205–53.

4. M. Hoyles, "The History and Politics of Literacy," in M. Hoyles, ed., *The Politics of Literacy* (London: Writers and Readers Publishing Cooperation, 1977), pp. 14–32.

5. Gitlin, "Media Sociology," p. 205; Aronowitz, "Mass Culture," p. 768.

6. Technological utopianism finds its most popular expression in Marshall McLuhan, *Understanding Media* (New York: Signet, 1963); technological fatalism is captured flawlessly in Jacques Ellul, *The Technological Society* (New York: Knopf, 1965). A critique of both these positions can be found in Henry A. Giroux, "The Politics of Technology, Culture, and Alienation," *Left Curve* 6 (Summer/Fall 1976): 32–42.

7. M.W. Apple, "Television and Cultural Reproduction," *Journal of Aesthetic Education* 12 (Oct. 1979): 109.

8. Christopher Lasch, *Haven in a Heartless World* (New York: Basic, 1977), pp. 93–94; Hans Peter Dreitzel, "On the Political Meaning of Culture," in Norman Birnbaum, ed., *Beyond the Crisis* (New York: Oxford University Press, 1977), pp. 83–138.

9. Gramsci, *Prison Notebooks;* an excellent representative sampling of Frankfurt school writers can be found in A. Arato and E. Gebhardt, eds., *The Essential Frankfurt School Reader* (New York: Urizon, 1978).

10. Bourdieu and Passeron, *Reproduction;* Bernstein, *Class, Codes, and Control,* vol. 3.

11. Dreitzel, "Political Meaning of Culture," p. 88.

12. Ewen, *Captains of Consciousness,* p. 202.

13. Braverman, *Labor and Monopoly Capital*; Ewen, *Captains of Consciousness,* p. 195.

14. T. McCarthy, *The Critical Theory of Jürgen Habermas* (Cambridge, Mass.: MIT Press, 1978), p. 37.

15. Hans Enzenberger, *The Consciousness Industry* (New York: Seabury, 1974).

16. Ibid., p. 16.

17. One critic claims that American society is characterized by a "falling rate of intelligence, one that represents a tendency rather than an iron law. Intellectual obsolescence annihilates memory and history so as to spur stagnating demand and production. The result is memoryless repetition—a social amnesia." Russell Jacoby, "A Falling Rate of Intelligence," *Telos* 27 (Spring 1976): 144.

18. Aronowitz, "Mass Culture," pp. 768, 770.

19. See D. Ben-Horin, "Television without Tears," *Socialist Review* 35 (Sept./Oct. 1977): 7–35.

20. Gouldner, *Dialectic of Ideology.*

21. Enzenberger, *Consciousness Industry*, pp. 95–128.

22. Gitlin, Media Sociology, p. 791.

23. Theodor Adorno, "Television and Patterns of Mass Culture," in *Mass Culture: The Popular Arts in America*, ed. B. Rosenberg and P. Manning White (New York: Free Press (1957), p. 93.

24. Aronowitz, *False Promises*, pp. 50–134.

25. Theodor Adorno, "Television and Patterns of Mass Culture," p. 484.

26. Norman Fruchter, "Movement Propaganda and the Culture of the Spectacle." *Liberation* (May 1971), pp. 4–17.

27. Fredric Jameson, "Class and Allegory in Contemporary Mass Culture: Dog Day Afternoon as a Political Film," *College English* 38 (April, 1977): 848.

28. Gitlin, "Media Sociology," p. 791.

29. Aronowitz, "Mass Culture," p. 770. See also D. Lazere, "Literacy and Political Consciousness: A Critique of Left Critiques," *Radical Teacher* 8 (May 1975): 20–21.

30. J. MacDonald, "Reading in an Electronic Age," in J. MacDonald, ed., *Social Perspectives in Reading* (Delaware: International Reading Association, 1973), pp. 24–27; Enzenberger, *Consciousness Industry*, pp. 95–128.

31. Gitlin, "Media Sociology," passim.

32. O. Negt, "Mass Media: Tools of Domination or Instruments of Liberation?" *New German Critique* 14 (Spring 1978): 70.

33. Examples of this tendency have been critiqued in Elsasser and John-Steiner, "An Interactionist Approach." Representative examples of positivist approaches to literacy in reading can be found in R.C. Calfee and P.A. Drum, "Learning to Read: Theory, Research, and Practice," *Curriculum Theory* 8 (Fall 1978): 183–250.

34. Giroux, "Beyond the Limits."

35. Quoted in Hoyles, *Politics of Literacy*, p. 78.

Chapter 7

1. Paulo Freire, *The Politics of Education* (S. Hadley, Mass.: Bergin & Garvey, 1985), p. 2.

2. Ibid., pp. 2–3.

3. J. Henriques et al., *Changing the Subject* (New York: Methuen, 1984).

4. Richard Johnson, "What Is Cultural Studies?" *Anglistica* 26 (1–2):11.

5. Roger Simon, "Work Experience," in David W. Livingstone, ed., *Critical Pedagogy and Cultural Power* (S. Hadley, Mass.: Bergin & Garvey, 1987), pp. 155–77.

6. Foucault, *Power and Knowledge.*

7. Peter McLaren, *Schooling as a Ritual Performance* (Boston: Routledge & Kegan Paul, 1986).

8. R. White and D. Brockington, *Tales out of School* (London: Routledge & Kegan Paul, 1983), p. 21

9. Mortimer Adler, *The Paideia Proposal* (New York: Macmillan, 1982), p. 42.

10. P. Cusick, *The Egalitarian Ideal and The American School* (New York: Longman, 1983), pp. 25, 71.

11. Ibid., p. 108.

12. W. Kerrigan, *Writing to the Point,* 2nd. ed. (New York: Harcourt, Brace, Jovanovich, 1979), p. 32.

13. Callahan, *Education and the Cult of Efficiency.*

14. I want to make clear that there is a major distinction between the work of John Dewey, *Democracy and Education* (New York: Free Press, 1916), in this case, and the hybrid discourses of progressive, educational reform that characterized the late 1960s and 1970s. The discourse of relevance and integration that I am analyzing here bears little resemblance to Dewey's philosophy of experience, in that Dewey stressed the relationship between student experience, critical reflection, and learning. In contrast, the call for relevance that abounds today generally surrenders the concept of systematic knowledge acquisition and uncritically privileges an anti-intellectual concept of student experience. For a critique of these positions, see Aronowitz and Giroux, *Education Under Siege,* and Giroux, *Ideology and Culture.*

15. Cusick, *The Egalitarian Ideal,* p. 55.

16. Ibid.; Theodore Sizer, *Horace's Compromise* (Boston: Houghton Mifflin, 1984).

17. Giroux and Purpel, *The Hidden Curriculum.*

18. Carl Rogers, *Freedom to Learn* (Columbus, Ohio: Charles Merrill, 1969).

19. Clyde Kluckhohn, *Mirror for Man: The Relation of Anthropology to Modern Life* (New York: McGraw-Hill, 1949).

20. P. Corrigan, "Race, Ethnicity, Gender, Culture: Embodying Differences Educationally—An Argument" (Unpublished paper, Ontario Institute for Studies in Education, 1985), p. 7.

21. R. Jeffcoate, *Positive Image: Towards a Multicultural Curriculum* (London: Readers and Writers Cooperative, 1979), p. 122.

22. M. Gollnick and P. Chinn, *Multicultural Education in a Pluralistic Society* (St. Louis: C.V. Mosby, 1983), p. 306.

23. Nathan Glazer, "Cultural Pluralism: The Social Aspect," in M. Tumin and W. Plotch, eds., *Pluralism in a Democratic Society* (New York: Praeger, 1977), p. 51.

24. Henry A. Giroux and Roger Simon, "Curriculum Study and Cultural Politics," *Journal of Education* 166 (Fall 1984): 226–38.

25. Simon, "Work Experience," p. 176.

26. Dell Hymes, "Ethnolinguistic Study of Classroom Discourse," Final Report to the National Institute of Education (Philadelphia: University of Pennsylvania, 1982); G. Kress and R. Hodge, *Language as Ideology* (London: Routledge & Kegan Paul, 1979).

27. Giroux, *Theory and Resistance in Education.*

28. Aronowitz and Giroux, *Education Under Siege.*

29. Giroux and Simon, "Curriculum Study and Cultural Politics."

30. The reproductive theiss in radical educational theory has been developed out of the work of Bowles and Gintis, *Schooling in Capitalist America,* and Giroux, *Theory and Resistance in Education.*

31. A major analysis of these discourses and the traditions with which they are generally associated can be found in Johnson, *"What Is Cultural Studies?"* I have drawn freely from Johnson's work in this section of the chapter.

32. Johnson, "What Is Cultural Studies?" pp. 64–65.

33. Apple, *Education and Power.*

34. Judith Williamson, *Decoding Advertisements* (New York: Marian Boyars, 1978).

35. Ariel Dorfman, *The Empire's Old Clothes* (New York: Pantheon, 1983), p. 149.

36. A. Touraine, *The Self-Production of Society* (Chicago: University of Chicago Press, 1977).

37. Johnson, "What Is Cultural Studies?"

Chapter 9

1. For a more detailed critique of the reforms, see Aronowitz and Giroux, *Education Under Siege;* see also the incisive comments on the impositional nature of the various reports in Charles A. Tesconi, Jr., "Additive Reforms and the Retreat from Purpose," *Educational Studies* 15 (Spring 1984): 1–11; Terence E. Deal, "Searching for the Wizard: The Quest for Excellence in Education," *Issues in Education* 2 (Summer 1984): 56–57; Svi Shapiro, "Choosing Our Educational Legacy: Disempowerment or Emancipation?" *Issues in Education* 2 (Summer 1984): 11–22.

2. For an exceptional commentary on the need to educate teachers to be intellectuals, see John Dewey, "The Relation of Theory to Practice," in John Dewey, *The Middle Works, 1899–1924,* JoAnn Boydston, ed. (Carbondale, Ill.: Southern Illinois University Press, 1977), [first published 1904]. See also Israel Scheffler, "University Scholarship and the Education of Teachers," *Teachers College Record* 70 (1968): 1–12; Giroux, *Ideology, Culture, and the Process of Schooling.*

3. See, for instance, Herbert Kliebard, "The Question of Teacher Education," in D. McCarty, ed., *New Perspectives on Teacher Education* (San Fransisco: Jossey-Bass, 1973).

4. Kenneth M. Zeichner, "Alternative Paradigms on Teacher Education," *Journal of Teacher Education* 34 (May–June 1983): 4.

5. Dewey, "Relation of Theory to Practice."

6. Jesse Goodman, "Reflection on Teacher Education: A Case Study and Theoretical Analysis," *Interchange* 15 (1984): 15.

7. Apple, *Education and Power.*

8. Patrick Shannon, "Mastery Learning in Reading and the Control of Teachers, *Language Arts* 61 (Sept. 1984): 488.

9. Scheffler, "University Scholarship," p. 11.

Chapter 10

The authors first presented sections of this chapter at "The Curriculum of Curriculum Conference" held at the School of Education, Michigan State University, during May 16, 17, and 18, 1984. We are especially grateful to Dean Judith E. Lanier and Professor Cleo Cherryholmes for their support.

1. Herbert M. Kliebard, "The Drive for Curriculum Change in the United States, 1890–1958. Part II, From Local Reform to a National Preoccupation," *Journal of Curriculum Studies* 11 (4): 273–86.

2. Freire, *Pedagogy of the Oppressed*; V.N. Volosinov, *Marxism and the Philosophy of Language* (New York: Hill & Wang, 1973).

3. Giroux, *Theory and Resistance.*

4. Roland Barthes, *Mythologies* (New York: Hill & Wang, 1972).

5. Bourdieu and Passeron, *Reproduction.*

6. Giroux, *Theory and Resistance.*

7. Gramsci, *Prison Notebooks.*

8. Aronowitz and Giroux, *Education Under Siege.*

Chapter 11

1. Our working definition of culture is taken from John Clarke et al., "Subculture, Culture and Class" in *Resistance Through Rituals,* Stuart Hall and Tony Jefferson, eds. (London: Hutchinson, 1976): "By culture we understand the shared principles of life characteristic of particular classes, groups or social milieux. Cultures are produced as groups make sense of their social existence in the course of everyday experience. Culture is intimate, therefore, with the world of practical action. It suffices, for most of the time, for managing everyday life. Since, however, this everyday world is itself problematic, culture must perforce take complex and heterogenous forms, 'not at all free from contradictions.' " pages 10–17.

2. This remark is based on the work of several members of the Group for Research into the Institutionalization and Professionalization of Literary Study (GRIP) who have been examining the relationship between the historical development of disciplines and their departmentalization. See also Thomas S. Popkewitz, "Social Science and Social Amelioration: The Development of the American Academic Expert," in *Paradigm and Ideology in Educational Research* (Philadelphia: The Falmer Press, 1984). pp. 107–28.

3. See Burton Bledstein, *The Culture of Professionalism: The Middle Class and the Development of Higher Education in America* (New York: Norton, 1976).

4. Paul Piccone, "Symposium: Intellectuals in the 1980's." *Telos* 50 (Winter 1981–82): 116.

5. Michel Foucault, *Discipline and Punish* Part Three, (New York: Pantheon). pp. 135ff.

6. Hubert L. Dreyfus and Paul Rabinow, *Michel Foucault: Beyond Structuralism and Hermeneutics* (Chicago: University of Chicago Press, 1982). p. 163.

7. Dreyfus and Rabinow, *Michel Foucault,* pp. 163–4.

8. See James Sosnoski's "The *Magister Implicatus* as an Institutionalized Authority Figure: Rereading the History of New Criticism." *The GRIP Report,* Vol. 1, (Oxford, Ohio: Research in Progress, circulated by the Society for Critical Exchange).

9. See David Shumway's "Interdisciplinarity and Authority in American Studies," *The GRIP Report,* Vol. 1.

10. See *New York Times,* August 13, 1984, p. 7. One wonders at the inclusion in this canonical list of *The Communist Manifesto:* a symptom of paranoia or cautious liberalism, or both?

11. See *PN Review* 10 (6); 4–5, a piece which is a quite typical expression of the new right's emergent views on the ideological relations of literature.

12. Cf. Anthony Giddens, *Central Problems in Social Theory* (Berkeley: University of California Press, 1983), pp. 150–51.

13. Giddens, p. 4.

14. Gramsci, *Prison Notebooks* (New York: International Publications, 1971), pp. 5–27.

15. Murray Bookchin, "Symposium: Intellectuals in the 1980's," *Telos* 50 (Winter 1981–82): 13.

16. Gramsci, *Prison Notebooks,* passim.

17. See Peter Hohendahl, *The Institution of Criticism* (Ithaca: Cornell University Press, 1982). pp. 44ff. and 242ff. for a discussion of this point.

18. Aronowitz, *False Promises,* p. 97.

19. Ibid., p. 111.

Chapter 12

1. Horkheimer, *Eclipse of Reason*; Theodor Adorno and Max Horkheimer, *The Dialectic of Enlightenment*, John Cumming, trans. (New York: Seabury Press, 1972); Walter Benjamin, *Illuminations*, Hannah Arendt, ed. (New York: Schocken, 1969).

2. Arthur Lothstein, "Salving from the Dross: John Dewey's Anarcho-Communalism," *The Philosophical Forum* 10 (1978): 55–111.

3. Jürgen Habermas, *Strukterwandel der Offenlichkeit* (Neuwied: Luchterhand, 1962); Marcuse, *One Dimensional Man*; John Dewey, *The Public and Its Problems* (New York: Henry Holt, 1927); Gramsci, *Prison Notebooks*.

4. Aronowitz and Giroux, *Education Under Siege*.

5. Giroux, *Theory and Resistance*.

6. Ernesto Laclau and Chantal Mouffe, *Hegemony and Socialist Strategy* (London: Verso, 1985), p. 190.

7. Goodman, "Reflections on Teacher Education," pp. 9–26.

8. Walter Adamson, *Hegemony and Revolution: A Study of Antonio Gramsci's Political and Cultural Theory* (Berkeley: University of California Press, 1980).

9. Henriques et al., *Changing the Subject*.

10. Ernest Mandel, *Late Capitalism* (London: New Left Books, 1975); John Brenkman, "Mass Media: From Collective Experience to the Culture of Privatization," *Social Text* 1 (Winter 1979): 94–109.

11. Peter McLaren, *Schooling as a Ritual Performance* (London: Routledge and Kegan Paul, 1986).

12. Cf. Cleo Cherryholmes, "Knowledge, Power, and Discourse in Social Studies Education," *Boston University Journal of Education* 165(4): 341–58; Manuel Alvarado and Bob Ferguson, "The Curriculum, Media and Discursivity," *Screen* 24(3): 20–34; Philip Wexler, "Structure, Text, and Subject: A Critical Sociology of School Knowledge," in Michael Apple, ed., *Cultural and Economic Reproduction* (Boston and London: Routledge & Kegan Paul, 1982), pp. 275–303. Ferdinand de Saussure, *Course in General Linguistics* (London: Fontana, 1974); Jacques Derrida, *Of Grammatology*, trans. Gayatri Chakravorty Spivak (Baltimore: Johns Hopkins Press, 1977); Michel Foucault, *Power and Knowledge: Selected Interviews and Other Writings*, ed. c. Gordon (New York: Pantheon, 1980); Jacques Lacan, *Ecrits* (London: Tavistock, 1977); Hans-Georg Gadamer, *Truth and Method* (London: Sheed and Ward, 1975); Roland Barthes, *Elements of Semiology*, trans. A. Lavers and C. Smith (New York: Hill and Wang, 1968); Jürgen Habermas, *The Theory of Communicative Action*, vol. 1 (Boston: Beacon Press, 1983).

13. Giroux and Simon, "Curriculum Study as Cultural Politics."

14. Johnson, "What Is Cultural Studies?" p. 11.

15. Laclau and Mouffe, *Hegemony and Socialist Strategy*, pp. 186–87.

16. Ibid., p. 176.

17. Benjamin Barber, "A New Language for the New Left," *Harper's Magazine* (Nov. 1986): 50.

18. Noam Chomsky, *Turning the Tide* (Boston: South End Press, 1986), p. 223.

19. Ibid.

20. Christopher Lasch, "Fraternalist Manifesto," *Harper's Magazine* (April 1987): 17–20.

21. Ernst Bloch, *The Philosophy of the Future* (New York: Herder and Herder, 1970), pp. 86–87.

22. Henry A. Giroux and Peter McLaren, "Teacher Education and the Politics of Engagement: The Case for Democratic Schooling," *Harvard Educational Review* 56(3): 213–38.

Chapter 13

1. For a detailed analysis of this issue, Henry A. Giroux, "Public Philosophy and the Crisis in Education," *Harvard Educational Review* 42 (May 1984): 186–94. Also see the insightful remarks of Charles A. Tesconi, Jr., "Additive Reform and the Retreat from Purpose," *Educational Studies* 15 (Spring 1984): 1–10.

2. See my detailed critical analysis of the limits of Marxist discourse on radical educational theory in Henry A. Giroux, "Marxism and Schooling: The Limits of Radical Discourse," *Educational Theory* 34 (Spring 1984): 113–35.

3. See Giroux, "Public Philosophy."

4. Allen Hunter, "In the Wings: New Right Ideology and Organization," *Radical America* 15 (1981): 129.

5. Stuart Hall, "Moving Right," *Socialist Review* 11 (Jan.-Feb. 1982): 128.

6. Miriam David, "Nice Girls Say No," *New Internationalist* (March 1984): 26; Miriam David, "Teaching and Preaching Sexual Morality: The New Right's Anti-Feminism in Britain and the U.S.A.," *Journal of Education* 166 (March 1984): 63–76.

7. Valerie Walkerdine, "It's Only Natural: Rethinking Child-Centered Pedagogy," in *Is There Anyone Here From Education?* Donald (London: Pluto Press, 1983), p. 87.

8. Stuart Hall, "Education in Crisis, in *Is There Anyone Here From Education?* p. 6.

Chapter 14

1. George S. Counts, *The Selective Character of American Secondary Education* (Chicago: University of Chicago Press, 1922), pp. 154, 156.

2. Oakes, *Keeping Track*.

3. Ibid., p. 21.

4. John Goodlad, *A Place Called School* (New York: McGraw-Hill, 1984).

5. Oakes, *Keeping Track,* p. 205.

6. Ibid., p. 92.

7. Ibid., p. 173.

8. Bowles and Gintis, *Schooling in Capitalist America*; Paul Willis, *Learning to Labour* (Lexington, Mass.: D.C. Heath, 1977); Bernstein, *Class, Codes, and Control,* vol. 3; Bourdieu and Passeron, *Reproduction*.

9. Martin Carnoy, "Education, Democracy, and Social Conflict," *Harvard Educational Review* 43 (1983): 402.

10. Oakes, *Keeping Track,* p. 205.

11. Ibid., p. 206.

12. Ibid., p. 210.

13. Ibid., p. 211.

14. R.W. Connell et al., *Making the Difference* (Sydney, Australia: Allen & Unwin, 1982), p. 193.

15. Ibid.

16. For an analysis of the various traditions that characterize the recent developments in radical educational theory, see Aronowitz and Giroux, *Education Under Siege,* and McLaren, *Schooling as a Ritual Performance.*

Chapter 15

1. Harold Entwistle, *Antonio Gramsci: Conservative Schooling for Radical Politics* (London: Routledge & Kegan Paul, 1979), p. 177.

2. Ibid., pp. 46, 47.

3. Karl R. Popper, *Objective Knowledge: An Evolutionary Approach* (Oxford: Oxford University Press, 1962).

4. Young, *Knowledge and Control.*

5. John Friedman, "The Epistemology of Social Practice: A Critique of Objective Knowledge," *Theory and Society* 6 (1978): 80.

6. Antonio Gramsci, *The Modern Prince and Other Writings* (New York: International Publishers, 1967), pp. 95–101.

7. Gramsci, *Prison Notebooks.*

8. Ibid., p. 30.

9. Ibid., pp. 32–33.

10. This issue is explored in depth in Marx Wartofsky, "Art and Technology: Conflicting Models of Education? The Use of a Cultural Myth," in Walter Feinberg and Henry Rosemont, Jr., *Work, Technology, and Education* (Urbana, Ill.: University of Illinois Press, 1975), pp. 166–85; Giroux, "Beyond the Limits of Radical Educational Reform"; Elshtain, "Social Relations of the Classroom."

11. Philip Simpson, "The Whalebone in the Corset: Gramsci on Education, Culture, and Change," *Screen Education* No. 28 (1978): 20.

12. Jerome Karabel, "Revolutionary Contradictions: Antonio Gramsci and the Problems of Intellectuals," *Politics and Society* 6 (1976): 172.

13. Gramsci, *Prison Notebooks,* p. 42.

14. Antonio Gramsci, "Socialism and Culture," in Paul Piccone and Pedro Cavalcante, *History, Philosophy, and Culture in the Young Gramsci* (St. Louis: Telos Press, 1975), pp. 20–21.

15. Entwistle, *Antonio Gramsci,* p. 92.

16. Ibid., p. 93.

17. Chantal Mouffe, "Hegemony and Ideology in Gramsci," in Chantal Mouffe, ed., *Gramsci and Marxist Theory* (London: Routledge & Kegan Paul, 1979), pp. 191–92.

18. Joseph V. Femia, "The Gramsci Phenomenon: Some Reflections," *Political Studies* 27 (1979): 478.

19. Mihaly Vajda, "Antonio Gramsci: Prison Notebooks Review," *Telos* No. 15 (1976): 151. See also Paul Piccone, "Gramsci's Marxism: Beyond Lenin and Togliatti," *Theory and Society* 3 (1973): 485–511.

20. Femia, "The Gramsci Phenomenon," p. 481.

21. Gramsci, *Prison Notebooks,* p. 481.

22. Ibid., p. 418.

23. Maxine Greene, "The Politics of the Concrete," *Social Practice* (June 1980); Henry A. Giroux, "Beyond the Correspondence Theory: Notes on the Dynamics of Educational Reproduction and Transformation," in *Ideology, Culture, and the Process of Schooling* (Philadelphia: Temple University Press, 1981).

Chapter 16

1. For example, see Dan Liston, "On Facts and Values: An Analysis of Radical Curriculum Studies," *Educational Theory,* 36:2 (1986): 137–52.

2. A typical example is Nicholas C. Burbules, "Radical Educational Cynicism and Radical Educational Skepticism," in *Philosophy of Education 1985,* David Nyberg, ed. (Urbana, Ill.: Philosophy of Education Society, 1986), pp. 201–5.

3. For example, see Robert R. Bullough, Jr., and Andrew D. Gitlen, "Schooling and Change: A View From the Lower Rung," *Teachers College Record* 87:2 (1985): 219–37. See also Robert V. Bullough, Jr, Andrew D. Gitlin, and Stanley L. Goldstein, "Ideology, Teacher Role, and Resistance," *Teachers College Record* 86:2 (1984): 339–58. These authors have a curious way of discovering problems that have a long tradition of radical analyses and then present them as if they have never been scrutinized in a similar critical fashion.

4. See, as one instance, Dan Liston, "Marxism and Schooling: A Failed or Limited Tradition?" *Educational Theory* 35:3 (1985): pp. 307–12. I have argued against this position in Giroux, *Theory and Resistance,* and Giroux, "Toward a Critical Theory of Education;" in this volume.

5. Philip Wexler, "Introducing the Real Sociology of Education," *Contemporary Sociology* 13:4 (1984): 408.

6. Terry Eagleton, *The Function of Criticism: From the Spectator to Post-Structuralism* (London: Verso, 1984); Welch, *Communities of Resistance.*

7. Ibid., p. 9.

8. Ibid., p. 107.

9. Ibid., p. 91.

10. Ibid., p. 98.

11. Ibid., p. 113.

12. Ibid., p. 112.

13. Anson Rabinach, "Between Enlightenment and Apocalypse: Benjamin, Bloch, and Modern German Jewish Messianism," *New German Critique* 34 (Winter 1985): 124.

14. Ernst Bloch, *The Principle of Hope, III* (Cambridge, Mass.: MIT Press, 1985), pp. 1366–67

15. An example of this type of discourse can be found throughout the work of C. A. Bowers. See, for example, *The Promise of Theory* (New York: Longman, 1984). Bowers's treatment of history as an unproblematic, unified discourse that is synonomous with a revered tradition has nothing in common with Enlightenment critics such as Adorno, Horkheimer, and Benjamin who believed that a liberating historical consciousness would selectively engage (not destroy) the continuum of history by brushing it against the grain to redeem its subjugated and repressed memories. Bowers wrongly argues that the Left's view of critical thinking directly translates into an uprooted individualism that denies the very notion of tradition. That critical thinking is a precondition for either collective

action or for a selective reading of the past appears to have escaped Bowers's attention. Such is the discourse of the political apologist.

16. This position is best exemplified in the most recent article by Nicholas C. Burbules, "Review Article—*Education Under Siege*," *Educational Theory*, 36:3 (1986): 301–13.

17. Burbules's position points to his own confusion over the nature of the interests that guide his own politics. This appears to be a continuous problem in much of his work. See Burbules, "Review Article," p. 309.

18. It is impossible to spell out the problems that need to be faced in calling for alliances with critical social movements. For a brilliant discussion of this issue, see Ferenc Feher and Agnes Heller, "From Red to Green," *Telos* 59 (Spring 1984): 35–44.

19. Bloch, cited in Anson Rabinach, "Unclaimed Heritage: Ernst Bloch's *Heritage of Our Times* and the Theory of Fascism," *New German Critique*, 11 (Spring 1977): 11.

20. Welch, *Communities of Resistance*.

21. Ibid., pp. 74–75.

22. Ibid., pp. 90–92.

23. Ibid., p. 26.

24. Ibid., p. 90.

25. Ibid., p. 15.

26. Ibid., pp. 82–83.

27. Michael Lowy, "Interview with Ernst Bloch," *New German Critique* 9 (Fall 1976): 37.

28. Michel Foucault, *Power/Knowledge: Selected Interviews and Other Writings, 1972–1977* (New York: Pantheon, 1980), p. 132

29. Ibid, p. 132.

30. The educational left is notorious for its reductionist treatment of ideology and Marxism. See Michael Dale, "Stalking a Conceptual Chameleon: Ideology in Marxist Studies of Education," *Educational Theory* 36:3 (Summer 1986): 241–57. See also Burbules's treatment of ideology-critique in Burbules, "Review article", p. 310. For a one-dimensional treatment of Marxism and education, see Francis Schrag, "Education and Historical Materialism," *Interchange* 17:3 (Autumn 1986): 42–52. Schrag's piece does have one virtue; it provides teachers and students with a classic example of how not to write about Marxism and education.

Index

RELATED BOOKS

LITERACY
Reading the Word & the World
PAULO FREIRE & DONALDO MACEDO
208 Pages

Critics Choice as one of the Outstanding Books for 1987
American Educational Studies Association

"Freire's provocative explanation of {literacy} could lead to a constructive 'dialectical debate' in the United States."
—*THE LOS ANGELES TIMES*

"At a time when popularizers of cultural literacy are prescribing a cultural canon for the purpose of prying open the 'closed minds' of American youth . . . LITERACY provides an articulate and courageous response."
—*HARVARD EDUCATIONAL REVIEW*

THE POLITICS OF EDUCATION
Culture, Power & Liberation
With a Dialogue on Contemporary Issues
PAULO FREIRE
240 Pages   Photo-Study of the author

"The book enlarges our vision with each reading, until the meanings become our own."
—*HARVARD EDUCATIONAL REVIEW*

A PEDAGOGY FOR LIBERATION
Dialogues on Transforming Education
IRA SHOR & PAULO FREIRE
224 Pages   Photos

"Thoughtful, humane, stimulating, and quite readable."
—*FUTURE SURVEY*

EDUCATION UNDER SIEGE
The Conservative, Liberal & Radical Debate over Schooling
STANLEY ARONOWITZ & HENRY A. GIROUX
256 Pages

" . . . a brilliant argument for a radical rethinking of education and democracy and surely one of the most important works of the decade."
—*EDUCATIONAL STUDIES*

THEORY & RESISTANCE IN EDUCATION
A Pedagogy for the Opposition
HENRY A. GIROUX
240 Pages

"Written with a verve and assurance. . . . There can be little doubt that this is an important book."
—*HARVARD EDUCATIONAL REVIEW*

CRITICAL PEDAGOGY & CULTURAL POWER
DAVID W. LIVINGSTONE & CONTRIBUTORS
368 Pages

" . . . a major addition to the literature on applied conflict theory in education."
—*EDUCATIONAL LEADERSHIP*

WOMEN TEACHING FOR CHANGE
Gender, Class & Power
KATHLEEN WEILER
192 Pages

CAREER PATTERNS IN EDUCATION
Women, Men & Minorities in Public School Education
FLORA IDA ORTIZ
196 Pages

ACADEMIC WOMEN
Working Towards Equality
ANGELA SIMEONE
176 Pages

THE MORAL & SPIRITUAL CRISIS IN EDUCATION
A Curriculum for Justice & Compassion in Education
DAVID PURPEL
192 Pages

BROKEN PROMISES
Reading Instruction in Twentieth-Century America
PATRICK SHANNON
240 Pages

EDUCATION & THE AMERICAN DREAM
Conservatives, Liberals & Radicals Debate the Future of
Education
HARVEY HOLTZ & ASSOCIATES
288 Pages   Illustrations

MODERN EDUCATION: ONE SIZE FITS ALL
CHANNELLED FROM THE BROTHERHOOD
BY MARY ELIZABETH CARREIRO
208 Pages

For free catalogue, write or call:

Bergin & Garvey Publishers, Inc.
670 Amherst Road
Granby, MA 01033
(413) 467–3113